THE WORSHIPFUL COMPANY OF GARDENERS OF LONDON

MASTER: C.R.S. Shrub-M-Coope

PRESENTED TO: Miss P Bosch

ROOT AND BRANCH

A History of the Worshipful Company of
Gardeners of London

ROOT AND BRANCH

A History of the Worshipful Company of
Gardeners of London

By
MELVYN BARNES
(Honorary Librarian to the Company)

Published 1994 by
The Worshipful Company of
Gardeners of London
London EC2A 4AR

© 1994 The Worshipful Company of Gardeners

ISBN 0 9523215 0 5

Printed by Manor Park Press Ltd, Eastbourne BN23 6PT.

CONTENTS

Preface 3
1. Introduction and Chronology 5
2. The Guilds and the City..16
3. The Company's Early History... 26
4. The Revival of the Company, and its Relations with the
   Corporation of London..47
5. Two Constitutional Issues 75
6. Personalities 79
7. The Honorary Freedom of the Company 88
8. Royal Occasions 92
9. The Company and the "Craft" or "Mystery" of Gardening 108
10. Foreign Relations 139
11. Charitable Activities...157
12. The Common Hall 173
13. Hospitality 176
14. Thomas Fairchild and the Fairchild Lecture 181
15. The Company's Collection...188
16. The Company's Library 196
APPENDIX A. Masters of the Company 199
APPENDIX B. Clerks, Beadles, Honorary Chaplains and
               Honorary Librarians..202
APPENDIX C. The Company's Scholars 206
APPENDIX D. Fairchild Lecturers...207
APPENDIX E. Inventory of Silver, Medals and Other Gifts..................210
APPENDIX F. The Company's Library 217
INDEX OF NAMES 227

ILLUSTRATIONS

(Between pages 74 and 75)

1. Freemen's Oath
2. Sir Edward Littleton
3. Heading of the Second Royal Charter, 9th November 1616
4. The Company's Coat of Arms
5. Lord Mayor's Day 1992 — presentation by the Master of a posy to the outgoing Lady Mayoress
6. Lord Mayor's Day 1992 — participation in the Lord Mayor's Show
7. The Gardeners' Company Window — West Crypt, Guildhall
8. The Queen's Coronation Bouquet — 2nd June 1953
9. A Basket of British Spring Flowers presented to Her Majesty The Queen to mark the 40th anniversary of her accession (1992)
10. The replica Coronation bouquet presented to Her Majesty The Queen at the former Royal Mint — 2nd June 1989
11. Flowers in St. Paul's Cathedral for the Royal Wedding of the Prince of Wales with Lady Diana Spencer — 29th July 1981
12. Replica of the silver-gilt casket given by the Company to Her Majesty Queen Mary to commemorate the Silver Jubilee in 1935 (Appendix E, item 47)
13. The admission of the Prince of Wales to the Livery of the Company at Highgrove, Gloucestershire — 12th June 1987
14. The Lord Mayor of London planting the last rose in St. Paul's Rose Garden — St. George's Day 1976
15. The Company's stand at the City of London Flower Show (1992)

(Between pages 138 and 139)

16. Flowers in the City 1989 — front page of publicity leaflet
17. Flowers in the City — Middle Temple, the Best Large Garden 1992
18. Flowers in the City — the Best Floral Street — 1st Award, 1992
19. John Tradescant the Younger (1608-1662)
20. 'Unconquerable'
21. The 1990 Ghent Floralies — King Baudouin and Queen Fabiola inspect the Company's exhibit
22. The 1990 Ghent Floralies — part of the English Spring Garden
23. Visit to Virginia — planting of a tulip tree in Richmond's Capitol Square (1982)
24. The Master David Howard greets Senior Past Master Geoffrey J. Gollin (1990)
25. Thomas Fairchild Citizen and Gardener 1667-1729
26. The Company's Golden Book (Appendix E, item 72)
27. The Master's badge and chain of office, the Company's ceremonial spade and chair back with the Company's Arms (Appendix E, items 30, 37, 59 and 92)

[2]

PREFACE

It is important to record the histories of the Livery Companies of the City of London, and to draw attention to their many achievements over the centuries for the crafts embodied in their names and for the benefit of society generally.

Many Livery Companies have published their histories, and the Worshipful Company of Gardeners has done so on more than one occasion. Charles Welch, Librarian of the Corporation of London and a prime mover in the Company's 1890 revival, produced in 1890 *A Brief Account of the Worshipful Company of Gardeners of London,* which he revised in 1900 as *History of the Worshipful Company of Gardeners*. Then in 1908 William Thomas Crosweller, Past Master of the Company, produced *The Gardeners' Company: a short chronological history 1605-1907 with an introduction,* which largely consisted of an annotated list of significant events in the Company's history, with their dates.

Furthermore in 1955, when the Clerk (Arnold Francis Steele) was going through the Minute Books for the purpose of compiling the Membership Register, it occurred to him that it would be useful to produce a history of the Company from its revival in 1890. His ideas were encouraged by the then Master, Sir Brunel Cohen, but the task proved time-consuming and it was not until 1964 that his *The Worshipful Company of Gardeners of London: A History of its Revival 1890-1960* was published, some years after he resigned the Clerkship in 1958.

In the 1980s, the task of updating the Company's history was accepted by Frank Steiner. There could have been no better choice, for Steiner had been closely involved with the Company as Clerk from 1958 to 1969 and again from 1973 to 1984, and he had also served the Corporation of London in prominent positions in the 1960s and 1970s. In his task, he was encouraged and assisted by Rear Admiral M.J. Ross (Master, 1983-84) and subsequent Masters, other members of the Court of Assistants throughout the 1980s, and by his successors as Clerk and their staff.

It was agreed by the Court of Assistants on 14th November 1991 that I should produce a new and complete history of the Company, based upon the Steele volume and the updated chapters provided by Frank Steiner. I have also taken into account the earlier works of Welch and Crosweller, and from non-Company sources I have added to the work of Steele and Steiner, as well as updating the researches of Steiner to cover the period since 1990.

In all of this, I have been greatly assisted by successive Masters – D.H.S. Howard, R.C. Balfour, D.E. Dowlen and E.M. Upward – as well as by Past Masters, the Clerk (Col. N.G.S. Gray) and members of the Company's Publications and Publicity Committee. My principal contact with the latter has been Past Master G.H. Denney, who has spent an enormous amount of time considering my drafts and referring passages to other members of the Company. Indeed, many people within and without the Company have provided comments and accounts of aspects of the Company's work, and it would therefore be impossible to provide a comprehensive list of acknowledgements here. I would, however, particularly record my gratitude to Past Masters D.M.H. Longman, D.A. Huggons and R.L. Payton for their invaluable suggestions, which have enhanced the text at various points. My thanks go also to colleagues at Guildhall Library.

I thank all concerned, and hope that this volume will now serve as a complete history of the Worshipful Company of Gardeners which is a suitable tribute to those – especially Welch, Crosweller, Steele and Steiner – who have done so much work on it previously and thus provided an admirable basis for my own efforts.

"To the Worshipful Company of Gardeners – may it flourish, root and branch, for ever."

Melvyn Barnes

CHAPTER 1

Introduction And Chronology

This history of The Worshipful Company of Gardeners is arranged in three parts.

Chapters 2-6 give a general introduction to the Guilds of the City of London, in order to place the Gardeners in context, and then recount the history of the Company and its connections with the Corporation of London. Chapters 7-14 deal with the Company's activities under several "topic" headings, and finally Chapters 15 and 16 draw attention to the special collections in the Company's possession.

In view of the wide-ranging roles of the Company, most particularly in the present century, it is felt that this is an effective and interesting way of presenting its history. It is accepted, however, that it might create difficulties for those requiring a straightforward chronological account of the Company, and the following selective "landmarks" are therefore intended to assist such enquirers and to lead into the text by providing page references against each chronological entry.

* * *

1345. First mention of the Guild in the City Corporation records, 24th August. A petition to the Mayor by the Gardeners of the Earls, Barons and Bishops and of the Citizens of the City to be allowed to continue to sell their produce "where they have been wont in times of old; in front of the Church of St. Austin, at the side of the gate of St. Paul's Churchyard". [29]

1605. On 18th September, after existing for centuries as a "mystery" or "fellowship", the Guild was incorporated by Royal Charter of King James I under the title of "The Master, Wardens, Assistants and Commonalty of the Company of the Gardeners of London". The preamble sets out the operations controlled by the Company, *viz* "the trade, crafte, or misterie of Gardening, planting, grafting, setting, sowing, cutting, arboring, rocking, mounting, covering, fencing and removing of plantes, herbes, seedes, fruites, trees, stocks, setts, and of contryving the conveyances to the same belonging". [30]

1606. On 1st July, Ordinances for the government of the Company were approved by the Lord Chancellor, the Lord Treasurer and the Lord Chief Justice of Common Pleas. These included a Grant of Livery to the Company. [32]

1616. On 9th November a further Royal Charter was granted by King James I, giving the Company powers of search for defective wares within the City of London and a radius of six miles thereof. [33]

1617. On 20th May a letter to the Lord Mayor of London from Sir Robert Naunton, Principal Secretary of State, on behalf of the King, drew attention to the Charter and requested that the entire Company, or at least as many as carried on their trade and dwelt within the City or within two miles thereof, might be admitted to the Freedom of the City. A petition was presented to the Lord Mayor to the same effect, but the Corporation did not comply until 1659. [34]

1632. On 29th June Sir Edward Littleton, Recorder of London, issued his Warrant to the King's Officers in London, Middlesex, Surrey, Kent and Essex, for the apprehension of any person using the trade of gardening in contempt of the Company's Charters. [36]

1634. On 3rd December King Charles I made a Royal Proclamation, to reform the many abuses committed against the Corporation of Gardeners. [37]

On 19th December, John Tradescant the Younger took up his Freedom of the Company. [134]

1649. Members of the Company maintained large market gardens outside the City and employed 1,500 men, women and children besides 400 apprentices. [37]

1659. On 28th July the second Charter (1616) was enrolled in the Chamber of London, with a proviso that no Livery be recognised until the Court of Aldermen should otherwise order. [39]

A Lease was granted by the City, giving the Company its usual place and standing in the new Herb Market in St. Paul's Churchyard, but the Company's markets were removed by the Court of Aldermen to Aldersgate Street and Broad Street in the following year. [38]

1668. On 25th February, an Order of the Court of Aldermen compelled all gardeners taking their Freedom by Patrimony in another Company to take their Freedom in the Gardeners Company also. [40]

This was amended by further Order in 1687. [40]

1675. The Company, on petitioning the City Lands Committee, was allotted sixty stations for members in the Gracechurch Street Market, by then known as the Woolchurch Herb Market. [39]

1681. The lease of land and property at Horsey Down (later Horselydown) in Bermondsey was mortgaged to the Company, and provided many administrative and financial problems until it was re-assigned in 1700. [42]

1704. Thomas Fairchild, gardener of Hoxton, took up his Freedom of the Company by Redemption. [181]

1722. Seven members of the Company (including Fairchild) claimed unsuccessfully to vote as Liverymen in Common Hall. [42]

1890. On 29th December, a Special Meeting of interested parties at 9 Old Jewry Chambers (the office of the Clerk, James Curtis) planned the revival of the Company after many moribund years. [47]

1891. On petition to the Court of Aldermen "the honour and privilege of the Livery of the City" (refused in 1659) was granted, the number of the Livery being fixed at 60. [50]

The Rt. Hon. Sir Joseph Savory, Bt., Lord Mayor of London, was elected Master of the Company. [49]

The present gold Master's badge was purchased. [51]

The Company's library was founded. [196]

1892. An Entertainment Fund was set up. [176]

1893. The scholarship scheme was instituted. [109]

1894. In honour of Mr. Alderman and Sheriff Marcus Samuel, a member of the Court, a car "emblematic of gardening" was provided for the Lord Mayor's Show. [62]

1895. The Company endowed a pension for a retired gardener through the Gardeners Royal Benevolent Institution. [157]

This year also saw the beginning of a long collaboration between the Company and the Metropolitan Public Gardens Association. [159]

1896. The first Honorary Freedom of the Company was conferred on the Hon. Alicia Margaret Tyssen Amherst (later Lady Rockley) in recognition of her work *The History of Gardening in England*. [88]

1897. A pension for an orphan was endowed through the Royal Gardeners Orphan Fund. [157]

W.T. Crosweller, a member of the Court, presented the badges of office of the two Wardens and the Clerk. [188]

1902. Mr. C.E. Osman, Master, presented a silver gilt chain for the Master's badge.[188]

Alderman Sir Marcus Samuel was installed as Master and subsequently elected Lord Mayor of London. The Company furnished a decorated car with banners and carriages for the Lord Mayor's Show. [62]

1903. Ernest Arthur Ebblewhite was elected Clerk. He remained in office until 1937, and much of the Company's progress during those years was due to his wisdom and energy. [82]

The Company's Charitable Fund was established. [157]

1905. A Warrant dated 9th June was issued by King Edward VII, enabling the Company to continue to bear its traditional Arms and Supporters which were duly exemplified by Heralds College. [57]

1906. "The Gardeners Company's Day" was founded for poor children, and continued until the outbreak of war in 1939. [160]

1908. In recognition of the benefit to the Company of Sir Edward Littleton's Warrant of 1632, the Company petitioned the Lord Mayor to be permitted to make a presentation of flowers, vegetables and herbs on the anniversary of the Warrant. This was granted, and the gift has since been made annually. [68]

1909. The Honorary Freedom was conferred on H.S.H. The Duke of Teck, President of the Royal Botanic Society of London, in recognition of his ten years' association with the work of that Society. [88]

In the Shrieval year of Liveryman R. Slazenger, the Company participated in the Lord Mayor's Show. [63]

1910. The Company petitioned the Court of Aldermen to increase the number of its Liverymen, either by removing the limitation completely or by granting an increase from 60 to 150, and in either case to grant to the Company a higher precedence in the list of Livery Companies. These requests were not approved. [59]

1911. The Company presented Queen Mary with her Coronation bouquet, and a silver gilt flower stand in the form of the Jacobean basket represented in the Company's crest. [92]

On petition to the Court of Aldermen, the limit on the number of Liverymen was increased from 60 to 100. [60]

The Company's connection with the lecture under the will of Thomas Fairchild (d.1729) was revived, and the lecture has since been delivered in Whit Week as part of its annual Guild Service. [185]

The Company paid an official visit to Holland, to study the economic conditions of horticulture, and especially bulb growing. [139]

Further visits to Holland by representatives of the Company occurred in 1950, 1970, 1975, 1978 and 1992. [146, 149, 152, 154]

1912. The Company supported an exhibition by the Royal Horticultural Society, which was opened by King George V. [160]

1913. A Common Hall Fund was set up. [173]

In June the Master and Clerk in personal audience presented to Queen Mary a replica of her Coronation bouquet. This presentation was made annually thereafter until the death of Queen Mary, but only in some years personally. [97]

The Company paid an official visit to Belgium. [139]

Further visits to Belgium by representatives of the Company occurred in 1931 and 1955, in addition to the regular visits to the Floralies Gantoises. [144, 147]

1914. The Company paid an official visit to France. [140]

Further visits to France by representatives of the Company occurred in 1920, 1959 and 1987. [144, 147, 153]

1915. The Court of Aldermen authorised an increase in the Livery from 100 to 160. [60]

1917. Sir Charles Hanson and George Rowland Blades being Lord Mayor and Sheriff respectively, the Company took part in the Lord Mayor's Show. [63]

1919. The Immediate Past Master and the Clerk visited Belgium, to investigate the effects of the War on horticulture. As a result, a sum of over £3,000 was raised by the Company. [142]

1920. The Court of Aldermen authorised an increase in the Livery from 160 to 250, which remains the limit today. [60]

1921. The office of Almoner was created. [162]

1923. The Company provided the bouquet on the marriage of The Lady Elizabeth Bowes-Lyon (now the Queen Mother) with the Duke of York. [99]

Similar bouquets were presented on the marriages of Princess Marina in 1934, the Duchess of Gloucester in 1935, Princess Elizabeth (now the Queen) in 1947, Princess Margaret in 1960, the Duchess of Kent in 1961, and Princess Alexandra in 1963. [99, 100]

This being the Shrieval year of Mr. (later Sir) Thomas Dron, the Company took part in the Lord Mayor's Show. [63]

1925. This being the Shrieval year of both Francis Agar and Charles Albert Batho, the Company took part in the Lord Mayor's Show with two landaus and the band of the 1st London Division Royal Engineers. [63]

1926. Alderman Sir George Rowland Blades, Bt. (later Lord Ebbisham) was elected Lord Mayor of London, the first in modern times whose Mother Company was the Gardeners Company. The Company took part in the Lord Mayor's Show in two motor landaulettes, decorated with streamers and rosettes in its colours, together with the band of the 1st London Division Royal Engineers. [64]

1933. The Honorary Freedom of the Company was conferred on Princess Mary, the Princess Royal. [101]

The Company was represented for the first time at the Floralies Gantoises (the Ghent Floralies). [145]

1935. The Honorary Freedom of the Company was conferred on Edward, Prince of Wales (later the Duke of Windsor). [102]

1936. In the Mayoralty of Past Master Sir George Broadbridge, the Company participated in the Lord Mayor's Show. [65]

At Company Dinners, the first appearance of "Gardeners' Pride". [180]

1937. The Company provided the Coronation bouquet of Queen Elizabeth (now the Queen Mother). As in the previous reign, an annual presentation has since been made on the anniversary of the Coronation, in some years by the Master and Wardens in personal audience. [97]

1943. E.A. Ebblewhite presented to the Company its Ceremonial Spade. [191]

1948. Past Master John Weir presented to the Company its Golden Book, to replace that donated by him in 1933 which had been destroyed by enemy action. [192]

The Cranfield collection of horticultural books was purchased, which considerably enhanced the Company's library. [197]

1949. The Company's Window Box Competition began, which by the 1960s had become greatly expanded into the "Flowers in the City" campaign. [118]

1950. Representatives of the Company visited Holland, during which the Master, Wardens and Clerk were received at Soestdijk Palace by Queen Juliana, who signed the Golden Book and was admitted to the Honorary Freedom of the Company. [146]

The Wardens and the Clerk attended the Annual Commemoration at Wye College, the beginning of a close association. [130, 166]

1950s. The Company gave many cups to local horticultural societies within its Charter area (six miles from St. Paul's), accompanied by grants to their prize funds – although there were many earlier examples from 1909, and extensively between the World Wars. [163]

1951. On the creation by the City Corporation of The Festival Garden – St. Paul's Garden – the three bronze heads for the fountains were given by the Company. [118]

1952. The Gardeners Royal Benevolent Institution (later Society) opened a residential home. The Company endowed a bed and afterwards made regular grants, and has since continued its support for the new home (Red Oaks, opened in 1973). [158]

1953. The Company presented to Queen Elizabeth II the Coronation bouquet which she carried in the procession to Westminster Abbey.[94]

1954. The Queen was graciously pleased to consent to an annual presentation of flowers on each anniversary of her Coronation, in some years by the Master and Wardens in personal audience. [98]

Inauguration of the London Teaching Hospitals Gardens Competition. [125]

Representatives of the Company visited Spalding at the invitation of the Tulip Time Committee. The visit resulted in the Company providing a silver trophy, awarded annually from 1956, "to the person, company or organisation who in the opinion of the committee had made the most outstanding contribution to Tulip Time over the year." The Company has continued to visit Spalding annually. [130]

Alderman H.W. Seymour Howard, Master of the Company in 1947, was elected Lord Mayor and the Company participated in the Lord Mayor's Show. [66]

1955. Inauguration of the London Non-Teaching Hospitals Gardens Competition. [125]
Representatives of the Company visited the Floralies Gantoises. [147]

1959. Inauguration of the London Church Gardens Competition. [126]

1960. Representatives of the Company visited Belgium for the opening of the Floralies Gantoises by King Baudouin, in the course of which His Majesty signed the Company's Golden Book. [147]

1962. The Honorary Freedom of the Company was conferred on King Baudouin of Belgium at the Palace of Laeken. [148]

1963. The Honorary Freedom of the Company was conferred on the Duke and Duchess of Gloucester, and the Duke was also admitted as an Honorary Liveryman. [103]

1964. Arnold F. Steele, Clerk to the Company from 1947 to 1958, published his book *The Worshipful Company of Gardeners of London: A History of its Revival 1890-1960* .[3]

1965. Representatives of the Company visited the Floralies Gantoises. [149]
The Company participated in the Lord Mayor's Show, jointly with the Metropolitan Public Gardens Association. [67]

1966. In the Shrieval year of Past Master Edward Howard, the Company participated in the Lord Mayor's Show. [67]

1967. First appointment of Stewards for the Master and Wardens. [179]

1968. A scheme was launched whereby the Company funded certificates to be awarded by horticultural associations, and this is still administered by the Gardeners Royal Benevolent Society on behalf of that Society and the Royal Gardeners Orphan Fund. [165]

1969. The Company provided for the Lord Mayor's Show a floral float, the theme of which was "Come to the City and See the Flowers". [67]

1970. Representatives of the Company visited Belgium for the opening of the Floralies Gantoises by King Baudouin, in the course of which Queen Fabiola added her signature to that of her husband in the Company's Golden Book. [149]

1971. Representatives of the Company visited Portugal, during which the Honorary Freedom of the Company was conferred on the President, H.E. Contra-Almirante Americo Deus Rodrigues Thomaz. [152]

The Company was accorded the right of planting its first official garden in the City of London in modern times, the Southern Garden of St. Dunstan in the East. [71]

The Honorary Freedom of the Company was conferred on King Gustav VI Adolf of Sweden. [90]

Sir Edward Howard, Bt., Master of the Company in 1961, was elected Lord Mayor of London. In honour of this the Company took part in the Lord Mayor's Show with a landau and a floral float. [67]

1972. The Company had the honour of providing part of the floral decorations at Barnwell Manor, on the occasion of the marriage of Prince Richard of Gloucester with Miss Brigitte van Deurs. [104]

The Master, accompanied by the Wardens and the Clerk, was received in audience by H.M. The Queen at Buckingham Palace on the occasion of her Silver Wedding. An exact replica of her wedding bouquet was presented to Her Majesty. [104]

1973. The Company had the honour of providing a floral set piece for the wedding breakfast at Buckingham Palace, on the occasion of the marriage of Princess Anne (now the Princess Royal) with Captain Mark Phillips. [104]

Representatives of the Company visited Germany, to study the vineyards of the Rhine. [152]

1974. The Court of Assistants passed a Resolution to the effect that the Court would welcome the Admission of ladies to the Livery. [76]

In the spirit of that Resolution and having regard to her lifelong interest in gardening, Princess Alice, Duchess of Gloucester was invited to become the first lady Liveryman of the Company. Her Royal Highness was invested with the Livery at a Court Meeting at Innholders Hall. [77]

1975. Representatives of the Company visited the Floralies Gantoises, in the course of which the Honorary Freedom of the Company was conferred on Queen Fabiola at Laeken Palace. [149]

1977. On the occasion of the Silver Jubilee of Queen Elizabeth II, the Master and Wardens presented a bouquet to Her Majesty in the garden of St. Paul's Cathedral. To commemorate the Silver Jubilee, the Master planted a magnolia tree in the garden of Queen Elizabeth the Queen Mother at Clarence House. [105]

1978. "The Gardeners' March" was composed. [180]

1979. The St. Paul's Cathedral Flower Committee was inaugurated, and since then the Company has subsidised festival flowers in the Cathedral. [128]

The City Flower Show was held for the first time, and included a Company stand. This was in the Royal Exchange, but has since become an annual September event in Guildhall. [121]

1980. Representatives of the Company visited the Floralies Gantoises. Through the efforts of the Company, Britain had an exhibit for the first time for many years, which received third prize in the international section. [150]

The Company participated with some forty Livery Companies in the Lord Mayor's Show, celebrating the theme "Livery, Leadership and Youth". [67]

1981. The Company was the principal provider of flowers for the decoration of St. Paul's Cathedral on 29th July, arranged by members of the Flower Committee on the occasion of the marriage of the Prince of Wales with Lady Diana Spencer. The Company also had the privilege of providing Lady Diana's wedding bouquet. [105]

To celebrate the Shrievalty of Liveryman Lady Donaldson, the Company participated in the Lord Mayor's Show. [67]

A Court Luncheon was held at the Savile Club to celebrate the admission of John Tradescant the Younger as a Freeman of the Company on 19th December 1634. The luncheon, now known as the Tradescant Lunch, has since been held by the Court each December. [137]

1982. At the invitation of The Garden Club of Virginia, members of the Company visited Richmond, Charlottesville, Williamsburg and other parts of Virginia, and could be said to have retraced the steps of John Tradescant the Younger, who made three visits to Virginia in the seventeenth century. [153]

1983. H.M. Queen Elizabeth the Queen Mother opened the Tradescant Garden, adjoining the Museum of Garden History in Lambeth, with which the Company had been associated. [136]

Dame Mary Donaldson, G.B.E., Liveryman, became the first lady Lord Mayor of London, and the Company participated in the Lord Mayor's Show with a coach flanked by tractors with decorated trailers. The Company arranged for a new rose to be named "Mary Donaldson" and presented to the Lord Mayor. [67]

1984. Representatives of the Company visited private gardens and nurseries in Jersey, as well as Government House. [132]

[14]

1985. Representatives of the Company visited the Floralies Gantoises. [151]

1986. On the occasion of the marriage of Prince Andrew (now the Duke of York) with Miss Sarah Ferguson, the Company presented a bouquet in the form of the initial "S". [106]

1987. The Honorary Freedom of the Company was conferred on Charles, Prince of Wales, who was also admitted as an Honorary Liveryman. [106]

1988. Representatives of the Company visited Italy, to study gardens near the North Italian lakes. [153]

Representatives of the Company visited the Glasgow Garden Festival, and were entertained by the Incorporation of Gardeners of Glasgow, with whom the Company has close links. In 1926 the Clerk had referred to his "discovery" of the Incorporation, and reported that its history and objects were similar to those of the Company. [155]

1990. Representatives of the Company visited the Floralies Gantoises, where the British exhibit won a special award from the Royal Belgian Horticultural Society. [152]

The recent increase in the number of Liverymen and Freemen closely involved in horticulture and gardening – both professionals and amateurs – enabled the Company to set up a Craft Committee and to offer other charities help and advice on garden projects, for which the Company provides assistance from its charitable funds. [137]

1992. The Company had the privilege of providing H.M. The Queen with a basket of British spring flowers on the 40th anniversary of her accession. [99]

Representatives of the Company visited the Floriade in Holland. A number of Liverymen were members of the working group for the British Garden at Zoetermeer, which won the premier award for outdoor exhibits. [154]

The Company participated in the Lord Mayor's Show of Sir Francis McWilliams, the Lady Mayoress being a Liveryman of the Company. [68]

CHAPTER 2

The Guilds and the City

The purpose of this Chapter is to provide a brief account of the Livery Companies, their origins and historical development, and the ways in which by time-honoured tradition they have been closely linked with the City of London and its governing body. It seeks to do no more than provide a context in which the succeeding Chapters, on the history and activities of the Worshipful Company of Gardeners, may be placed.

In order to appreciate the links between the Livery Companies and the Corporation of London, it is necessary firstly to understand the composition and nature of the latter. From this it becomes clear that the role of the Livery Companies in the life and governance of the City is of extremely long standing.

The Corporation of London

The Corporation of London is an ancient and unique institution, evolved from mediaeval times and not having changed to any real extent in more than seven hundred years. A Charter was granted by William the Conqueror, and even King John in 1215 bestowed the further concession of permitting the City to elect its own Mayor. To be precise and historically accurate, the Corporation of London consists of "The Mayor and Commonalty and Citizens" of the City.

The Mayor is the Lord Mayor, a title which has been used for many centuries. Before a person can become Lord Mayor, he or she must be elected an Alderman by the voters – an opportunity which does not occur regularly, since there is a fixed number of Aldermen and each is entitled to remain an Alderman until reaching the age of seventy. A person aspiring to the position of Lord Mayor must also have served a year as a Sheriff – of which there are two, changing annually, and candidates do not have to be Aldermen. The Livery Companies have a crucial role to play in the process of selecting a Lord Mayor, for the Liverymen annually elect the two Sheriffs. The Liverymen also annually nominate two candidates as Lord Mayor, from among those Aldermen who have served as Sheriff, with the Court of Aldermen making the final selection.

The Commonalty is the Court of Common Council, the body of elected members which is chaired by the Lord Mayor and is responsible – among other things – for the local government functions of the City in the same way as the Councils of the other thirty-two London Boroughs. The Common

Council today consists of twenty-five Aldermen and 132 Common Councilmen, the latter being subject to annual election by the voters. Since the mid-nineteenth century it has not been necessary for a member of the Common Council to be a Liveryman, but in practice it is usual for this to be the case. At the time of writing all twenty-five Aldermen are Liverymen, and of 132 Common Councilmen fewer than thirty are not Liverymen.

The Citizens are the Freemen of the City, and they are an integral part of the Corporation because all candidates for election to the Common Council must be Freemen. A member of a Livery Company has the right to apply for the Freedom of the City, and this right originates from a fourteenth century Ordinance that decreed that no person should be admitted a Freeman of the City unless he was of some "trade or misterie". Since 1835, however, it has also been possible to obtain the Freedom without the "intervention" of a Livery Company, and many people do so.

There are three modes of admission to the Freedom of the City which, like the Freedom of Livery Companies, can not be taken up until an applicant is twenty-one years of age. Firstly, Admission by *Patrimony* is available to any person born in lawful wedlock to a Freeman, providing that the applicant was born after his or her parent's own admission to the Freedom. Admission by *Apprenticeship* is available to a person who has been apprenticed to a Freeman by customary indentures, at the end of a term of service of not less than four nor more than eight years, provided that proof of faithful service is furnished and the apprentice is between the ages of fourteen and twenty-one. Admission by *Redemption* involves the payment of a small fee, except that persons on the Ward Lists of the City can be admitted free of charge.

Within the Corporation, there are two separate bodies with the power to grant the Freedom by Redemption. The Court of Aldermen considers all applications from persons presented by the Livery Companies, while the Court of Common Council considers those from persons without Livery Companies.

The Guilds or Livery Companies

Turning to the Livery Companies themselves, their Charters are obtained from the monarch but their grant of Livery since 1506 is awarded by the Court of Aldermen. That Court therefore decides whether or not a Company should be granted a Livery, and whether or not an increase in the number of a Company's Liverymen should be permitted, as well as dealing with amendments to a Company's Ordinances and Charters and with all matters connected with the Freedom of the City through a Livery Company. It will be seen in Chapters 3 and 4 that, in some of these respects, the Worshipful

Company of Gardeners was given a somewhat rough ride by the Court of Aldermen over several centuries of its existence, and that difficulties were not fully resolved until the Company's "revival" in 1891.

Membership of a Livery Company involves, in the first instance, being elected as a Freeman of the Company concerned. This is open to both men and women, although women are often known as "Freesisters". The modes of admission are essentially the same as those described above for admission to the Freedom of the City – by Patrimony (on attaining the age of twenty-one, and regardless of the candidate's trade or profession); by Servitude (normally after an apprenticeship of between four and seven years, although today this mode of admission is not significantly used in all Companies); and by Redemption, which since the eighteenth century has been a common practice resulting in many Companies attracting new blood from outside the ranks of their own trades and crafts.

There is also one special category of admission, the Freedom by Presentation, but this is awarded sparingly and without application by the candidate. It is usually reserved for those who have performed special services to the Company, or in some cases for persons whose membership would enhance the Company's prestige. As is clarified in Chapter 7, this is not to be confused with the Honorary Freedom of a Company, which is an extremely high honour rarely bestowed.

From the ranks of Freemen, a member is normally in due course called to the Livery. This can take some considerable time, particularly in those Companies where the number of Liverymen is restricted by their Charters or by decision of the Court of Aldermen. It should also be mentioned that there is no advancement for Freesisters in the case of those Companies which do not permit lady Liverymen, although happily this has not applied to the Gardeners since 1974.

The governing body of a Livery Company consists of its Master, Wardens and Court of Assistants. Depending upon the size of the Livery, a Liveryman can expect (often after many years) to have the opportunity to be elected to the Court of Assistants, from which is selected the Wardens who in most cases progress to the Mastership.

For readers seeking more detail of the fascinating history and practices of Livery Companies in general, several well-researched volumes have been produced over the years. One of these found particularly valuable by the present writer is Jennifer Lang's *Pride Without Prejudice: The Story of London's Guilds & Livery Companies* (Perpetua Press, 1975).

The late Sir Hugh Wontner, writing at the time as the 646th Lord Mayor of London, began his Foreword to Lang's book with the following words. "In no other city in the world is there a group of Companies, founded between the twelfth and the present century, not engaged in commerce, but each representing a different pursuit, occupation or trade, either still or originally carried on within the bounds of (that city). Only the very new Companies, such as the Guild of Air Pilots and Air Navigators, have obviously not been connected with the City, but it is an indication of the prestige attaching to these City Companies that those engaged in entirely modern pursuits, like flying, have sought and obtained permission from the City Fathers to establish a Company similar to the others."

Now, some eighteen years later, the validity of Wontner's words can be seen in the fact that since he wrote them another sixteen Livery Companies have been added to the list.

History of the Livery Companies

There are in 1993 one hundred Livery Companies functioning in the City of London, some of which were known to exist as Guilds for centuries before they received their first Charters from the Crown. The Butchers, for example, did not receive their Charter until 1606, yet John Stow's *Survey of London* (1598) recorded that "in the year 975 A.D. in the Ward of Farringdon, without the city walls, there are situated divers slaughterhouses and a Butchers Hall where the craftsmen meet". An early mention of a London Guild occurred in the case of the Weavers, whose dues to the Crown were recorded in the Exchequer Roll of 1130, and the same Roll refers to the "Goldsmiths of London" as if they were already an organised body. Before the end of the twelfth century the Bakers, Pepperers (later part of the Grocers), Clothworkers and Butchers were also mentioned, and there appear to have been associations of Turners, Cooks and Coopers.

Stories abound of other Guilds, some more fully documented than others, that would appear to demonstrate their extremely early origins, but it has long been accepted that the only reliable and consistent yardstick must be the date of their first Royal Charter. Using this measure, the oldest Livery Company is that of the Weavers (1184).

Nevertheless there is evidence that from even earlier times the various trades and crafts in the City of London formed themselves into Guilds. P.H. Ditchfield, in *The Story of the City Companies* (Foulis, 1926), said that some authorities trace a connection with the Roman Collegia and Sodalitates, but that there is a "fatal gap between the departure of the Roman legions and the coming of the Anglo-Saxon tribes which no historical evidence is able to bridge".

The Anglo-Saxons, when they settled on British soil, probably brought the Guild system with them. These were basically religious fraternities, associated with churches, monasteries and hospitals, and normally restricted to a specific neighbourhood. London crafts and trades were similarly linked with clearly defined areas, such as the Basketmakers in Pudding Lane, the Butchers in Eastcheap and the Drapers in Candlewick. It was therefore a natural transition for the Guilds to devote themselves not only to religious work, but also to encourage and assist the development of their crafts and to define and control standards of workmanship. Each exercised a monopoly in its own trade, which could only be carried out by becoming a member of the Guild.

Thus the Guilds came into being over a long period, and according to Ditchfield an enquiry in 1179 showed that there were no fewer than nineteen of them, but only four were trade Guilds. Some (such as the Weavers and the Saddlers) secured recognition by Royal Charter at an early stage, but others existed for many years before they were Chartered from the fourteenth century onwards. There developed a distinction between the trade Guilds and the craft Guilds, at least in respect of their prosperity – for in the Subsidy Roll of 1319, citizens assessed at the highest rates were trading as Drapers, Mercers, Grocers, Fishmongers, Skinners and Goldsmiths, whereas craftsmen such as Cordwainers, Coopers and Hosiers were less affluent.

The early religious connection is the explanation for the "livery" worn by members, which was based on the hooded robes and gowns worn by the various orders of monks. In due course the members, because of this apparel, were to become known as Liverymen and their associations as Livery Companies. The word "livery" originally meant not only the clothing, but the allowance of food and wine granted to their servants and dependants by the mediaeval monasteries, colleges and principal households. Today's gowns are not unlike those of the mediaeval monks, but the hoods have long since disappeared. As in early times, however, each Livery Company shows that it is a different "order" by the colour and design of its gown.

Embodied in the Charters of the Livery Companies were several legal rights which had a considerable effect upon the standards of their respective crafts, and one of the most important of these was the "power of search". This authorised a Company to inspect the goods handled by its members, and usually carried with it the right to confiscate goods of sub-standard quality or workmanship. Some Companies enjoyed this right in respect only of the City of London, while others had areas extending outside the City or were even able to apply it throughout the whole of England. It was a powerful means of control, and was intended to maintain such high standards that "foreigners" were unable to compete in the trades and crafts – although "foreigner" did not necessarily always have its present day meaning, and often referred simply to those who were not members of the Companies concerned. As well as confiscation of their goods and products, offenders frequently incurred punishment in the pillory and stocks.

On the one hand it could be said that these activities of the Livery Companies were the original "restrictive practices", so greatly criticised in the late twentieth century with its determination to let the market decide. On the other, there can be no doubt that it was a considerable influence upon the development and maintenance of high quality.

A further legal right of the Companies was to fix and control wages, and a strict hierarchy was applied. This ranged from apprentices to members of the Livery, and it must be remembered that this was long before the advent of trade unions. It was a system largely controlled by the master craftsmen and employers for their benefit, rather than in the interests of the lower strata.

Today the prosperity of some at least of the Livery Companies stems from another of their ancient legal rights, the "licence in mortmain", which gave them the right to hold land and property in perpetuity. Many rich Liverymen made gifts and bequests to their Companies in order to provide security for their dependants and heirs, rather than have their houses and lands commandeered by the monarch or the state. Even now, in spite of extensive damage or destruction in the Second World War, the financial security of many Livery Companies can be traced back to their position as unassailable freeholders in the City of London and elsewhere.

Very few of the Guilds received Royal Charters prior to the fifteenth century. They were, however, earlier recognised by the Mayor and Aldermen of the City of London, and had had their Ordinances approved by that body. According to Bryan Pontifex, in *The City of London Livery Companies* (Methuen, 1939), in 1437 the Court of Aldermen promoted an Act of Parliament insisting on all Charters granted to City Companies being presented to it for approval and enrolment.

The City records contain a reference in 1375 to the existence of twelve principal "misteries", but they are not named. It is possible that the composition of this group of pre-eminent Companies was not constant, and there is also no evidence that the order of precedence within the twelve was at that time firmly established. In the fifteenth century, on various ceremonial occasions, the so-called Great Twelve appear in various orders of precedence. Moreover, in the famous dispute-settling adjudication of 1484 that the Skinners and the Merchant Taylors should take precedence over each other in alternate years, it was not specified that they should rank sixth and seventh.

The accepted order of precedence appears to date from 31st January 1516, when the Court of Aldermen laid down an order for the Companies, then numbering forty-eight, so as to regulate their position in processions and for other purposes where seniority needed to be demonstrated. Although since that time there have been some amalgamations of Companies, the list of 1516 formed the basis of that accepted today. As will be seen from Chapter 4, several centuries later the Gardeners Company was ranked sixty-sixth in order of precedence, in spite of some reasoned argument that a higher position should have been accorded.

Today the Great Twelve, with the dates of their Charters, are: the Mercers (1393); Grocers (1345); Drapers (1364); Fishmongers (1364); Goldsmiths (1327); Skinners (1327) and Merchant Taylors (1326) alternately; Haberdashers (1448); Salters (1559); Ironmongers (1454); Vintners (1437); and Clothworkers (1528). The twelfth in the list of 1516, the Shearmen, later amalgamated with the Fullers to form the Clothworkers.

From the fifteenth century onwards, Livery Companies developed in number, power and influence, but there were also enormous financial pressures placed upon them at various stages in their history. Henry VIII, in keeping with his dissolution of the monasteries in the sixteenth century, confiscated monies that the Companies had acquired in support of their religious ceremonies and masses for their dead. The Tudors also saw the Companies as a conveniently organised network through which taxes could be collected from their Liverymen, and further taxes were raised through them for significant national events, whether the monarch was merry-making or war-making.

From the beginning of the seventeenth century a Company petitioning for a Royal Charter had to obtain a licence from the City beforehand, and failure to do so led to difficulties for many Companies including the Gardeners, as will be seen in Chapter 3. There was nevertheless a considerable increase in the number of Livery Companies acquiring Royal Charters, with or without the blessing of the City, for the Stuart Kings found it a convenient way of augmenting the Privy Purse. Taxes also remained a major problem, and Companies were brought almost to ruin by such costly factors as the colonisation of Ulster and the Civil War – to which was added the disaster of the Great Fire of London in 1666.

The health of the Livery Companies was put at an even lower ebb when Charles II, towards the end of his reign, sought to restrict the power of the City of London by transferring the control of the Companies to his nominees. His writ of *Quo Warranto* obliged them to surrender their Charters, or alternatively to prove their right to retain them, and against this pressure the Companies were powerless. It was necessary to pay a fine in order to receive new Charters, but this merely returned to them their time-honoured rights of control over their trades or crafts, whereas their Masters and Wardens were to be the King's men.

This would have proved an effective means whereby the Crown governed the Livery Companies, thereby severely reducing the considerable degree of independence from the Crown that the City of London had enjoyed for centuries, but the course of history was again changed by the death of Charles II in 1685. The policy was not vigorously pursued by his successor, James II, but it was not until the reign of William and Mary from 1689 that the Livery Companies fully recovered their powers.

It must have been a great relief in particular to the thirty-three Companies (including the Gardeners) that had only received their first Charters in the seventeenth century, and whose independence or survival might have been short-lived, as well as to those dating from earlier centuries. It also appears, by giving them a new lease of life, to have inspired them with renewed vigour.

By the eighteenth century, many of the most ancient Companies had weakened or lost their connection with their respective crafts or trades. Scientific and technological developments were making some crafts redundant, or alternatively were turning trades into industries by dramatically expanding the scale and methods of manufacture. There was no possibility, therefore, that the majority of Livery Companies could continue in positions of exclusivity, controlling and restricting activities which were no longer sustainable within the confines of the City of London.

As a result, many new craftsmen were not members of the appropriate Livery Company. Conversely, however, many Liverymen were from outside the crafts, since the system of admission by Patrimony had brought in successive generations who did not necessarily pursue the careers of their forefathers. This had the effect of bringing into the Companies new ideas for future developments which were not always directly craft-related. It also secured the position of many Companies as influential bodies in the City of London and its local government, as members of their Livery were important City figures. Their influence was similarly felt nationally, as until 1832 the privileges of a Liveryman included the right to vote in Parliamentary elections in the City.

There existed, however, a great divide between the rich and the poor Livery Companies. For those like the Mercers, who had been Chartered as early as 1393 and had a history of wealth and property, it was not difficult to continue to attract prominent newcomers to the Livery. Others were less prestigious or lacked the attractions of status and influence, and were also left at a financial disadvantage by the predations of the seventeenth century. Some were in danger of extinction, and indeed for a long period the Gardeners Company was virtually defunct until its revival in 1890.

The late nineteenth century saw a renewed interest and vitality among the Livery Companies. There might have been specific reasons for this in individual cases, sometimes directly related to changes and developments in the crafts from which they originated, and Chapter 4 recounts the circumstances in which new life was breathed into the Gardeners. There was, however, an over-riding factor which affected the Companies in general, and which saw them benefit because they suited the purposes of political expediency.

The rise of Liberalism was seen by the Tory party as a threat to the cherished institutions of England, and great benefit was therefore identified in swelling the ranks of the Livery Companies with those sympathetic to the Tory cause. By purchasing their Freedom in the Companies they could take a strong role in City politics, and this had the effect of expanding membership to such an extent that many Companies had to seek the approval of the Court of Aldermen to increase the number on their Livery.

It can not be suggested that the Livery Companies were themselves pursuing political ends, for they were merely taking understandable advantage of the motives of others and increasing their virility as a result. The Liberals, however, saw the dangers to themselves of what they perceived to be a rising Tory establishment that needed to be stopped in its tracks. Indeed Prime Minister Gladstone himself, in 1884, took direct action by appointing a

Royal Commission to enquire into the activities of the Livery Companies. No doubt to his chagrin, however, the matter backfired when a majority view was reached that the Companies were responsible bodies, managing the funds in their care for charitable purposes and for other socially desirable pursuits.

The attack by Gladstone, and their subsequent vindication, affected the Companies in ways which today can only be conjectural. It inspired them to new heights of activity, but it must also have brought home to them the fact that such attacks could only be based upon ignorance of their functions and motives. If they were seen by outsiders as political organisations, or quaint relics from a mediaeval age, or even as secret societies, then it was surely necessary to rectify such misapprehensions. Thus it was that some good came from Gladstone's persecution, and the Companies entered a new era of greater openness in which they wanted their positive values – whether in developing their crafts, in charitable work or in fields such as education – to be more visible to the general public.

Since 1947, twenty-one new Livery Companies have been formed and others have become incorporated, one of the preliminary steps towards full recognition. Taken as a whole, the Companies can be said to represent the wide range of professions and business interests operating in the City today. Companies such as the Goldsmiths, the Fishmongers, the Gunmakers, the Saddlers and the Vintners still regulate all or part of their traditional trades, and recently formed Livery Companies have tended to restrict their membership to people active in the field they represent. Some ancient Companies have proved themselves to be adaptable to the modern age – for example the Horners, Salters and Fanmakers have successfully embraced the plastics, chemical and air-conditioning industries respectively – while very new Companies such as the Information Technologists, the hundredth, are active in fields which the Liverymen of centuries past could never have imagined.

It is sad, therefore, that today there remains a lack of knowledge about the purposes and relevance of Livery Companies. To many people, these institutions derived from the ancient "crafts and misteries" are still themselves a mystery. They have survived the assaults of Kings and politicians, long ago and in more recent times, but in the minds of many they have survived only as strange bodies steeped in mystique and shrouded in ancient ceremonies and privileges. Their sterling work in today's world is insufficiently appreciated, and it is hoped that later Chapters in this book will play a small part in the necessary demystification, in respect of at least one such ancient yet modern Company.

CHAPTER 3

The Company's Early History

The previous Chapter attempted to place the Worshipful Company of Gardeners in context, by outlining the history of the Guilds and their relationship with the Corporation of London.

There is another context in which the Company could usefully be placed, the history of gardening itself, but that is virtually impossible since the topic is so vast. Many volumes have been written, and it may be of interest to note that the following contributions to the literature have been found useful by the present writer in acquiring a feel for the subject, and an understanding of how and why the Company played its significant role in the development of gardening in this country.

Hon. Alicia Amherst. *A History of Gardening in England.* Quaritch, 1895.

Julia S. Berrall. *The Garden: An Illustrated History from Ancient Egypt to the Present Day.* Thames and Hudson, 1966.

Mireille Galinou (Ed.) *London's Pride: The Glorious History of the Capital's Gardens.* Anaya, 1990.

Miles Hadfield. *A History of British Gardening.* Hutchinson, 1960 and Penguin Books, 1985.

John Harvey. *Early Gardening Catalogues.* Phillimore, 1972.

Blanche Henrey. *British Botanical and Horticultural Literature Before 1800.* 3 vols. Oxford University Press, 1975.

Edward Hyams. *A History of Gardens and Gardening.* Dent, 1971.

Dawn MacLeod. *The Gardener's London: Four Centuries of Gardening, Gardeners and Garden Usage.* Duckworth, 1972.

Ronald Webber. *The Early Horticulturists.* David & Charles, 1968.

Ronald Webber. "London's Market Gardens". In *History Today,* XXIII (12), December 1973.

This Chapter and succeeding Chapters therefore concentrate upon the history of the Company itself, although at various points it is appropriate to refer to aspects of gardening history – particularly in respect of the City of London – where this is useful in explaining the Company's involvement.

Early Gardens in London

London has been noted for its gardens from very early times. William

Fitzstephen, a historian and biographer in the reign of Henry II (1133-89), commented that the London citizens of his day had large and beautiful gardens surrounding their houses. An inquest was held in 1276, on one Adam Schot, who was killed by falling from a pear tree which he was attempting to climb to gather fruit, in the garden of one Laurence in the parish of St. Michael "Paternosterchirche". The value of the pear tree as a deodand was fixed at five shillings, a large sum in those days. In the same year King Edward I ordered pear trees for the Tower garden and for the royal garden at Westminster, which was noted for its profusion of roses and lilies.

The garden of the Earl of Lincoln (whose mansion was afterwards known as Lincoln's Inn) was also remarkable for its produce. The Earl's bailiff's accounts for 1296 show that it produced apples, pears, large nuts and cherries sufficient for the Earl's table. The vegetables grown were onions, garlic, leeks and beans. Hemp was also grown, and the cuttings of the vines were much prized. There were several varieties of pear trees, but the only flowers named are roses.

The Sovereign also had a garden within the City of London, as appears from a record in the eighth year of Edward II, 1315. On 11th June the Court of Aldermen granted to a hermit or anchorite, Sir Gilbert Hardyngham, a hermitage on London Wall near the King's garden.

In 1375, the lease of a garden in Tower Ward stated: "unto John Watlyngtone, serjeant, a garden situate in Tower Ward, near to Londonwal, which John Scot lately held; being between the garden which Geoffrey Puppe holds on the North side, and the garden which William Lambourne holds on the South ... for 30 years ... paying 10s. yearly". This was granted in the 49th year of Edward III by the Mayor (Sir William Walworth), the Aldermen and the Commonalty of London, and although there is no record of the size of the garden, the large rent suggests either that garden ground was difficult to procure in those early times or that the cultivation of garden produce was a profitable occupation.

The official residences at Guildhall, which were occupied by Corporation officers, had gardens attached. On 13th July 1444, Master John Clipstone, "Keper of the Liberary atte Guyldehalle", petitioned the Court of Aldermen "that he may be made so sure of his lyflode, housyng and easement of the gardyn which he hath for that occupacion atte this day, that he be not hereafter putte away therefro ne noo part thereoff". It is gratifying to know that the Court, in consideration of Clipstone's merits and diligence, duly granted his request.

The Bridge House, near St. Olave's Church in Southwark, possessed a fine garden with an arbour, fountain and ponds, which was the scene of many an entertainment at which the Mayor, Aldermen and other distinguished guests refreshed themselves after the annual auditing of the Bridge Master's accounts. The cost of such a feast in 1423 was £4 19s. 6d.

Apart from the extensive and well-kept gardens attached to religious houses in the City, such as the Charterhouse, most of the Livery Company halls had gardens belonging to them. Those of the Drapers and Grocers, and the garden at Girdlers Hall with its famous mulberry tree, were of particular note. The Merchant Taylors' garden stretched from Threadneedle Street to Cornhill, and an account of 1572 mentioned a "bowllynge alley, terras, erbes for the garden and for furnishing of knottes". Some details of the expenditure of a Company are provided by the records of the Pewterers, who paid 39s.3d. in 1486-87 for the construction of a frame for their highly prized vine. This expense appears actually to have been borne by Walter Walsh, the senior Warden for that year, who added the following note to the account:

"Shewing vnto you all my Gode and loving Brethyrn as Tuchyng of all this Cosste tht is done ffor helpe and comfort of you and so all apon the seyd vyne I yevyde you all ffrely and God ys Blessing and myne".

As an appendix to the account there is a list of the expenses of laying out the garden and bowling green attached to the Hall, which again appear to have been borne by the same generous donor.

On the question of market gardeners in the City, one of the few to be mentioned by name was one Cawsway in the reign of Henry VIII (1509-1547). John Stow's *Survey of London* (1598) mentions that three brothers called Owen had taken over a field in Houndsditch for a foundry, and that the part they did not require had been made into a garden by Cawsway who "served the market with herbs and roots". Stow also refers to a garden at the Minories, near Tower Hill, which had originally belonged to a nunnery of the order of St. Clare and had been taken over by Henry VIII in 1539. Other evidence of market gardening in or near the City is found in the Gardeners Company's own records, which show that John Markham (Upper Warden in 1605 and Master in 1607) was a market gardener in Clerkenwell and that his sons, Moses and Tobias, carried on the business; and that Thomas Oaker was a market gardener in Shoreditch.

In those days, many of the religious orders had garden land. The Greyfriars, for example, had a large space extending from Newgate to St.

Martin-le-Grand, and the land of St. Helen's was at the Bishopsgate end of St. Mary Axe. The Austin Friars had a garden enclosed on one side by London Wall, covering the area from there to Lothbury, Broad Street and Coleman Street. Such gardens satisfied the needs of the monks for flowers, vegetables and fruit, and any surplus was sold in the markets.

The Petition of 1345

The ancient Company of Gardeners has experienced varying fortunes in the course of its long career. Little enterprise appears to have been shown by its founders in the advancement of gardening as an industry, and the jealousy felt by English craftsmen against "foreigners" was strongly shared by the Gardeners Company of London. These prejudices, embodied in national legislation and in the Ordinances of the Company, retarded the introduction of new and improved methods of cultivation. No master was permitted to employ a journeyman who had not been apprenticed to a Freeman of the Company, and the number of each Freeman's apprentices was strictly limited.

The first record in the archives of the Corporation of London relating to a Guild of Gardeners is dated 24th August 1345 when, in the reign of Edward III, a petition was presented to John Hamond, Mayor, by the Gardeners of the Earls, Barons and Bishops and of the Citizens of the City of London. The purpose was "to suffer and to maintain that the said gardeners may stand in peace in the same place where they have been wont in times of old; in front of the Church of St. Austin, at the side of the gate of St. Paul's Churchyard in London: there to sell the garden produce of their said masters, and make their profit, as heretofore they have been in their wont to do; seeing that they have never heretofore been in their said place molested, and that as they assert, they cannot serve the commonalty, nor yet their masters as they were wont to do: – as to the which they pray for redress".

St. Austin's or Augustin's Church is on the north side of Watling Street and the east side of Old Change, near the east end of St. Paul's Cathedral. It was rebuilt after the Great Fire of London (1666), the church of St. Faith being united to it.

It is curious that the petitioners did not include the gardeners of the monastic foundations, which were so numerous within the City. The reason for this was probably that the produce of their gardens was little more than sufficed for the needs of the religious communities. The Earls, Barons and Bishops, on the other hand, had town mansions in the City and its suburbs, the gardens of which were maintained at considerable cost and must have proved a notable embellishment to the City.

The petition was considered by the Mayor and several Aldermen, including Roger de Depham, Simon Fraunceys and John de Caustone, assembled in the Chamber of Guildhall. They resolved, however, that "the place aforesaid ... is such a nuisance to the Priests who are singing Matins and Mass in the church of St. Austin, and to others both clerks and laymen, in prayers and orison there serving God, as also to other persons passing there both on foot and horseback; as well as to the people dwelling in the houses of reputable persons there, who by the scurrility, clamour, and nuisance of the gardeners and their servants there selling pulse, cherries, vegetables, and other wares to their trade pertaining, are daily disturbed...".

As a result it was ordered that "the gardeners of the City, as well aliens as freemen, who sell their wares aforesaid in the City, should have, as their place, the space between the south gate of the Churchyard of the said church and the garden wall of the Friars Preachers at Baynard's Castle, in the said city: and so they should sell their wares aforesaid in the place by the said Mayor and Aldermen thus appointed for them, and nowhere else". This order apparently did not affect the sellers of fruit, leeks, onions and garlic, whose stations continued to be kept in West Cheap (Cheapside) and on Cornhill.

Thus the Mayor and Aldermen arrived at a pragmatic solution to the problem by moving the gardeners to a new station, where they doubtless soon secured a successful trade. It is probable, however, that some of their former business was lost as a result of their removal from the great stream of traffic coming into the City from its western entrance at Ludgate.

The Gardeners continued to exist for centuries as a fellowship. In addition, the large immigration of Flemings and Frenchmen in the beginning of the sixteenth century gave a great impetus to the art of gardening in England, and surnames such as Lambert, Cambrey, Vanhee, Avis and Campion (which appeared in the Company's records in the seventeenth century) probably belonged to the descendants of some of these immigrants.

The First Royal Charter

The records of the Gardeners between 1345 and 1605, when they were incorporated by the Royal Charter of King James I of 18th September 1605 as "The Master, Wardens, Assistants and Commonalty of the Company of the Gardeners of London", do not appear to have survived.

At the time of the incorporation of the Company the word "gardener" had a very wide meaning, and embraced such trades and occupations as botanist, florist, forester, fruiterer, fruit-grower, garden implement dealer, greengrocer, herbalist, horticultural sundriesman, horticulturist, landscape gardener, market gardener, nurseryman, plant merchant, seedsman and sower.

A Company or Society of Fruiterers existed in London before 1605, and had probably become a fellowship out of the "Free Gardeners" which had existed since the reign of Edward III. They were incorporated in 1606, and became known as "The Master, Wardens and Commonalty of the Mystery of Fruiterers of London", but their records went back to 1292 when "Gerin the Fruter" was selling fruit. The first members of the incorporated Guild were fruiterers or sellers of fruit in the City of London and suburbs, and they were entrusted with the duty of victualling and serving the citizens with good and wholesome fruit. It is nevertheless clear that the Gardeners, who were incorporated five months earlier, were selling fruit in the London markets and continued to do so until after the restoration of Charles II. William Clarke, the first Renter Warden of the Fruiterers Company, was probably that same William Clarke who was a member of the Court of the Gardeners Company in 1616.

The preamble to the Gardeners' first Charter sets out the operations controlled by the Company as "the trade, crafte, or misterie of Gardening, planting, grafting, setting, sowing, cutting, arboring, rocking, mounting, covering, fencing and removing of plantes, herbes, seedes, fruites, trees, stocks, setts, and of contryving the conveyances to the same belonging". It also states that certain ignorant and unskilful persons who had taken upon themselves to practice the said trade, not having been apprenticed thereto, had sold dead and corrupt plants, seeds, stocks and trees. To prevent these abuses the gardeners in the City of London and within six miles thereof were incorporated under the above style into one body politic, with powers to plead and be impleaded, to acquire and demise lands, to have a Common Seal and to make Ordinances for their government.

These powers were to be exercised under a Master, two Wardens and twelve Assistants. Thomas Young was appointed as the first Master, and John Markham and Thomas Worrall (or Morrall) the first Wardens. The twelve Assistants were Henry Banburye, Robert Heechcock, Mark Hench, Richard Martyn, John Mortimer, Thomas Weston, William Barbor, John Richardes, John Heyward, John Tucker, Richard White and Bartholomew Lambert (or Lumbert).

It is of interest that not only did the Charter contain the usual reservation to the Sovereign of the power to revoke it if at any time "it shall be justly and truly found by experience and so lawfully proved that this our grant shall be inconvenient and not fit to be continued any longer", but that it could also be revoked upon a certificate in writing to that effect by the Lord Mayor and Court of Aldermen given to the Lord Chancellor or Lord Keeper of the Great Seal of England and enrolled in the Court of Chancery. So great were the powers of the City, in whose Chamber the Charter was duly enrolled.

The Ordinances of 1606

On 1st July 1606 the Ordinances for the government of the Company were approved by the Lord Chancellor, the Lord Treasurer and the Lord Chief Justice of Common Pleas, in pursuance of the Ordinances of Corporations Act 1503. These were in great detail (thirty-nine items in all), but perhaps the most important was that which created a Livery of the Company, to membership of which the Court could call any Freeman of the Company upon payment of 6s.8d. "towards the buying of some plate and other necessaries for the use of the Company", and of 3s.4d. to the Clerk and one shilling to the Beadle – refusal to pay these sums being punished by a fine of 26s.8d. Refusal to serve on the Livery was punishable by a fine of five marks.

The Ordinances limited the number of apprentices who could be serving at the same time to four each for the Master and the Wardens, three for members of the Livery and two for Freemen, and prohibited a time-expired apprentice from working for anyone not a member of the Company for seven years unless authorised by the Court. There was also a prohibition against anyone not a member of the Company carrying on the "art or mystery of gardening" within the Company's Charter area.

The Ordinances provided for "quarterage" payments by members of six pence per quarter. Quarterly Courts were held, beginning at the early hour of 8 a.m. in summer and 9 a.m. in winter; a fine of four pence was imposed upon every latecomer, and anyone leaving the Court without permission was fined 2s.6d. Each Liveryman was required to come in his livery to the burial of any Liveryman or his wife within the City or six miles thereof, and was forbidden to leave before the rest under a penalty of 3s.4d. The Beadle was to be paid twelve pence by the executors of the deceased, for summoning members of the Livery to attend.

Freemen and Liverymen also incurred penalties if they privately or openly chose to "revile or misuse with evil speeches or words of reproach" the Master, Wardens or Court, or if they showed disobedience to those officers or sat in a Court or Common Hall "not in decent apparel".

The approval of the Court of Aldermen to the Ordinances was needed, and there is no record that this was applied for at the time. At any rate it was not forthcoming if applied for, possibly because the Company did not apply to that Court for approval of its action in 1605 in petitioning the King for a Royal Charter before taking that step.

The Second Royal Charter

For some years the Company carried on under the Charter, but it does not seem to have been altogether satisfactory as the powers granted proved insufficient to enable them to repress the specified deceits and disorders.

In 1616 the Company decided to apply to the Crown for more ample authority, and petitioned the King for a renewal of the Charter, "with amendment of those defects and with such other necessary provisions as" the King should "think most fit and convenient". This was granted on 9th November 1616, and it increased the Court from twelve to twenty-four Assistants, and prohibited any person inhabiting the City or within six miles thereof ("other than such of our subjects as shall garden for their own household use and private spending") from using or exercising the "art or mystery of gardening" within that area "either in places privileged or not privileged" without the licence of the Company.

It further forbade any person not a member of the Company from selling garden produce except at such accustomed times and places as the foreign bakers and other "foreigners", not Freemen of the City, sold their wares. This was upon pain of forfeiture of the goods sold, such forfeitures to be distributed amongst the poor of the place where made. It also gave the Company for the first time powers of search and seizure of "unwholesome dry rotten deceitful and unprofitable wares", within the area of the Company's chartered activities. This was the main object of the second Charter, the Sovereign "desiring nothing more than the general good and welfare of our loving Subjects and that all deceits sleights and ill practices of what sort so ever may be as much as in Us is subverted and taken away".

In 1618 the members, with the consent of the Court of Chancery, incurred a tax of three hundred pounds to cover the cost of the second Charter and its attendant legal costs.

The Company now had ample powers of self-government, and some control over the trade. They were not, however, in favour with the City authorities, and there still remained the need to obtain the approval of the Court of Aldermen to the Livery constituted by the Ordinances of 1606. This would procure for the Gardeners complete powers to regulate their craft, and full admission to the status and privileges of a duly constituted trade Guild of the City of London. It is not clear how the misunderstanding between the Gardeners and the Court of Aldermen arose, and it probably stemmed either from the opposition of other crafts to their incorporation or from disapproval of the Company's action in approaching the King for a Charter without the sanction of the Court of Aldermen.

In the event, the Company decided to approach the Aldermen by seeking the intervention of King James himself. This was effected on 20th May 1617, when Sir Robert Naunton, the King's Principal Secretary of State, wrote from Holyrood House to the Lord Mayor. He stated that the King, having incorporated the Company of Gardeners and being solicited by them to give his Royal recommendation to the City, had directed him to state that as their admission to the Freedom could be no way more prejudicial to the City than that of the other Companies which had been voluntarily accorded by the City, but would rather tend to the reformation of any disorders amongst them and an increase of regular obedience, he requested that the entire Company might be admitted, or at least as many as carried on their trade and dwelt within the City or within two miles thereof. Should any inconvenience of importunity induce the Lord Mayor to the contrary, His Majesty desired to be forthwith informed fully thereof.

Armed with this recommendation, the Company presented a petition to the Lord Mayor in the following terms:

To the right honorable the Lord Maior of the Cittie of London, and to the right Wortt the Aldermen and Common Councell of the same.

The humble petition of the Maister Wardens and Assistants of the Companie of Gardeners London.

Humblie beseechinge that yee will the rather for the reasons and inducements heere vnder written, be pleased, that such of their said Corporation as dwell in London, or within one or two miles onelie of the same trade Maie bee admitted into the ffreedomme of this most honorable Cittie, for which they shall accordinge to theire dueties praie for ye ever florishinge estate of the same &c.

The Inducements are these.

1. It appears by the Records of the Cittie that there were free Gardiners of London verie many yeares sithence.
2. The letters pattents of theire corporation, dated in the thirde yere of his Maiesties raigne that nowe is, were then inrolled in the Chamber of London.
3. Some of theire Corporation were then sworne freemenn of the cittie, when they were so incorporated.

4. They shall contribute towardes all Taxes and Levies of ye Cittie.
5. They shalbe subiect to all the Orders and Ordinaunces of the Cittie for the exercise of theire Trade, and the price of their daielie laboures And they are further willinge, that the Cittie shall assesse the price of theire daies workinge from tyme to tyme.
6. The freedome gives to them noe priviledge or libertie which they had not before concerninge the exercise of their trade, but makes them subiect to the orderinge of the Cittie, howe farr, and in what manner they shall vse the liberties which the kinge hath graunted vnto them for the best good of the cittie.
7. They can hurte noe Companie in London, for theire Life is altogether in the ffieldes or Gardens And so desirous of Libertie and Ayer, that they will not be tied to a Shopp, nor, are they capeable of anie other trade.
8. They desire not (neither can ye freedome give them power) to restraine any forreyners to bringe into the Cittie anie such comodities as they sell, for the fundamentall lawes of this land give to all men whatsoever, libertie soe to doe in regard that they bring victuall wholesome and according to the lawes.
9. They take awaie the dunge and noysomnes of the cittie.
10. They imploye thowsandes of poore people, ould menn, women and children, in sellinge of theire Commodities, in weedinge in gatheringe of Stones &c., which would be otherwise verie burdensome to the cittie, and suburbes thereof.
11 They desire the freedome but for such onelie which dwell within one or two miles of the cittie, beinge but fewe, whereas they are incorporated for vj miles compasse about the cittie.
12. The cittie hath graunted the like formerlie and this is the least preiudiciall to them of anie yt ever they graunted.
13. The Companie of Gardiners will vndertake that yf they maie be admitted accordinglie, the prizes of anie thing which they sell, shall rather heereafter fall then exceede the prizes which they have formerlie borne, according to the disposition of the seasons.

The City authorities, however, did not see fit to comply with the prayer of the petition until 1659, and then only in part.

By 1622 the membership of the Company had reached five hundred, and in that year Court of Chancery proceedings were started against the Master (John Grene), Wardens (James Burley and Thomas Newman) and the Court of Assistants. The action was brought by Thomas Cambrey, John Dixon, John Mold, Richard Melton, Thomas Mason, and thirty-three other "poor gardeners", who complained of certain abuses and of the levying of money. The case lasted until the end of the following year, at a cost of over four hundred pounds, and in settlement the Company agreed that only such of their Freemen as were "on the Livery" should be summoned to meetings.

From about the 1630s meetings were held in Freemasons Hall, later Masons Hall in Masons Avenue, for which an annual rent of ten pounds was paid. This continued until Christmas 1665, when the Company moved to Joiners Hall at an annual rent of eight pounds, but both Halls were destroyed in the following year in the Great Fire of London. Most of the Company's records were lost, though happily the two Royal Charters and a few manuscripts were preserved.

Sir Edward Littleton's Warrant

The next event of interest was on 29th June 1632, when Sir Edward Littleton, Recorder of London, issued a Warrant to "All Bailiffs, Constables, Headboroughs and all other His Majesty's Officers and Ministers within the City of London and Counties of Middlesex, Surrey, Kent and Essex".

It appears from the preamble that the need for Littleton's Warrant arose from the old story of "divers stubborn headstrong and wilful persons ... which do use the said trade Craft and Mystery of Gardening" in contempt of the Company's Charters, and who obstinately refused to be "ordered, guided and governed by the Master and Wardens".

Littleton's Warrant directed those officers to whom it was addressed to aid and assist the bearer in the apprehension of the culprits and to bring them before the Recorder or some other Justice of the Peace, so that there might be taken security with sufficient sureties for their personal appearance before the Master and Wardens at their Common Hall to answer their contempts and disobedience.

The Warrant was of great service to the Company and continued in force until 1640, when Littleton became Lord Chancellor, but it was not renewed by his successor and Littleton died in 1645.

While it remained in force, however, the Warrant was seen as official support for the maintenance of a "closed shop" for the members of the Gardeners Company. In 1633, they were able to refuse membership to the gardeners of Fulham, Kensington and Chelsea, on the grounds that they were really only husbandmen, and had not served the apprenticeship required by the Company. The Company was uncomplimentary toward those who "pretend themselves to be Market Gardeners and to furnish the Market with Eatables", and who "take a piece of Ground, but for want of Judgement how to crop and manure the same as requisite, they in a few years run out of their Stock of ready Money, disappoint their Landlords of their Rents and leave the ground in a worse condition than they found it".

The Royal Proclamation of 1634

On 3rd December 1634, King Charles I issued a Proclamation "for reformation of the many abuses committed against the Corporation of Gardners". This referred not only to competition from non-members of the Company, but also said that "some of the said Company are become contemptuous, refusing to observe those things that conduce to their publike welfare", and others had commenced and threatened to commence divers suits against the Company for executing their Ordinances by confiscating bad stock and punishing offenders.

This Proclamation commanded "that no person or persons whatsoever, whether Denizon or Stranger, not having served as Apprentice or Apprentices, to a Freeman of the said Company, by the space of seven yeares, and not having beene by them admitted into their Societie, do henceforth presume to take upon him or them, the Art or Science of Gardening" within the Company's Charter area nor "offer any discouragement, or opposition to the said Company, for search by them duely made, or for taking away, cutting, burning, or destroying of any dead, corrupt, unwholesome and bad plants". It also enjoined all Freemen of the Company to observe and perform the provisions of the Letters Patent and Ordinances, and required the Master and Wardens to admit satisfactory apprentices to the Freedom. Finally, it commanded the Lord Mayor and the Justices of the City and of the four Counties mentioned in the Recorder's Warrant "to be aiding, helping, and assisting to the said Master, Wardens, and Company".

The Recorder's Warrant of 1632 and the Royal Proclamation of 1634 seem to have stemmed the unfair competition from which the Company had suffered, as well as materially increasing its prosperity. In fact by 1649 members of the Company maintained large market gardens outside the City on the south bank near Tower Bridge, and employed 1,500 men, women and children in addition to four hundred apprentices, the land being divided amongst the members with a maximum of ten acres for each.

Then in 1650 there was a significant example of the Company asserting its privileged position, by taking action in the Mayor's Court against one Rowland and other gardeners acting in contempt of the Company. These unqualified men sold "one fruit for another", dealt in "corrupt and unwholesome trees, plants, seeds and stocks", and sold "ordinary trees and flowers for extraordinary". This was settled in 1651 in the Company's favour, on an undertaking not to prejudice the City by engrossing etc., and on promising to "admit them that sow" to the Freedom in the same way as apprentices. The term "engrossing" at that time referred to the practice of buying up the whole or the majority of a commodity for the purpose of "regrating" – that is, selling at an unreasonable profit as a result of cornering the market.

The site of the activities of members of the Company was changed by the City Corporation from time to time down the years. We have seen how in 1345 they were ousted, apparently for no good reason, from the front of St. Austin's Church. In 1659 there is a record that the City Lands Committee leased to the Company its "usual place and standing" in the new Herb Market in St. Paul's Churchyard (probably the site assigned to the Fellowship in 1345), and removed the costermongers who had been obstructing the passages there. The Gardeners gave up their morning standing in Gracechurch Street and their stalls in Cheapside, where they had sold fruit, flowers, herbs, roots, plants and other garden commodities.

In 1660 the Court of Aldermen removed the Company's markets to Aldersgate Street and Broad Street, but the latter was soon given up as inconvenient. The former was similarly not a bed of roses, as in 1661 the Court of the Company resolved to petition against the "costermongers hagglers forestallers and other rude people" who interfered with its Aldersgate Street market, and against the "foreign" gardeners who had set up a rival fruit and vegetable market in Gracechurch Street.

After consideration, in 1662 the Court of Aldermen allowed the Company "and other country people" to retain the daily use of Aldersgate Street market from 4 a.m. to 7 p.m. in summer and from 6 a.m. to 5 p.m. in winter. They were to stand in two rows on both sides of the street – the Gardeners and their widows next to Aldersgate; the other country people (with herbs, fruits, flowers, roots, etc.) next to them; the Fruiterers and costermongers next to them again; and the carts and wagons (with turnips, carrots, beans, peascods, etc.) between the Half Moon Tavern and the Barbican. The annual charge for keeping the market clean was fixed at ten shillings per standing of six square feet for every "Incorporated Gardener", and for others one penny per day with two pence for each cart.

Even in those days the problem of traffic congestion seems to have worried the Corporation, as one paragraph of the report lays down "That no person whatsoever that shall bring herbs roots or fruits or other commodities to their several standing in the market in wagons or carts shall suffer the said wagon or cart to stand longer in the said Market than while the same may be unladen", and there was a similar provision for water-borne produce.

The Gracechurch Street market, despite its occupation by "foreigners", was found to be an ancient one and permitted to continue. Its predecessor was the Stocks Market or "les Stokkes", on the site of the present Mansion House, which had been used since early in the fourteenth century. In 1675 the Gracechurch Street market (by then known as the Woolchurch Herb Market) had become a busy trading centre, and on petition to the City Lands Committee, the Company obtained sixty stations for its members. They seem to have been still there in 1751, when in a survey of the City the market is called the Leadenhall Herb Market. There is, however, no record of any further change or of when a formal central market was given up.

The Enrolment of the Second Charter

For some reason, or by oversight, the Royal Charter of 1616 had never been enrolled in the records of the City, and the petition of 1617 only referred to the 1605 Charter. In 1659 the Company sought to have this rectified, and submitted a petition to the Lord Mayor and Court of Aldermen "to have their Charter enrolled for the better regulation of their trade and Company".

On 20th July 1659, the petition was considered by a Sub-Committee consisting of Lord Tichborne, Alderman William Thomson, Alderman Joseph Fredericke, Alderman Tempest Milner and the Common Serjeant (Henry Proby), and their report to the Lord Mayor and Court of Aldermen stated: "That upon perusal thereof and hearing the Petitioners' reasons of their desires we conceive the admittance of the said Company into the Body of the City will be an especial encouragement and assistance to them for the well regulating of their Society and without any inconvenience to the state of this City And are therefore of opinion that their said Charter be enrolled accordingly by Mr Town Clerk and the Chamberlain of London to take notice of them to be Citizens and Gardeners of London to all intents and purposes..."

The sting was in the tail of the report, which continued: "saving only this limitation That they shall have no Livery of their Company for choice of Mayors Sheriffs or Members for Parliament unless this Honourable Court shall hereafter by their positive Order in writing grant and allow the same."

With this significant proviso, the Company's second Charter (1616) was enrolled in the Chamber of London on 28th July 1659.

In a further petition to the Court of Aldermen regarding admission to the Freedom of the City, lodged in 1668, it was stated that although the Company was incorporated and "enrolled a Company of this City" it had "but one member who is a Citizen and Gardener of London only, so that unless some speedy remedy be applied that Corporation must unavoidably sink having no members who are Freemen of this City to support and govern it". The remedy agreed to by the Aldermen was that "all persons who shall follow the trade of a Gardener and, being capable, shall come and will receive and take his and their Freedom of this City by patrimony in any other Company shall also be obliged at the same time to take their Freedom in the Gardeners Company, and that such as shall refuse to conform here untoo shall by Mr. Chamberlain be denied their Freedom", and similar provision was made for the Freedom by Servitude. Thus were the fortunes of the Company saved from extinction for the time being, on 25th February 1668.

By 1687, however, the order of 1668 had not been observed or its observance had long been discontinued. This led to a further petition by the Master and Wardens, but they met with a rebuff. The report of the Committee of Aldermen found that the order of 1668 "as it is penned is according to the strict interpretation of the words impracticable and could not be pursued by the custom of this City, for that by the Custom no person can be made free by service or patrimony in any other Company than that to which they were bound or wherein their fathers had their Freedom at the time of their birth; but that if in any case any person desire his Freedom in any other Company it can be by redemption only". Accordingly the Committee recommended that all persons following the trade of Gardener who were capable of their Freedom by service or patrimony in any other Company might on due proof of their qualification be made free of the City by redemption in the Gardeners Company, "without any fine to be paid in respect to the meanness of the said Trade".

This would not have been an infringement of the custom of the City. It was nevertheless a far different position from that under the 1668 Order, and though there is no record of just how adversely it may have affected the Company, it would seem to have jeopardised its position.

In 1690, in the Mastership of John Hurles, a Committee was appointed to deal with a dispute about the Company's periodical searches in the markets. This Committee met at St. Dunstan's House, the Cross Keys in Fleet Street, the Cock at Amen Corner, the Butchers' Arms in Newgate Market, the White Lion, the Dolphin in Lombard Street, and at "Captain Edgar

[40]

Cuper's". It proved not to be a short-lived matter, and troubles in the markets continued well into the 1690s.

At this time, the Company's problems were further compounded by the fact that hundreds of country labourers were moving into the London area to work on the grounds of Hampton Court and Kensington Palace, and on the gardens of the Duke of Beaufort and the Earls of Chesterfield, Sunderland, Rutland, Bedford, Devonshire and Craven. At one time as many as five hundred were employed, with only ten "able masters" and forty other professed gardeners, many of whom afterwards posed as gardeners. Thus the Company not only faced continuing difficulties with controlling the markets, but it appeared to have little influence over the employment of recognised gardeners in the seats of power.

In 1701 the Company, possibly despairing of enlisting the sympathy of the City Fathers, sought to obtain an Act of Parliament to enforce its Charters as they found that gardeners could go outside the Charter area and defy the Ordinances.

By that time the "mystery of gardening" included potagery, or kitchen herbs and salads; florilege, or flowers, evergreens, etc; orangery, or foreign plants grown in "stoves" or hothouses; sylvia, or the planting of avenues, lawns, etc; botany, or the study and knowledge of plants; nursery work, or the propagating and raising of all greens, fruit trees, and trees for avenues, fit for planting out; and designing or making of grounds, parterres, etc.

It was proposed to extend the Company's influence over the whole of England and Wales; to incorporate ten garden designers, 150 noblemens' gardeners, 400 gentlemens' gardeners, 100 nurserymen, 150 florists, twenty botanists, and 200 market gardeners; and to establish a system of technical correspondence, employment agencies and supervision of all gardeners and apprentices. Sadly, however, this major initiative by the Company was not accepted.

Meantime, in 1684 Charles II had declared the Charters of the City of London and of all Corporations in England, including those of the City Companies, to be forfeited. It was not until the news of the advent of William of Orange that James II restored their ancient franchises, and in 1690 one of the first acts of William and Mary was to pass an Act of Parliament annulling the *Quo Warranto* proceedings of Charles II. The Court of Aldermen thereupon reinstated the Livery Companies, but no mention was made of the Gardeners Company, whose Livery it did not recognise.

Notwithstanding the refusal of the Court of Aldermen to recognise the Livery granted by the Company's Ordinances under the 1605 Royal Charter, several attempts were made by members of the Company to exercise the Livery vote in Common Hall. Thus it is recorded that in 1710 Humphrey Batt unsuccessfully put forward a claim, and in 1722 John Cockson, Thomas Fairchild, John Goodwell, William Helm, Matthew Mash, Thomas Pool and John Taylor were no more successful.

In 1720 a number of Freemen, who were also Freemen of the City, petitioned the Court of Aldermen against the Court of Assistants, alleging neglect of their duties, and that several Assistants were not Freemen of the City. The petition was referred to the Recorder and the Common Serjeant, who took evidence and examined the Company's Charters, but no orders were made.

The Horselydown Saga

At this point, it is of interest to relate the history of another aspect of the Company's activities – the administration of a specific area of land, the story of which stretches from 1645 to 1700 and beyond.

It is recorded that in 1645 the City Corporation granted to William Byers, Citizen and Leatherseller, a lease in Horsey Down (later Horselydown) in Bermondsey of land forming part of the Bridge House Estate – the ancient City trust, the income from which maintained the four City bridges over the Thames free of all cost to the ratepayers (and still does so). The site was near the old Artillery Ground, which was enclosed in 1639 and later covered by St. John's Church.

In 1681 the lease was mortgaged to the Company for £160 at six per cent, and six members of the Company acted as trustees: of these only two were "gardeners" (one at Bermondsey and the other at St. Martin-in-the-Fields), one was a "citizen and clothworker", and each of the others (including Humphrey Goodspeed, afterwards Master) were described as "citizen and merchant taylor".

In 1685, the mortgagor being in default, the Company brought an ejectment action and recovered possession of the land. The tenements were in a ruinous condition and Thomas Murrey, Renter Warden, began to repair them. Byers died in debt, and his widow renounced administration – although later, in 1693, she gave a bond to the Master (Hugh Berry) and the Wardens for twenty-two pounds advanced.

The management of the land and buildings appears to have given a good deal of trouble and expense, with Humphrey Goodspeed (the Master) in 1686 paying for building materials, ground rent, tithe and hearth-tax, and Robert Chandler (the Master) and Humphrey Goodspeed in 1688 paying for cleansing the sewers. Then in 1689 there was a further financial liability, when Horselydown incurred a tax under the "Act for the Granting of a present Aid to Their Majesties".

In 1691, in the Mastership of Thomas Cooke, a new Horselydown Committee of six members of the Court was appointed; three were gardeners at Southwark, Stepney and Battersea, and the others were Freemen of the Companies of Leathersellers, Vintners and Haberdashers. More expense followed in 1692, with a tax "towards the Carrying on of a Vigorous War against France", and in 1694 the Court of Sewers for Surrey ordered the Company to "wharf and amend" the sewers. In 1699, in the Mastership of Francis Ballard, payments included the cost of one thousand new tiles and a tax "for Disbanding Forces, Paying Seamen, and other Uses".

The Company had to face a further complication in 1700, arising from the fact that the late Sir William Inwood of Cobham had retained a financial interest in Horselydown as a result of earlier dealings with the Byers family. His widow, Dame Katherine Inwood, having married the Revd. William Weston of Cobham, had died and left him administrator of the Inwood estates. Weston took proceedings in Chancery against the Company and, on a settlement of all accounts, the Horselydown lease was assigned to him. Thus ended the Company's fifteen years' administration of the property and, in spite of the loss of rents from tenants, it must have been something of a relief to the Master and Wardens. In any case, in 1714 the lease granted by the Corporation of London came to an end, and Horselydown reverted to the Bridge House Estate.

Eighteenth and Nineteenth Century Minutes
The earliest extant Minute Book of the Company commences in 1764 and the first entry, relating to the meeting on Whit Wednesday, records the election of Aaron James as Master and William Simpson as Upper Warden. Charles Wainhouse was appointed Upper Beadle, with salary fixed at four pounds, and the Clerk was George Stubbs.

These early minutes throw little light on the Company's activities. They do, however, record the amounts received for quarterage (6d. per quarter), absences (2s.6d. per time), bindings (14s. each, rising later to 21s.6d.), the admission of freemen (30s.), and Livery fines (one guinea and later 29s.6d.).

On outgoings, they record the salaries of the Clerk (one guinea per Court) and the Beadle (one pound per Court), "rooms and expenses" and Chamberlain's fees on bindings. One item appears regularly, "exceedings at dinner", being the difference between the cost of Court Dinners and members' contributions thereto – a salutary reminder that a deficit on the Entertainment Account is nothing new.

The Quarterly Courts were held at venues as various as Guildhall Coffee House, North's Coffee House, the Clerk's residence in Parliament Street (Westminster), The Pauls Head and the Kendal Tavern in Fleet Street.

In 1776 Richard Wortley was elected Master, but in May 1777 it is minuted that "not having (after due notice given to him) taken upon him the said office and been sworn...and not having attended the duty of that office since his election, Resolved that the said Richard Wortley do forfeit and pay...the sum of 5 marks of lawful money of England in pursuance of the Byelaw in that respect". Notwithstanding this default, he was re-elected Master at that Court.

It is of interest to note that Edward Hipkins, whose descendants gave rise to a point concerning the legitimacy of the Company's revival over a century later, was elected Under Warden in 1777. He does not appear to have proceeded further, and he died in 1787.

In 1779, five hundred copies were printed of *A State of the Company's mode of transacting business, fees, fines, etc.*, compiled by the Clerk, George Stubbs.

About this time attendances at the Court began to decline, and in July 1782 no-one attended; in October 1782, only the Master and Wardens were present; in January 1783, only two Assistants; and in April 1783, again there was a nil attendance. While in January and April 1784 there were similarly unattended Courts, the situation afterwards improved somewhat for a time.

In June 1795 there was a change of Clerk, with George Stubbs the Younger (who was already a Court Assistant) succeeding his late father. The latter had been elected to the Livery in May 1780 and to the Court in June 1781 and was Under Warden in 1784-85 and Upper Warden in 1785-86, but he did not proceed to the office of Master. George Stubbs the Younger became Master in May 1801, though he had not served as a Warden, and was re-elected in 1802.

CHAPTER 3

There is a gap in the minutes between September 1807 and November 1816, when Francis Bligh Hookey was elected Clerk on the death of George Stubbs the Younger. In the early 1820s interest in the Company declined; at the May 1822 Court only the Clerk was present, and in several subsequent years the number attending was only two or three. Hookey, after some sixteen years which must have been somewhat discouraging, gave notice of his resignation in July 1832 and was succeeded in June 1833 by John Finch. Clearly Finch was unable to revive interest in the Company, however, for only two persons attended the Court in May 1836 and then the situation further deteriorated.

At the Election Courts from 1837 to 1840 inclusive, there is the melancholy entry "no member present"; in 1841 three members turned up, in 1842 only one, and from 1843 to 1853 it is recorded each year that there was "no member present although summoned".

There was a further change of Clerk in 1853, with Charles Shepheard succeeding John Finch. After a break in the minutes from 1854 (again a nil attendance), it is recorded in 1872 that "Mr Beaumont Shepheard was substituted for Mr Charles Shepheard as Clerk" – apparently in spite of there being no-one present to elect him! This is the last entry, ending the first 270 years of the Company's history since it received its first Royal Charter from King James I.

The last occasion in this period on which the minutes set out the names of members of the Court was at the Election Court of 1835, when among the Assistants were William John Hipkins, Henry Izzard Hipkins and William James Hipkins. The Hipkins family was later to be cited as a factor which saved the Company from legal extinction, by preserving the "apostolic succession" during the interregnum, although it was not until some years after the revival of the 1890s that the importance of the link was recognised.

We have seen that the Company in its earliest days was composed of working gardeners, although some of the leading members had in their employ several apprentices and journeymen. With the phenomenal increase in the price of land within the City of London, which dated from the early years of the nineteenth century, the art of practical gardening virtually ceased in the City. Even the few open squares which remained, and the disused churchyards, were so neglected during this money-making period as to become not only eyesores but potential health hazards. The love of gardening, which the citizens had when they lived over their own shops within the City, was transferred to their suburban homes.

[45]

At the same time, the craft itself experienced an almost complete transformation and development. The number of scientific gardeners greatly increased, instead of being limited as formerly to a select few in the employment of noblemen and others of wealth. Much was done by the Royal Horticultural Society (founded 1804 as the Horticultural Society; Royal Charter 1861) and other institutions to improve the cultivation of garden produce, and an enormous literature sprang up to bring a knowledge of the best methods of culture within reach of all but the poorest. In the City itself, the retailer gave way to the wholesale merchant, and the world's seeds, plants and garden necessities were received and distributed under the shadow of Bow Bells.

The Worshipful Company of Gardeners, by the late nineteenth century, had long ceased to enforce their rights of control over the London members of the craft. The Company instead began to seek a wide sphere of influence in endeavouring to promote the best interests of the horticultural art by rewards and encouragement, rather than by the repressive measures of a bygone age.

CHAPTER 4

The Revival of the Company, and its Relations with the Corporation of London

The revival in the fortunes of the Worshipful Company of Gardeners dates from the end of 1890, when steps were taken to secure the co-operation of the officials and leading Fellows of the Royal Horticultural Society in the promotion and extension of the Company's usefulness.

A Special Meeting held at 9 Old Jewry Chambers, on 29th December 1890, was attended by Major George Lambert (Chairman), Mr. John Chester and Mr. Charles Welch, with Mr. James Curtis (the Clerk). The minutes do not clarify the capacity in which these three persons attended, and they were not Liverymen of the Company at that stage. In fact a complete list of the Company dated 1900-1901 shows no Liverymen or Assistants elected before 1891 – although it must be remembered that the Company's Livery was not officially recognised by the Court of Aldermen before then, so these three and others could have been working "unofficially" in the interests of the Company by 1890. It has to be assumed, however, that for some time the Company had been virtually defunct, and that 1890 saw a gathering of men who were interested in reviving it and who also wanted to bring in others of like mind. This would explain the fact that, soon afterwards, many people were simultaneously elected to the Freedom, the Livery and even to the Court of Assistants.

So what is known of those attending the meeting on 29th December 1890? The minutes reveal little, although it is known that Charles Welch was the Librarian of the Corporation of London. It is not even clear how and when James Curtis became Clerk, but from a much later minute (11th February 1931) it can be adduced that he succeeded Beaumont Shepheard, whose duties since 1872 cannot have been other than nominal. It is far from certain, however, that Curtis immediately succeeded Shepheard when the latter resigned the Clerkship in 1890, only that the meeting of 29th December appeared to have the power to elect (or re-elect) Curtis as Clerk. All this suggests again that the triumvirate and Curtis, perhaps with the continued support of Shepheard, were the only people at that time who assumed any responsibility for the Company. Any further information about them, as contained in the following paragraphs, has had to be largely derived from sources other than the Company's records.

James Curtis was a solicitor, and the venue of the meeting was his office, which appears to have become the Company's base at that time. It is recorded in a later minute that he was also Clerk to the Paviors, Tin Plate Workers and Horners Companies.

Major George Lambert was a member of the family firm of goldsmiths, silversmiths and jewellers situated at 11/12 Coventry Street, W. In the Gardeners Company, he became Renter Warden in 1892, Upper Warden in 1893 and Master in 1895.

John Chester was a barrister residing at 1 New Court in the Temple, with chambers at 23 Old Square in Lincoln's Inn. He was admitted to the Livery in 1891, but does not appear to have progressed further.

Beaumont Shepheard was not present at the meeting, but his likely influence upon the revival of the Company should not be underestimated, as his family had been prominent and hard-working on behalf of the Livery for many years and continued to be so. Charles Shepheard was Clerk to the Fletchers (1853-70), and for roughly the same period he was also Clerk to the Gardeners (1853-72); although he was the Fletchers' Renter Warden in 1872 and Upper Warden in 1874, he did not become Master. His son, Alfred James Shepheard, succeeded him as Clerk to the Fletchers (1870-90) and was Master of that Company in 1895. Charles Shepheard's other son, Beaumont, succeeded him as Clerk to the Gardeners (1872-90), then succeeded his brother Alfred James as Clerk to the Fletchers (1890-1906). Beaumont was in turn succeeded as Clerk to the Fletchers by his own son, Percy Beaumont Shepheard, in 1906.

Beaumont Shepheard, who was certainly one of the prominent names at the time of the revival of the Worshipful Company of Gardeners, did not fade into the background when he resigned as the Company's Clerk in 1890. He served as a member of the Court of Assistants, and became Master in 1894. Neither did he relinquish his connection with the Fletchers when he resigned as their Clerk in 1906, as he was their Master from 1918 to 1921.

The Shepheards were solicitors, and Beaumont practiced in the family firm with offices at 31/32 Finsbury Circus in the City, as well as with a partner at 1 King Street in Kensington. He was also active in the Corporation of London, and in 1882-83 and again in 1890-91 he served as the Corporation's Under-Sheriff (a role that is today combined with the salaried post of Secondary at the Old Bailey). As such, he would have been in close contact with the Lord Mayor and the Aldermen, and it is not unreasonable to suppose that he was influential in securing the interest of Lord Mayor Sir Joseph Savory in becoming Master of the Company in 1891 – an election which gave great impetus to the Company's revival.

The Special Meeting on 29th December 1890 discussed "the desirability of taking more active steps to develop the Company so as to extend its usefulness", and they forthwith elected Charles Welch and the Revd. William Wilks (Vicar of Shirley and Honorary Secretary of the Royal Horticultural Society) to the Freedom and Livery and to the Court of Assistants without payment "in recognition of special and meritorious services rendered by them to the Company". They also elected (or re-elected) James Curtis as Clerk and Solicitor; resolved that Major George Lambert and Mr. Ex-Sheriff George Burt take up their Freedom and be elected on the Livery and the Court of Assistants; that Mr. John Chester and Mr. George Rowland Blades be presented with the Freedom and Livery of the Company without payment in recognition of special (but unspecified) services rendered by them; and that Archdeacon Frederick William Farrar be invited to be the Honorary Chaplain to the Company.

At the next meeting, on 2nd February 1891 (with the Revd. William Wilks in the chair), the Clerk reported that the Lord Mayor of London had expressed willingness to become Master. Sir Joseph Savory (1843-1921), a great supporter of the Livery, was a Goldsmith, a Clockmaker, a Shipwright and a Poulter; indeed he served three separate years as Master of the Clockmakers, firstly in 1889-90. During his Lord Mayoral year of 1890-91 he was created a Baronet, and while still Lord Mayor he not only became Master of the Gardeners (1891-92) but began a second year as Master of the Clockmakers. He served as Conservative M.P. for the Appleby Division of Westmorland from 1892 to 1900, and in 1912-13 was Master of the Clockmakers for a third time.

The Gardeners accordingly resolved in 1891 that Sir Joseph Savory be presented with the Freedom and elected to the Livery, the Court and as Master without payment – surely the speediest promotion in a Livery Company's history!

Elections followed thick and fast. The admission of Colonel John Thomas North to the Freedom and Livery and to the Court was reported, and it was resolved that Sir Trevor Lawrence (President of the Royal Horticultural Society), Nathaniel Newman Sherwood (proprietor of Hursts, wholesale seedsmen), Edwin Frederick Fitch, Robert Gordon Mullen, Mr. Under-Sheriff Beaumont Shepheard and Major Alexander McKenzie

(Superintendent of Epping Forest) take up their Freedom and be elected to the Livery and to the Court. Robert Gofton-Salmond was elected to the Court later that month, when Sir Trevor Lawrence was elected as Upper Warden and the Revd. William Wilks as Renter Warden.

Sir Trevor Lawrence (1831-1913) had become President of the Royal Horticultural Society in 1885, and had brought to it a determination to improve the Society's fortunes and standing. His collection of orchids and other plants, at Burford near Dorking, was renowned. The Revd. William Wilks (1843-1923), Secretary of the Royal Horticultural Society, was similarly an experienced gardener rather than a theorist – although he described his seven acres at Shirley near Croydon as "The Wilderness", he carried out much fine work including the selection and breeding of the Shirley strain of poppies, and his work in fruit-growing resulted in a cooking-apple being named after him. It was clearly felt in 1891 that two such energetic and knowledgeable men could be most valuable in assisting the revival of the Worshipful Company of Gardeners.

There was then a lull until 6th April 1891, when Messrs. Philip Crowley (Treasurer of the Royal Horticultural Society), Richard Clout, Henry Frederick Tiarks, Constant Edward Osman and George William Burrows were elected to the Livery and the Court, and an "exhaustive scheme was submitted by Sir Trevor Lawrence and others for making the Company more practically useful to the trade and occupation of gardeners".

The time was now ripe for the Lord Mayor, Sir Joseph Savory, to take up his office as Master. He did so at the Court Meeting at Mansion House on 10th April 1891, and on Whit Wednesday as prescribed by the Ordinances the Master and Wardens were duly re-elected.

Several new Freemen were elected to the Livery including George Fergusson Wilson, Britain's most successful cultivator of lilies. Wilson's estate, Oakwood at Wisley, later became the nucleus of the Royal Horticultural Society Gardens, although at that time they were still at Chiswick. Sadly the revival of the Company came too late for him to make a major contribution, however, for he died in 1902.

The Recognition of the Livery in 1891

The acceptance of the Mastership in 1891 by the Lord Mayor gave a great fillip to the Company's fortunes, and priority then needed to be given to securing recognition of the Company's right to a Livery, which had been granted in 1605 by the first Charter of James I. The petition requesting "the honour and privilege of the Livery of the City" was presented to the Court of Aldermen in 1891, and it recited the Charters and Ordinances and included the fact that under the Ordinances there was no limitation in the number of the Livery. Then, somewhat prematurely, it continued: "The Company is now and has for some time past been engaged in a comprehensive plan for developing the Art of Gardening in this Country and for affording technical instruction and practical training to those engaged in the occupation of gardening".

The Court of Aldermen does not appear to have questioned the nature and state of the Company's "comprehensive plan", or the legal position of the petitioners as members of the Company, and on 12th August 1891 the Clerk was notified that the Court had agreed with the report of its Committee for General Purposes, which recommended "that the Company should be created and made a Livery Company of this City". The terms included the fixing of the Livery fine at twenty guineas, the number of the Livery at no more than sixty, and that no person should be admitted without first producing a copy of his Freedom of the City.

The recognition of the Livery of the Company did not escape attention in Parliament. James Rowlands, the National Liberal Member for East Finsbury, drew attention to the matter and asked "whether as a result of that decision the sixty new Liverymen will become electors of the City of London and whether Her Majesty's Government will take such legislative steps as are necessary to prevent the manufacture of fagot votes". Rowlands could not have been entirely averse to the Livery Companies, however, since he was himself a Freeman of the Goldsmiths!

Irrespective of this caustic comment, the Company had achieved full recognition as a Livery Company of the City of London in all respects, and had at long last overcome its historic differences with the Court of Aldermen. At a meeting of the Company's Court held on 16th December 1891, a design by Mr. George Edwards for a Master's badge was accepted, and a staff head for the Beadle was ordered to be provided.

It is clear, therefore, that events moved very swiftly to secure the Company's revival, transforming it in just a few months from a moribund Company to one of great vibrancy and promise. What is more, the leading lights recruited to the Company during 1891 were prominent people in the field of horticulture and in City life. There is no precisely recorded reason for all this to have happened, but it is likely to have been a happy combination of factors. The time was right, and the right people were involved.

The circumstances of the time were opportune. There was clearly much to achieve in the field of horticulture, whereas so many of the other Livery Companies originated from crafts and trades which by the late nineteenth century were dead or dying. This is not to deny that other Companies still saw a future for themselves, in many cases with largely social and charitable objects, and of course there were privileges to be upheld in order to preserve the ancient rights of Liverymen to exercise their votes and influence the civic City.

In the case of the Gardeners, however, there was also the fact to which attention was drawn at the end of the previous Chapter. The Company's original function, controlling the activities of London members of their craft, had long disappeared and had probably resulted in the Company losing its way for very many years. Now, however, there was a new challenge in sight – to achieve, by rewarding and encouraging the best practices, the highest standards in the horticultural field.

It was also a time of emerging civic pride and rapidly developing municipal government. This must have been a considerable incentive to many people, inspiring a will to breathe new life into the less active Livery Companies and to restore them to their former positions of importance in the City. Moreover, the failure of Gladstone's assault on the City Guilds could have provoked a backlash, a resurgence of popular interest, and a renewed determination that the Guilds should survive and find new roles for themselves.

There was another necessary factor, however, and fortunately the Gardeners were not found wanting in this respect. The time was right, but the right people also had to be there, willing and able to secure the Company's revival. Beaumont Shepheard has already been mentioned, the interest of the highest officials of the Royal Horticultural Society was forthcoming, and people active in national and local government were recruited. Of the latter, the role of Charles Welch must have been significant. Not only had he been the Guildhall Librarian of the Corporation of London since 1888, but his involvement in City affairs was prodigious and he had a passionate interest in researching the history of the City and its institutions. It is unlikely that such a man would meekly accept the decline and eventual demise of a Livery Company in which he was interested, and not at all surprising that he was among that small band of men who gathered together on 29th December 1890 to get the revival under way.

So the position and rights of the Worshipful Company of Gardeners were clearly re-affirmed, by decision of the Court of Aldermen, in 1891.

The Company was ranked as 66th in order of seniority among the Livery Companies, but the rationale of this placing is not clear as some Companies which were incorporated after the Gardeners (in one case a century later) are senior to it in order of civic precedence. In the report of the Commission on Municipal Corporations (1837) the Company is listed as 70th, but several Companies appear to have dropped out between then and 1891, namely the Combmakers, Silkthrowers, Silkmen and Pinmakers.

The Company's gratitude to Sir Joseph Savory for his help in securing recognition of the Company's Livery proved to be rather short-lived, as in January 1896 it was minuted that he had refused to pay the Entertainment Fee of five guineas, which had been imposed in December 1892, but had expressed his willingness to contribute to any scheme for promoting the interests of the Company. Having regard to this it was resolved that he be asked to contribute twenty guineas to the Scholarship Fund, but sadly on 14th May 1896 a letter was read tendering his resignation as a member of the Court, "as apparently my views do not accord with those of other members of the Court".

Meanwhile, in December 1891 the Court had thought it time to lay down an order of precedence for future elections, as follows:

Master	Alderman Sir Joseph Savory, Bt.
Upper Warden	Sir Trevor Lawrence, Bt., M.P.
Renter Warden	The Reverend William Wilks, M.A.

Assistants:

1. Beaumont Shepheard
2. Major George Lambert
3. Colonel John Thomas North
4. Ex-Sheriff George Burt
5. Nathaniel Newman Sherwood
6. Edwin Frederick Fitch
7. Robert Gordon Mullen
8. Charles Welch
9. Major Alexander McKenzie
10. Ex-Sheriff Sir William Farmer
11. Robert Gofton-Salmond
12. Philip Crowley
13. Richard Clout
14. Henry Frederick Tiarks
15. Constant Edward Osman
16. George William Burrows
17. Lionel Smith Beale
18. George Fergusson Wilson
19. Ex-Sheriff Thomas Clarke
20. Frederick George Ivey
21. Alderman Marcus Samuel
22. Alfred Barker
23. George Corble
24. Henry Wood

And so things went for several years with elections to the Freedom, Livery and Court, and elections to office at the annual Common Hall on Whit Wednesday.

The Minute Book contains the first list of members entitled to vote for the election of Members of Parliament, which is dated 1893-94 and consists of thirty-two names.

The Arrival of Ebblewhite

James Curtis resigned from the Clerkship in January 1894, on his appointment as Registrar of the Marylebone County Court. In recognition of the valuable services he had rendered in the resuscitation of the Company, he was unanimously elected as an Honorary Member of the Court of Assistants.

Curtis was succeeded by Mr. Assistant Robert Gofton-Salmond, who later resigned from the Court and retained the office of Clerk until his death in 1902. For some months the duties of Clerk were discharged by Col. Thomas Davies Sewell, an Honorary Member of the Court, until January 1903. Then the new Clerk, Ernest Arthur Ebblewhite, began a long and fruitful tenure which lasted until 1937.

Ebblewhite had been a Freeman of the Company since 1894, and was keenly interested in antiquarian studies. On his election, it transpired that he doubted the legality of the method of the Company's revival in 1890 and the standing of those who had brought it about. At his first Court he raised various points which suggested that the Court had not adhered to the provisions of the Charter and Ordinances, some of which were referred to a special committee for report.

Ebblewhite showed that of sixty-four members purported to have been elected to the Livery since 1890, only eleven were qualified. Eighteen were Liverymen of other Companies before election, and had therefore not complied with the requirement of the Court of Aldermen when it granted the Company recognition as a Livery Company of the City. This had stipulated that no Liveryman of another Company should be admitted to the Livery of the Gardeners Company without being translated "openly" before the Court of Aldermen. A further thirty-five had been admitted to the Livery before taking up their Freedom of the City, again contrary to the requirements of the Court of Aldermen, but twenty-nine having since done so were eligible for election.

If all these irregularities were put in order, the Livery would then have been four over the maximum permitted. This was overcome by the doubtful expedient of recommending that as the eighteen members whose Mother Company was another Company would not be returnable as Gardeners in either the Common Hall or Parliamentary Lists rendered by the Clerk, until they were translated, they should not be counted as on the strength of the Livery, but that as far as possible their precedence in the Company should be maintained.

The Hipkins Succession

At the same Court, Ebblewhite presented a petition to the Master, Wardens and Court by Joseph William Hipkins, praying to be admitted "on special grounds" to the Freedom of the Company. The petitioner, born in 1830 and therefore in his seventies, was the great-grandson of Edward Hipkins senior, who had been admitted to the Freedom of the Company in 1759 and served on the Court from 1771 until his death in 1787. This Edward Hipkins had two sons, Edward junior and George, who became Freemen of the Company by Patrimony in 1781 and 1788 respectively and proceeded to the Livery in 1802 and 1794 respectively. Edward Hipkins junior had three sons – Joseph (the father of the petitioner), who came of age in 1818 and was entitled to his Freedom by Patrimony, but having been bound apprentice to a Stationer, took up his Freedom in that Company by Servitude; and William John and Henry Izzard, who took up the Freedom of the Gardeners Company by Patrimony in 1805 and 1822 respectively and were both elected to the Court in 1834. William James, son of William John, was admitted to the Company in 1827 and elected to the Court in 1835. Henry, also a son of William John, took up his Freedom in 1838 when he was described as "of Horselydown, waterman".

So the chain was broken by the petitioner's father, Joseph Hipkins, who died in 1860. The petitioner had taken up his Freedom of the City in 1859 without the intervention of a Livery Company, and in the words of the petition "is desirous of being recorded in your Worshipful Company, with the Freedom, Livery and Court of which so many members of his family have been actively associated since the reign of King George III".

It would be interesting to know how Joseph William Hipkins came into contact with the Company, but it was nevertheless a fortuitous event. If there was any need to show some legal continuity between the pre-1830 Company and its revival, here it was – the "missing link", but for the unfortunate lapse of his father in preferring the Stationers Company. The son was immediately elected to the Freedom by Presentation, and it was resolved that he be recorded in the Chamber of London at the Company's expense. He was admitted to the Freedom out of Court a few days later, and elected to the Livery and to the Court two months later without payment of fees on election as Assistant. Thereafter he does not appear to have taken an active part in the Company's affairs, and he resigned on account of ill health in May 1904 and died the following month. The admission of his son to the Freedom by Redemption followed his own on the next day, so preserving the family connection.

It appeared from the Report of a Committee in 1906, appointed to consider the compilation of a History of the Company, that one John Bowes had been admitted to the Freedom of the Company and taken up his Freedom of the City in or about 1770. His descendant, Charles Cuthbert Bowes, is recorded in the minutes as having been admitted to the Freedom by Redemption in November 1891 (but without any reference to the previous connection of his family with the Company), and as having declined election to the Livery in 1909, dying some time between 1935 and 1937.

If the Hipkins link was not considered sufficient to preserve the "apostolic succession" between the old and the revived Company, the Bowes family might have filled the bill. We shall never know, however, whether the historic and civic connection of the Bowes family from 1770 to 1891 was ever ascertained.

The Company's Arms

Notwithstanding the new-found relevance of the Hipkins family, other qualms were felt about the legality of the Company's revival. The indefatigable Ebblewhite had discovered in 1905 that the Company's Armorial Bearings, although delineated in the margin of the second Charter granted in 1616, were not lawfully borne, as they had not been granted by that Charter and were not registered at the College of Arms.

In spite of Ebblewhite's assertion, it must have been clear that the Company's Arms had been generally recognised from an early date. In 1677, *London's Armory* was produced by Richard Wallis, citizen and "arms painter" (or Painter-Stainer). This included the full armorial bearings of the Company, although the caption and motto had slight differences of spelling from those accepted today – with the Company described as the "Gardiners" and the motto as "In the swet of thy brows shalt thow eat thy bread".

It is also of note that Wallis appears to depict the Arms of the various Companies in order of precedence throughout his book, if one can assume that as the "Great Twelve" appear in their proper order those following them are also in the order accepted at the time (1677). Indeed Wallis's first thirty-three Companies are in the order of precedence accepted today (except that the Armourers and Brasiers and the Cutlers are for some reason reversed).

Beyond that point there are variations when compared with today's order, although this is largely explained by the fact that various Companies have amalgamated or ceased to exist since Wallis's time. In view of the dissatisfaction expressed by the Gardeners in 1910 with the position accorded to them in 1891, it is of interest that they were ranked at 71st by Wallis, compared with the 66th position of 1891. Their "rivals", the Fruiterers, were ranked at 45th by Wallis and retain that position today. All of which goes to prove that the order of precedence has no particular connection with the dates of Royal Charters, since the Weavers (with the earliest Charter, 1184) were ranked 44th by Wallis and are 42nd today.

On the question of the right of the Gardeners to bear Arms, Ebblewhite proposed to resolve all doubt by obtaining from the Earl Marshal a Patent of Confirmation of the Arms, Crest and Motto, and a Patent of Supporters at a cost of £131 10s, and the question arose whether in addition to this the Company should first obtain a Royal Warrant at an additional cost of £54 13s. Some members were unhappy about the expense, which the Master described as "perhaps superfluous in relation to the question of Armorial Bearings only", but "in answer to a question...the Clerk stated that as such a Royal Warrant would contain recitals of (1) the Company's two Charters (2) of its exercise of the power to make Ordinances (3) of its perpetual succession and (4) of its right to a Common Seal". The Clerk "was of the opinion that it would be most desirable for the Company to have such a document as well as the two Patents with its muniments".

In accordance with this advice, a petition was sealed in Common Hall on 12th April 1905, in the reign of Edward VII. On 29th May a letter was received by Somerset Herald intimating that "the King has signified His Pleasure that the prayer of the Petition be complied with". This prompted a telegram to the King at Windsor, despatched on 14th June, which read: "The Company of Gardeners in Court assembled at the Albion Tavern Aldersgate Street desire humbly to congratulate your Majesty on the success of the Garden Party at Windsor today and ask permission to humbly thank your Majesty for having graciously acquiesced in the prayer of their Petition as to the continued use of their Armorial Bearings."

There is no apparent connection between the two events mentioned in the telegram, but the announcement that the matter was finally sealed was made at a Common Hall of the members of the Company on 18th September 1905, which was the 300th anniversary of the grant of the first Charter. The Master reported that a Royal Warrant dated 9th June 1905 and Warrant of the Earl Marshal dated 27th July 1905 had been received. The actual Grant of Arms and Grant of Supporters were dated 8th September 1905, exemplified by Heralds College with the following heraldic description:

> "*Arms* – On a shield representing a landscape, the figure of a man, habited about the body with a skin, delving the ground with a spade, all proper. *Crest* – On a wreath, argent and vert, a basket of flowers and fruit, proper. *Supporters* – On either side a female figure proper, vested argent, wreathed about the temples with flowers, and supporting on the exterior arm a cornucopia proper. *Motto* – In the sweat of thy brows shalt thow eate thy bread."

If there were ever doubts as to the validity of past proceedings, therefore, they were dispelled by this evidence of royal goodwill toward the Company.

The Researches of Ebblewhite

Much of the above clarification and regularisation of the Company's position and practices resulted directly from the researches of the new Clerk, Ernest Arthur Ebblewhite. Indeed he must have undertaken considerable work with great speed and vigour on taking up his duties in 1903, and probably earlier. At his first Court he reported upon an exhaustive search which he had made for the Company's early records to the end of the seventeenth century, "which had remained unclaimed for a considerable period in the custody of the Corporation of the City of London". He had retrieved them and proposed to have them cleaned, translated, sorted and bound. This work was not completed until January 1914, at a cost of fifty guineas.

To these ancient documents (or copies of some of them) he added the results of his own laborious research into the history of the Company and its early members, together with his contemporary records during his Clerkship, making a series of sixteen large bound volumes covering the period 1616-1934 with some very large gaps. These volumes are now in the custody of the Corporation of London at Guildhall Library, for safe keeping for future generations.

Ebblewhite had also discovered in the vaults of Guildhall a substantial chest with several locks, which had been bought in accordance with the Byelaws of 1606, and had had it cleaned and restored. It appears from a picture in the Minute Book, reproduced from the *City Press*, to have been a very fine coffin-shaped box with a domed top and iron bands. Sadly its present whereabouts are unknown, though it is mentioned in a Company inventory of 1918.

Another oak chest was traced and restored, but has since disappeared.

This was marked "AL 1675", but bought by the Clerk, James Curtis, in Lowestoft in 1891. There was also at one time a third oak box in the care of the Clerk, with an inscription on the front:

               Worshipful Company of Gardeners

Robert Bagley	Master	
George Ives	Upper Warden	1817
John Gaywood	Under Warden	

The Petitions of 1910, 1911 and 1920

An attempt to improve the Company's seniority was made in 1910, with which was coupled a request to increase the number of Liverymen. A lengthy petition to the Lord Mayor and the Court of Aldermen was prepared, and by resolution of the Company on 15th March 1910 was signed and Sealed on 2nd May by the Master (Charles Bayer), the Upper Warden (E.A. Strauss), the Renter Warden (Sir Horace Brooks Marshall) and the Clerk (E.A. Ebblewhite).

The petition related the history of the Guild from 1345, referring to the Royal Charters and quoting relevant extracts from the Ordinances and the various orders of the Court. There was also reference to the admission of Freemen into the Livery of the Company "for the space of over two hundred years, the last admission being in the year 1806", and to the Company not being cognisant of its existing rights at the time of the 1891 petition.

Then follow several paragraphs referring to the Fruiterers Company, which had received its Royal Charter in February 1606 – five months after the Gardeners Company – and which, it was alleged, had been formed out of that Company's predecessors, the Society of Free Gardeners of London. The Charter or Constitutions of the Fruiterers Company established a Livery and empowered them to call an unlimited number of Freemen to such Livery, and it was stated in the petition that the Clerk of that Company had reported to the Court of Aldermen in 1724 "that he knew of no other authority for such Livery but ... these privileges have been regularly allowed to the said Company of Fruiterers without any special Order or grant by your Worshipful Court and your Petitioners submit that this case should be taken as a precedent for dealing with the present Petition". What irked the Gardeners Company was that in 1687, after the restoration of the ancient franchises of the City of London by James II, the Livery Companies were reinstated and the Fruiterers were placed 33rd on the list of seniority and were at the time of the petition 45th as against the Gardeners' ranking of 66th.

The petition prayed for a recognition of the Company's ancient Livery with an unlimited number conferred by the Constitution of 1606 or, alternatively, an increase from sixty to 150, and in either case the recognition or grant of a higher precedence than was at that time conceded to the Company. The reference to the Fruiterers Company, however, provoked a counter-petition from them asking the Court of Aldermen to reject the Gardeners' prayer, and on 20th September 1910 the Town Clerk wrote that the Court of Aldermen had that day "decided that the prayer of the Company's Petition be not complied with". There was apparently an informal intimation that if another petition were presented later, praying merely for an increase in the Livery, it would be favourably entertained.

In June 1911 Alderman Sir Horace Brooks Marshall was elected Master, and on 12th October the further petition was presented. This was supported by Alderman Sir Joseph Savory, and in February 1912 the Master reported that the Court of Aldermen had authorised an increase from sixty to 100 by Order of 5th December 1911. This limit was further increased to 160 in January 1915, but the question of the Company's place in the order of precedence seems never to have been raised again and friendly relations with the Fruiterers remained unimpaired.

By 1920 the membership of the Livery had so increased that it was decided to petition the Court of Aldermen for an increase from 160 to 250. In fact the petition had to confess that "the present number is and has been for some time past up to that number (160) and has at times exceeded it". It continued tactfully, "Your Petitioners have received applications from many persons, Horticulturalists, Merchants of the City of London, and others of good repute, for admission to their Livery and Your Petitioners believe that an increase ... would be for the benefit of the Company of Gardeners, would interest many in the history of the ancient Corporation of the City of London and the valuable work done by the Livery Companies, and extend the number of those who desire the preservation of the privileges of the Corporation and of the Liverymen of the City".

The petition also asked for an increase in the Livery Fine from twenty guineas to forty guineas. Sponsored by Alderman Sir Marcus Samuel (Lord Mayor and Master in 1902-03), the prayer of the petition was granted on 11th May 1920 – and the limit on the Livery remains at 250 today.

The Mastership and the Mayoralty

Following Sir Joseph Savory, the Worshipful Company of Gardeners has had seven Masters who have been Lord Mayor of London:

Sir Marcus Samuel (1853-1927) – Liveryman 1891, Knighted 1898, Master 1902-03 and Lord Mayor in the same year, created a Baronet in 1903, Baron Bearsted of Maidstone in 1921 and 1st Viscount Bearsted in 1925.

Sir Charles Cheers Wakefield (1859-1941) – Liveryman 1906, Knighted 1908, Lord Mayor 1915-16, created a Baronet in 1917, Master 1918-19, created Baron Wakefield of Hythe in 1930 and 1st Viscount Wakefield in 1934. Wakefield was also at various times Master of the Cordwainers, Haberdashers and Spectacle Makers.

Sir Horace Brooks Marshall (1865-1936) – Liveryman 1901, Knighted 1902, Master 1911-12, Lord Mayor 1918-19, and created 1st Baron Marshall of Chipstead in 1921.

Sir George Rowland Blades (1868-1953) – Liveryman 1890, Master 1912-13, Knighted 1918, created a Baronet in 1922, Lord Mayor 1926-27, created 1st Baron Ebbisham of Cobham in 1928, and served as Unionist M.P. for the Epsom Division of Surrey 1918-28. Blades was for many years the Father of the Company, and served also as Master of the Haberdashers and the Stationers.

Sir George Thomas Broadbridge (1869-1952) – Liveryman 1926, Knighted 1929, Master 1934-35, Lord Mayor 1936-37, created a Baronet in 1937 and 1st Baron Broadbridge of Brighton in 1945, and served as Unionist M.P. for the City of London 1938-45.

Sir (Harold Walter) Seymour Howard (1888-1967) – Liveryman 1930, Master 1947-48, Lord Mayor 1954-55, Knighted 1955 and created a Baronet at the end of his term of office as Lord Mayor.

Sir (Hamilton) Edward (de Coucey) Howard (b.1915) – Liveryman 1947, Master 1961-62, succeeded to the Baronetcy on the death of his father (Sir Seymour Howard) in 1967, Lord Mayor 1971-72, and created Knight Grand Cross in 1972.

Four other Liverymen have also served the office of Lord Mayor:

Sir Charles Augustin Hanson (1846-1922) – Liveryman 1913, Lord Mayor 1917-18, created a Baronet in 1918, and served as Coalition M.P. for the Bodmin Division of Cornwall 1916-22.

Sir Charles Albert Batho (1872-1938) – Liveryman 1921, Knighted 1926, Lord Mayor 1927-28, and created a Baronet in 1928. Batho was Master of the Paviors in 1919-20.

Sir Stephen Henry Molyneux Killik (1861-1938) – Liveryman 1922, Knighted 1923, Lord Mayor 1934-35, and created Knight Grand Cross and Knight Commander in 1935. Killik was sometime Master of the Fanmakers.

Dame (Dorothy) Mary Donaldson (b.1921) – Liveryman 1975, Lord Mayor 1983-84, and created Dame Grand Cross in 1983. Dame Mary was made an Honorary Freeman of the Shipwrights Company in 1985.

This makes a total, with Savory, of twelve members of the Company who have held the highest civic office since the revival of 1890, which is a proud record.

In addition to the above, in the same period, at least twenty-one members of the Company have served the office of Sheriff of the City. Furthermore, and excluding those who became Sheriff, some forty members of the Company have served on the Court of Common Council. Of the latter, it is noteworthy that David Howarth Seymour Howard is not only the third generation of his family to have become Master of the Company (1990-91), but is also the third generation to have been elected a Common Councilman for the Ward of Cornhill (1972), and he succeeded his father as Alderman of that Ward in 1986.

The Company has also been a popular Livery for senior officers of the City Corporation, and indeed in recent years two have served successively as Master. Edwin George Chandler (Master, 1988-89) was City Architect throughout the 1960s and 1970s, and afterwards a Common Councilman and Deputy of his Ward; whereas Gordon Herbert Denney (Master, 1989-90) served the Corporation for over thirty years, and was Deputy Chamberlain at his retirement in 1989.

The Company and the Lord Mayor's Show
This close association with the City Corporation has also been reflected in the Company's participation in the Lord Mayor's Show on many occasions.

The first was in 1894, with a car "emblematic of gardening" in honour of Alderman and Sheriff Marcus Samuel, who was on the Company's Court of Assistants. Then in 1902, when Master of the Company, Samuel was elected Lord Mayor, so it was thought that the Company should make a special effort to celebrate. The Lord Mayor and Sheriffs Committee, which is responsible for organising the Show each year, provided two bands to lead the Company's contingent, which consisted of a floral car emblematical of gardening and floriculture with banners and carriages. This brought an enthusiastic and congratulatory letter of thanks from the Lord Mayor. In the same year, incidentally, Liveryman Sir Horace Brooks Marshall was a Sheriff, and he was to become Master in 1911 and Lord Mayor in 1918.

CHAPTER 4

In 1907, when Charles Cheers Wakefield was Sheriff, the Court again offered to provide "a floral motor car", but the Lord Mayor and Sheriffs Committee replied merely "offering to make arrangements for the Company to attend in the procession with their own band, banners and carriage". It was decided to take no further action in the matter.

The Company made up for its rather peevish behaviour two years later, however, when in 1909 Liveryman R. Slazenger was Sheriff. The Master (Charles Bayer), with Past Masters Tasker, Shepheard and Sherwood, wearing their robes and badges, Tudor hats and buttonholes in the Company's colours, and accompanied by the Beadle decked in a silk sash, rode in a landau drawn by four bay horses decorated with rosettes also in the Company's colours, and escorted by two postillions and a footman. The Company's four banners were carried in the procession. Afterwards the Master, who had borne the cost, presented to the Company the Beadle's sash and three-cornered hat, the four leather flag holders and seven rosettes.

Strangely it appears that the Company did not participate in the Lord Mayor's Show of Sir Charles Cheers Wakefield in 1915, particularly as he was Renter Warden at the time. But in the Lord Mayor's Show of Liveryman Charles Augustin Hanson in 1917, when Past Master George Rowland Blades was the "lay" Sheriff, the Renter Warden (Panajotti Teofani) and Past Master Beaumont Shepheard, with five members of the Court chosen in seniority, wearing Livery robes and hoods and Tudor hats, and the Clerk, rode in two carriages with the Beadle and his staff and sash. Then sadly in 1918, in the Mayoralty of Past Master Sir Horace Brooks Marshall, the Company was squeezed out by "the unusually large dimensions of the naval and military display".

The Company declined to participate in 1921, the year in which Liveryman H.J. de Courcy Moore was Sheriff, while in 1922 Sheriff S.H.M. Killik was a very new Liveryman. Then in 1923, when Mr. (later Sir) Thomas Dron was Sheriff, the Master (Victor Brown), Upper Warden (J.H. Solomon), Immediate Past Master (G.H. Thompson) and another Past Master, with the Clerk and Beadle, rode in a carriage and pair.

In 1925, both Sheriffs were members of the Company – Francis Agar being a Past Master, and Charles Albert Batho having been elected to the Court in June of that year. It was accordingly felt that exceptional arrangements were required, and a special Court was convened. It was decided that the Company should "be represented by a car designed in an artistic manner to illustrate the trade, craft, or mystery of Gardening, and that Mr. Edward

[63]

Piper be requested to supply the car and decorations (in accordance with his design) at a cost not exceeding £70, and that a band of music be provided at a cost not exceeding £22 10s." – the band to be that of the 1st London Division of the Royal Engineers. Two landaus were to be hired, each drawn by a pair of horses, decorated with the Company's rosettes, and carrying in one the Master (W.T. Roberts), the Wardens (Sir John Young and R.J. Sainsbury) and the Clerk, in robes and Tudor hats with the Beadle on the box; and in the other, four members of the Court chosen by seniority and to be preceded by two commissionaires to bear the Company's banner. The gracious offer of the Fruiterers Company to supply fruit for the decoration of the car was accepted, and subscriptions from members of the Court and the Livery amounting to £62 10s helped to defray the cost of this imposing cavalcade.

The Company's efforts on this occasion brought a joint letter from the Sheriffs, who stated:

"We feel that we should recognise the extraordinary generosity of the Gardeners Company, to which both of us are so proud to belong, in connection with the car which was such a distinguished feature of the Lord Mayor's Show. It is the opinion of both of us that probably never has such a distinguished tribute been paid to the members of any Company who have occupied the official position we now hold, and the execution of it reflects the greatest credit on everyone concerned, both on the part of those who conceived the idea and those who executed it."

The following year, 1926, was even more noteworthy for the Company. It was recorded in the minutes that "probably for the first time in the history of the Company a 'Citizen and Gardener' was to be installed as Lord Mayor and that the Master, Wardens and Clerk were to be present at the Installation Ceremony in Guildhall and at the preliminary luncheon at the Mansion House: and further that the Lord Mayor Elect (Sir George Rowland Blades, M.P.) and the Lord Mayor and Sheriffs Committee had invited the Court to attend in the procession on 9th November. The Master and Wardens had informed the Remembrancer that the Company's tribute to the popularity of our Past Master would consist of the Band of the 1st London Division of the Royal Engineers, the banner of the Company's Arms borne by two commissionaires, and two motor landaulettes decorated with streamers and rosettes of the Company's colours, containing the Master (Sir John Young), the Wardens (R.J. Sainsbury and G.E.W. Beeson), the Immediate Past Master (W.T. Roberts), two Assistants, the Clerk and the Beadle."

Perhaps the expense of these two years was the reason for a resolution moved in Court by Past Master Sir Francis Agar – who disavowed any intention of criticising the action of the Master and Wardens in issuing appeals – "That in future the expenses in connection with the Lord Mayor's Procession shall be met from the funds of the Company instead of by asking for individual subscriptions from either members of the Court or the Livery". The resolution was carried, possibly because the 1926 appeal only realised some thirty-seven pounds.

In February 1927, "The Clerk reported that he had represented to the Town Clerk that this Company was the Lord Mayor's Fellowship and in the Lord Mayor's Procession went afore all other Fellowships in accordance with the programme of the Remembrancer; that following the Order of the Court of Aldermen of 10th April 1484 'the Fellowship of the same Mayor shall after the old custom of the said City go afore all other Fellowships in all places within the said City during the time of the Mayoraltie of the Mayor so chosen'". He had therefore asked the Town Clerk how he should advise the Court as to the Company's precedence during the current year, but the Town Clerk had replied that it was ordered by the Court of Aldermen in 1706 that "from henceforth no Company whereof the Lord Mayor for the time being shall be a member shall have or pretend to have any precedency on that account except on the Lord Mayor's day". This was a true Ebblewhite touch, combining his zeal for the Company's prestige with his passion for historical research, which in this case went somewhat awry.

It does not appear that the Company participated in the Show in 1927, when Assistant Sir Charles Albert Batho was Lord Mayor. In fact there is no further record in the minutes until 1932 when W. Lacon Threlford, who had become a member some five years previously, was the "lay" Sheriff. The minute is laconic, the matter being merely recorded as: "Communications – Letters were received from . . . the Lord Mayor and Sheriffs Committee (inviting the Company to take part in the Lord Mayor's Procession – declined)".

There is the usual hiatus in the records, owing to the destruction of the Company's Minute Book running from January 1934 to April 1941. It is worth noting, however, that in 1933 the Upper Warden (Sir George Broadbridge) was a Sheriff, and that the Lord Mayor in 1934 (Sir Stephen Henry Molyneux Killik) was a Gardener.

In spite of the absence of records, an amusing story is told of the Show of 1936, the year of Past Master Sir George Broadbridge's Mayoralty, when the Company was represented by a decorated car carrying the Master (A.N.

Pitts), the Upper Warden (Lt.Col. S.S.G. Cohen), Assistant F.J.B. Gardner, the Chaplain and the Clerk, in their gowns and Tudor hats. Prior to the procession, breakfast was served in Bakers Hall, which was then the Common Hall of the Company. According to Ebblewhite the traditional breakfast should have been boiled mutton and port wine, but bacon and eggs were served instead. When he saw that the Chaplain (the Revd. Tom Wellard) had consumed no less than five eggs, Ebblewhite drily protested that he would be egg-bound during the procession.

There is no record that the Company celebrated the Shrievalty of Alderman Sir Howard Button, who was Renter Warden in 1942-43 but who died in 1943 without succeeding to either the Mastership or the Mayoralty. Then in 1943 Liveryman Gervase Wood was elected the "lay" Sheriff, and in 1944 Seymour Howard (who was on the Court of Assistants) filled the same position. There is, however, no mention in the minutes of any participation by the Company in the Lord Mayor's Show on either occasion, although there were resolutions of congratulation to the Sheriffs.

Seymour Howard was elected an Alderman in 1945, and duly became Lord Mayor in 1954. This occasion again saw the Company represented, and the day began in the Guildhall Art Gallery with the presentation of addresses by various bodies with which the Lord Mayor was connected. That from the Company, engrossed and illuminated on vellum, read:

"To the Right Honourable The Lord Mayor – Alderman Harold Walter Seymour Howard. We, the MASTER WARDENS ASSISTANTS AND COMMONALTY of the COMPANY OF GARDENERS OF LONDON wish to offer to Your Lordship our heartfelt congratulations and good wishes on the day on which you assume the high and historic office of LORD MAYOR OF LONDON. Remembering that the Gardeners Company is your Mother Guild, of which you were Master in 1947-8, we feel special pride and satisfaction at your elevation to the Chief Magistracy of the City, the acme of a distinguished career of public service in the City and elsewhere, which we have followed with immense interest and admiration; we hope that you and the Lady Mayoress may be blessed with health and strength to carry out the manifold and arduous duties of the Office which you are undertaking. We further desire to express our thanks for all you have done in the past for the Company's welfare, and feel assured that your interest in it will continue undiminished. Our heartfelt wish is that you and the Lady Mayoress may enjoy a happy and brilliant year of office."

In the procession of 1954 was the ceremonial spade borne by a member of the Livery on foot, followed by a car with the Master (Sir Brunel Cohen), the Wardens (Lord Nathan and Donald Byford) and the Clerk. The car was decorated with flowers and had across its bonnet the banner with the Company's coat of arms, presented in 1895 by Maj. George Lambert, then Master.

In 1965, in the Mastership of A.J.D. Robinson, it was agreed that the Company should participate in the Lord Mayor's Show as a joint venture with the Metropolitan Public Gardens Association. On this occasion the Lord Mayor, Sir Lionel Denny, had no special connection with the Company. When the Company participated in 1966, however, it marked the Shrievalty of Past Master Edward Howard during the Mastership of Maj.Gen. K.C. Appleyard.

The Company provided, for the Lord Mayor's Show of 1969, a floral float with the theme "Come to the City and See the Flowers" – which was not surprising, since the Master that year was F.E. Cleary. While the Lord Mayor (Sir Ian Frank Bowater) was not of the Company, the Gardeners' involvement was therefore most appropriate in view of Cleary's enormous enthusiasm for the "Flowers in the City" campaign, as covered in Chapter 9.

On the occasion of the Mayoralty of Past Master Sir Edward Howard, in 1971, the Master (J.L. Stevenson), the Wardens (Bishop R.W. Stannard and N.A. Royce) and the Clerk rode in a horse-drawn carriage with the crest of the Company displayed on its doors. There was also a float with an exhibit divided into two sections, depicting "Work in the Garden" and "Leisure in the Garden", and it is recorded that financial contributions to the float had been made by the Metropolitan Public Gardens Association, the London Gardens Society and the London Flower Lovers League.

Again in 1980 there was no special connection with the Lord Mayor, Col. Sir Ronald Gardner-Thorpe, but the Company (in the Mastership of L.J. Reddall) participated with some forty Livery Companies in celebrating the Show's theme "Livery, Leadership and Youth". Then in 1981 the Company took part again, in the Mayoralty of Sir Christopher Leaver, this time to mark the Shrievalty of Liveryman Lady Donaldson, with a carriage transporting the Master (R.L. Payton), the Wardens (J.G. Keeling and R.Adm. M.J. Ross) and the Immediate Past Master (L.J. Reddall).

In 1983, in Dame Mary Donaldson's procession, the Master (R.Adm. M.J. Ross), the Wardens (P.D. Marriner and W.P. Maclagan) and the Clerk again rode in a horse-drawn carriage. On this occasion, however, the carriage was flanked by two small tractors drawing decorated trailers. They were escorted on foot (as in 1980) by members of the "Young Gardeners", at that time a flourishing self-regulated organisation of Liverymen and Freemen of the Company under the age of thirty-five, together with relatives of members of the Company and invited boys and girls. On the route, the walkers distributed flowers and vegetables to the onlookers.

One of the unique features of Dame Mary Donaldson's Mayoralty was particularly apt, given her association with the Gardeners Company. Her year of office was marked by the naming of a new salmon pink rose, "Mary Donaldson", bred by Cants of Colchester and selected by the Master (R.Adm. M.J. Ross) with the advice of Liveryman R.C. Balfour (then President of the World Federation of Rose Societies).

In 1991 the Master (R.C. Balfour) inaugurated a tradition of presenting the incoming and outgoing Lady Mayoresses and their companions with posies of roses, herbs and other flowers as they joined their coach in Guildhall Yard.

By its contribution to the Lord Mayor's Show, the Company has continued to reflect the fact that it is an important part of the life of the City. Most recently, in the 1992 Show of Sir Francis McWilliams, a foot escort was provided for the Lady Mayoress's coach, in recognition of the unusual fact that on this occasion the Lady Mayoress was a Liveryman of the Company. Led by the Upper Warden (E.M. Upward), this consisted of members of the Company and their families dressed in period costume, depicting the story of gardeners and gardening over the past four hundred years and bearing flowers, herbs and garden produce. A decorated trolley, carrying a "Flowers in the City" campaign banner, and a barrow completed the escort.

The Annual Presentation

Another longstanding example of close links with the City is the Annual Presentation to the Lord Mayor, a ceremony which originated from a suggestion in December 1907 by Charles Bayer, then Renter Warden. This was approved by the Court, who petitioned the then Lord Mayor (Sir John Bell) for permission to make the gift.

The petition is set out in the minutes of 24th March 1908 and recited the Company's Royal Charter of 1605, the approval of the Byelaws by the Lord Chancellor, Lord Treasurer and Chief Justice in 1606, and the further Royal Charter of 1616. It also stated that by reason of the opposition of unqualified persons the Company had experienced difficulty in carrying out the provisions of its Charters, and had in 1632 petitioned the Lord Mayor for a redress of their grievances. As a result Sir Edward Littleton, the Recorder, had on 29th June 1632, by direction of the Lord Mayor, issued his Warrant which had greatly contributed to the usefulness and prosperity of the Company and protected the Freemen in carrying on their trade in the London markets. The prayer of the petition was for leave to allow the Master, Wardens and Clerk to present to the Lord Mayor for the time being, annually on 29th June, a basket containing specimens of flowers, vegetables and herbs.

The response to this petition was a very appreciative letter from the Lord Mayor, written in his own hand on 14th April 1908, giving the requested permission and promising to ask his successors "to continue on their part the observance of this agreeable and pleasant practice". The first presentation was duly made on 1st July 1908 by Sir Thomas Dewar, the Master, and was contained in a gilt basket – the whole in the form of the Company's arms. In addition, an old English bouquet containing no fewer than forty flowers which were popular in 1632, and a second bouquet containing forty of the finest orchids known to the gardening world, were presented to the Lady Mayoress.

After the presentation the Master, Wardens and Clerk lunched with the Lord Mayor and Lady Mayoress – a practice which continued until 1984, and which must surely have been one of the most agreeable occasions of a Master's year. For many years the ladies of the Master, Wardens and Clerk were included in the invitation, and the lunch took place in either the private dining room or the Long Parlour at Mansion House. On one such occasion, the Lord Mayor informed the Master that the Gardeners were the only Livery Company to have the privilege of lunching "en famille" at Mansion House on a regular basis.

For some years past the presentation has taken the form of a smaller selection of garden produce, together with a cheque for the Lord Mayor's Charity. The luncheons have not been resumed since 1984, but sherry is served after the presentation.

The presentation in 1925 was particularly interesting, as it was attended by Major and Mrs. Francis Manley Lowe. Mrs. Lowe was a descendant of Sir Edward Littleton, the Recorder who had played such a significant role in the Company's history in 1632, and to commemorate the occasion Major Lowe presented to the Company a print of R. White's engraved portrait of Littleton.

Attacks on the City

It is a sad fact that, from time to time, the historic traditions of the City of London and its Livery Companies have come under attack. On such occasions, the civic City has always received the strong support of the Livery.

In March 1948, the Lord Mayor sent to all Livery Companies a circular regarding the Representation of the People Bill. The Court of the Gardeners responded by passing a resolution, calling for the retention of the separate representation of the City in Parliament and a special provision enabling the business community to record their votes for their business premises instead of where they reside. A successful protest against a similar Bill had been made in 1917, as announced in a somewhat flamboyant statement issued by a Committee of Livery Companies in the following terms:

"In spite of bitter opposition, the betrayal of our cause by those who should have been foremost in the fight for liberty, and widespread apathy . . . the City of London Livery Companies have obtained a signal triumph: (1) The historic Livery Vote has been retained; (2) The honour of the Livery Companies, which had been so unworthily impugned, has been triumphantly vindicated."

In 1977, and again in 1991, there were further attacks on the City and particularly on the Corporation of London. In the former case the Greater London Council (subsequently itself abolished), and in the latter case the Labour Party, campaigned for the abolition of this local authority which for many centuries had been inextricably linked with the Livery Companies. Still the Corporation survives.

Some City Connections Since 1960

In the period since 1960, the Minute Books have recorded numerous instances which indicate the prominent role played by the Company in City affairs. In some cases it is not easy to distinguish clearly between those activities relating to the "craft and mystery of gardening" and those identifying the Company with the City, which has led to some inevitable overlap with Chapter 9.

In 1964, reference was made at a Court meeting to the forthcoming City Festival of Flowers. The Lord Mayor, Sir James Miller, was acting as Patron and a number of eminent people with premises in the City were acting as Vice-Patrons, and the Master expressed the hope that all members of the Court would do everything possible to encourage flowers in the City during the Festival. Later that year the Court agreed to make a financial contribution to the decoration of the garden attached to St. Andrew by the Wardrobe, organised by the Metropolitan Public Gardens Association for the Festival.

In February 1965, the Master (M.J. Thurston) reported that Liveryman Harry Wheatcroft had offered a gift of one hundred roses to be presented by the Company to the City Corporation. These roses were planted in accordance with the suggestion of the City Architect, Liveryman George Chandler, in the Whittington Garden on the north side of Upper Thames Street.

The Lord Mayor's residence, Mansion House, became a topic on the Company's agenda in 1968, when the Master (L.H. Kemp) suggested that the roof garden was by no means suitable for such a prominent building. After devoting much time to the project, he prepared designs and plans which finally resulted in considerable improvements being made. As Past Master, Leslie Kemp not only sponsored the scheme but also provided the furniture. Following his Mastership of 1971-72, J.L. Stevenson presented five teak tubs. These gestures, and indeed the overall idea, were symbolic of the Company's regard for the City and for the office of Lord Mayor, for it was the expressed hope that the residents of Mansion House might be enabled to enjoy their short periods of leisure in a busy year in pleasant surroundings, while the roof garden might serve also as a reminder of the activities and interests of the Company.

In June 1971, it was reported to the Court that Past Master F.E. Cleary (Chairman of the Trees, Gardens and Open Spaces Committee of the Corporation) had asked the Corporation to secure a plot of land within the City as a garden which the Company could supply with plants, trees and shrubs. The request had been approved, and the Company had been allocated the Southern Garden of St. Dunstan in the East, the ruined Wren church at Eastcheap.

Liveryman Peter Stagg, the Corporation's Superintendent of Parks and Gardens, had indicated that he would be pleased to co-operate with the Company in preparing a plan and scheme for planting. Donations were invited from members of the Company to meet the initial costs of this extensive garden, which was duly opened on 13th October 1971 and has since been maintained by the Corporation of London.

Then in 1972 occurred an opportunity for the Company to create a very concrete and positive link with Guildhall itself, when the Corporation decided to reinstate the West Crypt, which had not been in use since its destruction in the Great Fire of 1666. It had been suggested that certain of the Livery Companies might make themselves responsible for the stained glass windows to be incorporated in the renovation, and the Gardeners readily agreed to take one as their own. Donations to cover the cost were made by 110 members of the Company, and the stained glass window was presented at Mansion House to the Lord Mayor (Past Master Sir Edward Howard) at the end of his Mayoralty in October 1972. The West Crypt was formally opened on 16th February 1973 by Sir Edward's successor as Lord Mayor, the Lord Mais, who unveiled the Company's window. The overall collection of Livery Company windows was officially installed by Lord Mayor Sir Hugh Wontner, on 8th April 1974.

The description of the Company's window states:
"At the centre are the full arms, supporters, crest and motto of the Company. Below is the shield of its illustrious member, the reigning Lord Mayor, together with some of the City regalia. Gardening is the most popular of all forms of recreation. It is also the most ancient since, as the arms of the Company show, it relieved the tedium of Adam in Paradise. The background of the window therefore shows seasonal flowers, with butterflies and birds, including the 'Gardener's Friend', the robin. At the head of the window are rain and sunshine, the latter represented in the form of a sunflower, as a compliment to the Company. In the centre of the window is England's emblem, the rose."

One of the many open spaces maintained by the Corporation of London, the churchyard of St. Bartholomew the Great, received the Company's special attention in 1973. To commemorate the 850th anniversary of the foundation of the Priory and Hospital of St. Bartholomew, the Company presented a ten year old English yew tree which was planted by the Master (Bishop R.W. Stannard).

In 1976, a decision by the Court of Common Council directly affected one of the Company's own rules. It had been resolved to permit the Freedom of the City of London to be acquired by Patrimony through either parent, which led the Company to follow suit. It would be manifestly in accordance with the spirit of the times, it was felt, if the right to the Freedom of the Company by Patrimony were made available to any person born in lawful wedlock if either parent at the time of birth had already been admitted to the Freedom of the Company.

The City of London Jubilee Garden was opened in Cavendish Court, adjoining Devonshire Square, on 27th June 1977. The Company had supported the appeal launched by the Metropolitan Public Gardens Association, of which Past Master F.E. Cleary was Chairman, to raise the necessary funds. This was a true community effort, with contributions from the London Silver Jubilee Committee, Livery Companies, Ward Clubs, societies, business firms and friends of the City of London. The opening ceremony was performed by the Lord Mayor, Commander Sir Robin Gillett, and the Garden was subsequently maintained by the Corporation – though sadly it is no longer in being, and today the site is occupied by an electricity substation.

In 1978 the Company agreed to share the cost, with the Metropolitan Public Gardens Association, of laying out and maintaining a piece of land to the west of St. Mary Somerset. This church, except for its tower, was destroyed in the Second World War. The garden was duly completed, and opened by the Lord Mayor (Sir Kenneth Cork) on 22nd November 1978. Trees were planted by the Master (D.A. Huggons) and the Chairman of the Metropolitan Public Gardens Association (Past Master F.E. Cleary).

Frank Steiner

When considering relations between the Company and the Corporation in the 1960s and 1970s, mention must be made of the active role played by Frank Nathaniel Steiner, who served two periods as Clerk to the Company (1958-69 and 1973-84).

Steiner was also Clerk to the Fletchers Company for a period from 1971, linking both Companies like his predecessors Charles and Beaumont Shepheard, and he was elected an Honorary Liveryman of the Fletchers in 1977. As recently as 1991, he served as Master of the Fletchers. In the case of the Gardeners, his devotion to the Company was recognised in 1969 when he was awarded the Honorary Freedom and elected an Honorary Liveryman.

Steiner's service to the Corporation of London began in 1962, with his election as a Common Councilman for the Ward of Bread Street. Together with F.E. Cleary, he ensured that environmental matters were high on the agenda and that the Corporation worked closely with the Company in the beautification of the City. He held various Chairmanships, and reached the pinnacle of achievement as a Common Councilman – in 1977 he was elected Chairman of the City Lands and Bridge House Estates Committee, and therefore Chief Commoner of the Corporation, and on 3rd March 1977 the Court of the Gardeners passed a unanimous resolution of congratulation.

West Ham Park

Finally, it is worth recording the role that members of the Company have played in the control and management of West Ham Park, an estate of seventy-seven acres situated in what is now the London Borough of Newham. The Park was conveyed to the Corporation of London in 1873, to be held on trust in perpetuity as "open public grounds and gardens for the resort and recreation of adults and as play grounds for children and youth".

It is administered by a Committee of Managers of which eight are elected by the Court of Common Council from among its members, four by the heirs-at-law of John Gurney (former owner of the estate) and three by the Parish of West Ham. Of the Common Councilmen serving over the years on the Committee, many have been Liverymen of the Gardeners Company and in recent years the Chairman has been Liveryman and Common Councilman Mrs. Janet Owen.

West Ham Park serves as the headquarters of the Corporation's Parks and Gardens Department, of which the Superintendent in recent decades has been successively Liveryman Peter Stagg and Freeman David Jones.

1. Freemen's Oath.

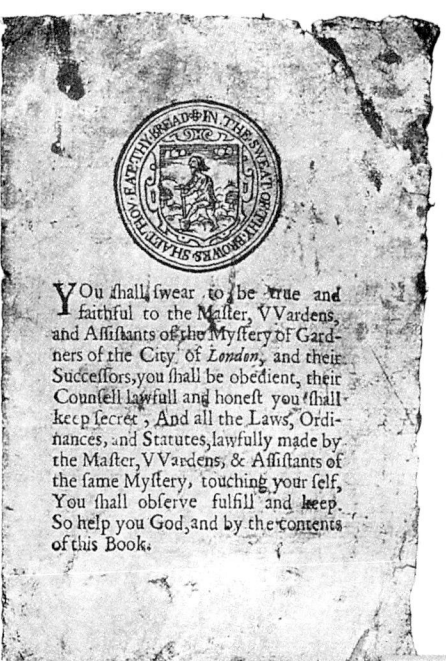

YOu shall swear to be true and faithful to the Master, VVardens, and Assistants of the Mystery of Gardners of the City of *London*, and their Successors, you shall be obedient, their Counsell lawfull and honest you shall keep secret, And all the Laws, Ordinances, and Statutes, lawfully made by the Master, VVardens, & Assistants of the same Mystery, touching your self, You shall observe fulfill and keep. So help you God, and by the contents of this Book.

2. Sir Edward Littleton.

3. Heading of the Second Royal Charter, 9th November 1616.

4. The Company's Coat of Arms.

5. Lord Mayor's Day 1992 — presentation by the Master of a posy to the outgoing Lady Mayoress.

6. Lord Mayor's Day 1992 — participation in the Lord Mayor's Show.

7. The Gardeners' Company Window — West Crypt, Guildhall.

8. The Queen's Coronation Bouquet — 2nd June 1953. Copy of a painting by Anna Zinkeisen reproduced by gracious permission of Her Majesty The Queen and with acknowledgement to The Medici Society Ltd, London.

9. A Basket of British Spring Flowers presented to Her Majesty The Queen to mark the 40th anniversary of her accession (1992).

10. The replica Coronation bouquet presented to Her Majesty The Queen at the former Royal Mint — 2nd June 1989.

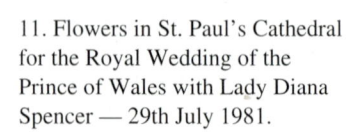

11. Flowers in St. Paul's Cathedral for the Royal Wedding of the Prince of Wales with Lady Diana Spencer — 29th July 1981.

12. Replica of the silver-gilt casket given by the Company to Her Majesty Queen Mary to commemorate the Silver Jubilee in 1935 (Appendix E, item 47)

13. The admission of the Prince of Wales to the Livery of the Company at Highgrove, Gloucestershire — 12th June 1987.

14. The Lord Mayor of London planting the last rose in St. Paul's Rose Garden — St. George's Day 1976.

15. The Company's stand at the City of London Flower Show (1992).

CHAPTER 5

Two Constitutional Issues

In the past thirty years, two matters relating to the Company's constitution brought significant change. They are considered in some detail here, because they may be said to have contributed greatly to the enhanced stature and reputation of the Company.

In the 1960s, it was becoming a worrying fact that the Court tended to have a far larger proportion of Past Masters than Assistants below the Chair. This was a situation which could only worsen, since the Court was limited in number to twenty-four (in addition to the Master and the two Wardens), and Past Masters were normally re-elected to the Court. Clearly it would have to be resolved, if the Company wished to provide a satisfactory line of promotion and satisfy the ambitions of younger Liverymen.

The nettle was finally grasped at the Court Meeting held on 19th October 1966, when Past Master Edward Howard moved a successful resolution that no more than twelve Past Masters should serve on the Court. This would mean that a vacancy on the Court would occur at least once each year, when one of the Assistants was elected Renter Warden. A less positive effect of the change, however, might have been that the experience and knowledgeable counsels of Past Masters would be lost to the Court if there were no vacancies for them. It was therefore also agreed that the title of Senior Past Master could be bestowed at the discretion of the Court on a Past Master, and that a Senior Past Master would be accorded all the privileges and rights of a member of the Court except the entitlement to vote. A Senior Past Master would not be counted as a member of the Court, and would not therefore occupy one of the twenty-four places.

This was a far-sighted approach, and a clear demonstration that the Company was in favour of progress rather than ossification. A few years later, however, there was another issue to be faced and another nettle to be grasped. It was one which would test not only the Company's readiness to accept change, but its attitude toward modern thinking.

In the Autumn of 1973, there arrived on the Clerk's desk an application for the Freedom (by Redemption) and Livery of the Company. It had been duly proposed and seconded by two Liverymen, in accordance with the regulations laid down by the Court. Both Liverymen happened to be Past Masters of the Company, one an Alderman and the other a member of the

Court of Common Council, and both had known the applicant for some years. The application was therefore completely in order, but it had one unusual feature in that the applicant was a lady.

Lady Donaldson, the wife of a High Court Judge who later became a Lord Justice of Appeal and Master of the Rolls, had in 1966 been elected a Common Councilman for the Ward of Farringdon Without. This was perhaps not surprising, since the Ward contained a large number of barristers as electors and Sir John and Lady Donaldson had residential premises in Essex Court in the Temple. Nevertheless her election was unique, since it made her the first lady to serve on the Court of Common Council.

On receipt of the application, the Clerk approached the Master (N.A. Royce) and was told to arrange for the applicant to appear before the next meeting of the selection committee. This duly occurred, and after the interview objections were voiced – not concerning the suitability of the applicant, but the principle of ladies becoming Liverymen. The Charters gave no guidance, because the Interpretation Act of the last century had laid down that words of the male gender were deemed to include the female. Although for many years ladies had been admitted to the Freedom of the Company by Patrimony, Servitude and Redemption, there was no precedent within the Gardeners Company for the admission of ladies to the Livery.

Consideration of Lady Donaldson's application was adjourned, but the Court proceeded in due course to tackle the principle which that application had raised. It soon became time to test the water, and on 5th June 1974 Past Master G.J. Gollin moved "That this Court would welcome the admission of ladies to the Livery". After discussion the motion was carried by fourteen votes to two, with three abstentions.

The following month there was a further long and full discussion, and it was unanimously agreed that the Court would invite H.R.H. Princess Alice, Duchess of Gloucester (already an Honorary Freeman of the Company since 1963) to become the first lady Liveryman. Pending her decision on acceptance, it was decided that no further action would be taken in connection with applications from ladies.

Her Royal Highness having graciously agreed to accept the offer of the Livery, the Court proceeded in September 1974 to approve the arrangements for her admission, including the substitution of the word "Sister" for the word "Brother" in the phrase "a full Brother Admitted" appearing in the declaration made by new Liverymen.

There then followed a lengthy discussion on the resolution of 5th June 1974. Among points resolved were that the decision should be made as widely known as possible within the Company, and that the Master should refer to it in his speech later that day at the Harvest Thanksgiving Reception. It was also agreed that lady Liverymen should be invited to become Dining Members, but that only male guests be permitted to attend the Livery Banquet (later to become merged with the Ladies Banquet, to which the restriction to male guests obviously never applied) and Court Dinners. The underlying reason for this decision was in order not to affect adversely the importance and impact of Ladies Banquets, and in fact the arrangement appears to have worked well.

Her Royal Highness duly became the first lady Liveryman at a Court Meeting held at Innholders Hall on 28th October 1974, when she honoured members of the Court by lunching with them after the ceremony and by responding to the toast to the Company's first lady Liveryman. A Court Meeting held following the luncheon saw the election to the Livery of Alice Carton, wife of the Master and daughter of the late Past Master Marcel Porn, and Janet Sheppard (later Owen), sister of the Upper Warden (David Longman) and daughter of Past Master Martin Longman. These ladies were already free of the Company by Servitude and Redemption respectively. There followed the election to the Freedom (by Redemption) and Livery of Lady Donaldson, while at the same Court it was agreed that all persons (male or female) admitted to the Livery should be designated Liverymen.

Within the next five months, four more ladies were elected to the Livery, and other Livery Companies in the next few years followed the example of the Gardeners. Miss Sylvia Tutt became the first lady to be Master of a Livery Company, the Chartered Secretaries and Administrators, although since that time Princess Anne (now the Princess Royal) has been Master of more than one Company.

So by the 1980s the barricades of male exclusivity within the Livery Companies of the City were breached, but were not down. A significant male bastion remained – the City Livery Club, described in its leaflets as "the Club for the Livery", which is situated in Syon College on Victoria Embankment. When the number of ladies in the Livery of Gardeners reached a meaningful proportion of the total, the Clerk (Frank Steiner) took action. He was then a Council Member of the Club, and pointed out on more than one occasion that it must either admit lady Liverymen to membership or alter its advertising, since it could not be "the Club for the Livery" if it excluded a growing number of the Company of which he was Clerk. This was to no avail, for the Council still refused to admit ladies, even as guests at lunch.

The year 1983 saw the turning point, when Lady Donaldson was elected Lord Mayor and was also created a Dame Grand Cross. The Lord Mayor had always been Patron of the City Livery Club, and the Patron could hardly be denied membership. Her election to membership followed almost immediately, and ladies were thereafter permitted to lunch as guests. Many ladies have since become Liverymen of those Companies that would admit them, and members of the Club in their own right – but even today, many Livery Companies still refuse to admit ladies.

CHAPTER 6

Personalities

It is patently obvious that the strength and success of a Livery Company lies in the sum total contributed in loyalty and active participation by its members, officers and staff. Yet it is always possible to single out those who have made a special contribution, whether by the sheer length of their involvement or by their specific attention to particular areas of the Company's activities.

In attempting to do so, the historian runs at least two risks. The first is that persons of prominence at one particular time, or who may even be remembered many years after, are often sadly forgotten in the long term. Thus it is possible for extensive coverage of any one person in a historical survey to be thought strange in years to come. The second problem is that the converse also applies, and there is the inevitable risk of causing offence to contemporary and recent personalities – who might indeed have made sterling contributions to the Company – by omitting them from consideration.

This Chapter, then, is very selective indeed, and it opens with some consideration of those who tend to be described as the "Grand Old Men".

George Rowland Blades

George Rowland Blades (1868-1953) was Knighted in 1918, created a Baronet in 1922 and 1st Baron Ebbisham of Cobham in 1928. He was for many years the Father of the Company, having been elected to the Freedom and Livery on 29th December 1890 and to the Court on 26th October 1903.

Blades was a man of very many parts. In City life, he was "lay" Sheriff (1917-18), Alderman for the Ward of Bassishaw (1920-48) and Lord Mayor (1926-27), and also served as H.M. Lieutenant for the City of London. His Livery service was not confined to the Gardeners, as he served as Master of both the Haberdashers and the Stationers, and his work for charitable organisations included Dr. Barnardo's Homes, the Primrose League, the City of London Savings Committee, and Christ's Hospital. He was a Fellow of the Society of Antiquaries, a Deputy Lieutenant of Surrey, a J.P. for the County of London and Surrey, and President of the Federation of British Industries (1928-29).

In politics, Blades was Unionist M.P. for the Epsom Division of Surrey from 1918 to 1928 and Treasurer of the Conservative Party from 1931 to

1933, and perhaps of interest to present-day readers is the fact that he was a member of the Channel Tunnel Committee of 1929. Among his international honours, he was a Grand Officer of the Legion of Honour, a Grand Officer of the Crown of Italy, a Grand Officer de l'Ordre de la Couronne (Belgium), and an Officer of the Order of the Nile.

In the case of the Worshipful Company of Gardeners, the admission of Blades to the Livery in 1890 was irregular, as in 1903 the new Clerk (E.A. Ebblewhite) pointed out that Blades had not taken up his Freedom of the City. This was rectified by his readmission after doing so, and until the later years of his life were clouded by illness he continued to take a lively interest in the Company, which he served as Master in 1912-13. The Company's official visit to Belgium in 1913, led by Blades, helped to establish the tradition whereby the Company made many worthwhile international links.

Robert Inigo Tasker

One of the most remarkable records of service to the Company was that of Sir Robert Inigo Tasker (1868-1959), who succeeded Lord Ebbisham as Father of the Company on the latter's death in 1953. He was elected to the Freedom and Livery in July 1897 and to the Court in November 1897, and was Master in 1908-09 and again in 1939-40 following the death in office of S.H. Baker. He was also a member of the Paviors and the Fanmakers Companies.

Tasker received his Knighthood in 1931. In his professional life he was a Fellow of the Incorporated Association of Architects and Surveyors, and the Association's President from 1927 to 1929, as well as serving as Honorary Surveyor to many charitable institutions. His public service included a long period as a J.P. for the County of London from 1910, as Unionist M.P. for East Islington from 1924 to 1929, as Unionist M.P. for Holborn from 1935 to 1945, and as a Member of the London County Council from 1910 to 1937.

Notwithstanding his long period of sixty-two years' service to the Worshipful Company of Gardeners, it was rare until just before his death in February 1959 for Tasker to miss a Court Meeting. So active was he that in November 1955, at the age of eighty-seven, he presided as Senior Past Master in the absence of the Master (Lord Nathan) at a dinner of Liverymen and Freemen held at Mansion House to celebrate the 350th anniversary of the Company's first Royal Charter. In that year it was recorded that in the previous nine years he had attended thirty-seven out of forty-five Courts held.

On 12th June 1957 it was resolved that:
"The Court wishes to pay an affectionate tribute to their much respected colleague Sir Robert Inigo Tasker, T.D., D.L., J.P., the Father and Senior Past Master of the Company, on the forthcoming 60th anniversary of his admission to the Freedom of the Company on 6th July 1897. The members feel that a Diamond Jubilee would be a notable occasion in the case of any member, and is particularly so in the present case. Throughout his 60 years' membership of the Company, and in spite of the pressure of his manifold public activities, which included 27 years' membership of the London County Council (of which he was chairman in 1930-1) and membership of the House of Commons from 1924-9 and again from 1935-45, Sir Robert Tasker has always given freely of his time to the welfare of the Company, which he has twice served as Master, and has played a great part in the revival of its fortunes. The members of the Court wish to place on record their deep gratitude to him for all his services to the Company, and, in assuring him of the affection in which he is held by all the members of the Company, to express the hope that they may have the benefit of his wise counsel and his genial personality in the years to come."

In May 1958, Tasker tendered his resignation from the Court on the grounds of age and ill health. After his long service to the Company this could hardly be refused, although he had been told on previous occasions when he had considered resigning that his was "a life sentence". The difficulty was surmounted by his election as an Honorary Assistant, but he died just a few months later.

Thornton-Smith and Gollin
Another record of long service to the Company was that of Ernest Thornton-Smith (1881-1971), who became Father of the Company and was very active in its affairs. He was elected in June 1927, and was Master in 1938-39.

Thornton-Smith served with the Ministry of Food from 1917 to 1919, and in the 1930s was Chairman of the National Mark Egg and Poultry Trade Committee, the Government Director on the National Mark Egg Central Board, and the Minister of Agriculture's representative on the Pig Marketing Board. He was a Fellow of the Institute of Directors and a Fellow of the Royal Society of Arts, and his charitable work was prodigious – including Our Dumb Friends League, the Hospital for Women in Soho, the Middlesex Hospital, the Blue Cross and the Friends of St. John.

Given these facts, it is perhaps strange to describe him as a gentleman of leisure and a country squire. He was a great public benefactor, however, and in the 1960s gave considerable lands in Sussex and Cornwall to the National Trust.

Among many kindnesses to the Worshipful Company of Gardeners, he presented in 1939 the charming statue of Queen Anne in Queen Anne's Gate, Westminster, which suffered the indignity of being bricked up during the war but has for many years given pleasure to lovers of Georgian London. Since the early 1970s, the care and maintenance of the statue has been undertaken by the Department of the Environment.

Following Thornton-Smith's death in 1971, the longest serving member of the Company was Geoffrey Joseph Gollin (1901-92). An engineer by profession, Gollin worked first in the 1920s on diesel engines and then turned to his lifelong work on continuous combustion. Immediately before the Second World War he worked on combustion systems for the Whittle jet engine, and throughout the War he played a significant role in developing a British liquid-fuel rocket in parallel to the German V2. Throughout his life, Gollin also devoted himself to a wide range of charitable and social concerns – including the Scout movement, girls' education and the history of London.

Gollin's service to the Worshipful Company of Gardeners was phenomenal. He was elected in 1928, and served as Master in 1958-59. At the time of his death in 1992 he had overtaken Ebbisham and Tasker, with his magnificent total of sixty-four years' service to the Company.

Ernest Arthur Ebblewhite

Turning from notable and long-serving members to a notable and long-serving Clerk, there is one name that appears in these pages more frequently than any other – that of Ernest Arthur Ebblewhite. While it is necessary to avoid repetition, a history of the Gardeners Company would be deficient if it did not draw together a picture of the remarkable man who was its Clerk for thirty-four years, and to whom so much credit for developing its position in the civic life of the City was due.

Ebblewhite (1867-1947) was a Barrister at Law (Middle Temple) and a Fellow of the Society of Antiquaries, who first applied for the Clerkship on the resignation of James Curtis in 1894. He was not successful, and the post was occupied by Robert Gofton-Salmond until 1902. Ebblewhite then applied again and, in the face of opposition from a strong list of ten candidates, he was elected at the age of only thirty-five.

Throughout these pages, it is demonstrated how industriously he applied himself to putting the Company's affairs into order – although he was already Clerk of the Tin Plate Workers Company (1894-1937), which must have occupied much of his time. He was the bureaucrat *par excellence*, in the most complimentary sense of the term, and he brought to the work a correctness and a bent for historical research which was to prove invaluable on countless occasions.

Even so, it is impossible to dispel the feeling that in those early times – and perhaps throughout subsequent decades – there were many occasions for irritation in the Company's higher echelons. Ebblewhite had to meet any suggestion of cutting corners and any impulsive proposal for ill-considered action, and he did so by skilful use of research, rules and protocol. It was to his credit, and to the Company's benefit, that he used the same incisive skills when dealing with other organisations with which the Company had relations.

Members of the Court must have been shaken by the Agenda for Ebblewhite's first Court Meeting only ten weeks after he had assumed office, the minutes of which take up fifteen pages. It covered advice on future elections to the Court, long-standing irregularities in the admission of members to the Livery, the formation of a separate Charitable Fund, the finances of the Entertainment Fund, a report on the discovery of early records of the Company, and the presentation of the petition of Joseph William Hipkins to be elected and recorded in the City Chamberlain's Office as a member of the Company.

As recorded in other Chapters, Ebblewhite kept up the pressure, crossed swords with the Royal Horticultural Society over the scholarships and with the Guildhall Librarian over the Company's library, instigated and carried through the petition to the King for leave for the Company to continue to bear its ancient arms, and was mainly responsible for the Company's visits abroad.

In the course of his period of office he received many honours, not the least being his election as Master of the Ironmongers Company in 1928, and to the Presidency of the Fellowship of Clerks of Livery Companies (of which he was one of the founders) in the same year. He was Mayor of Hornsey in 1908, and became a Justice of the Peace of Middlesex in 1909. Company directorships, and charitable work in hospitals and schools, also added to his busy life.

In 1914 the King of the Belgians conferred on Ebblewhite the

Decoration Speciale Agricole 1st Class, in 1919 he was made a Chevalier of the Order of the Crown of Belgium, and in 1921 he was promoted to Officer of the Order. In 1925 he became an Esquire of the Order of St. John of Jerusalem, and in 1929 was promoted to be a Commander of the Order. Then in 1929 he received the honorary degree of Doctor of Laws from Sheffield University, and the Honorary Fellowship of the Royal Horticultural Society.

For the last six years of his tenure as Clerk to the Gardeners Company, he was also Clerk to the Framework Knitters (1931-37) as well as the Tin Plate Workers, and was Master of the Parish Clerks Company in 1941-42.

The Court decided in 1927 to mark the twenty-fifth anniversary of Ebblewhite's election as Clerk, and in response to an appeal to members "a substantial sum" was raised. A cheque was presented to him, with an album containing the following address: "To Ernest Arthur Ebblewhite Esq., J.P., F.S.A., – The Master, Wardens, Assistants and Commonalty of the Company of Gardeners of London express to you their congratulations and best thanks on the completion of your 25 years work as Clerk of the Company and ask you to accept as the result of their personal subscriptions the accompanying cheque and this album in appreciation of your services."

This was signed by the Master, Wardens, thirteen Past Masters, eleven other members of the Court, 110 Liverymen and twenty Freemen – surely evidence that rarely, if ever, has a Livery Company been more devotedly and successfully served by its Clerk.

In 1943, long after his resignation as Clerk, Ebblewhite presented the Company with its ceremonial spade. This further example of his devotion, and his indefatigability in fulfilling ambitions for the Company, is more fully covered in Chapter 15 (item 59).

Frederick Ernest Cleary

Finally, it is appropriate to pay tribute to a more recent figure who did so much in the best interests of the Company. It is suggested above that Ebblewhite deserves much of the credit for improving the Company's position in the civic life of the City of London, and the same can surely be said of Frederick Ernest Cleary (1905-1984).

Cleary's interest in the Livery was not restricted to the Gardeners, for in common with Ebblewhite he was closely connected with the Tin Plate Workers. It was his Mother Company, of which he was Master in 1964.

CHAPTER 6

A Fellow of the Royal Institute of Chartered Surveyors from 1929, Cleary founded Haslemere Estates Ltd., was its Chairman from 1943 to 1983, and also founded and Chaired the City and Metropolitan Building Society from 1948. One of the major concerns of Haslemere Estates, not surprisingly in view of his personal interests, was the restoration of old buildings in London in a manner friendly to the environmental needs of the locality.

It is significant that in his autobiography *I'll do it Yesterday* (Carlos Press, 1979) he wrote: "With environmental changes in view, therefore, I became a member of the Hornsey Borough Council . . . (where) my single-minded concentration on Hornsey's beautification earned me the nickname Amenity Cleary." Later, his similar concentration in the City led to his nickname Flowering Fred. While a member of Hornsey Borough Council, Cleary wrote the book *Beauty and the Borough* (St. Catherine Press, 1949), which described his work in adding to the amenities of streets and buildings.

He was Chairman of Hornsey Town Planning Committee, and in 1951 was Deputy Mayor of the Borough. Then in 1959 he was elected in the City of London as Common Councilman for the Ward of Coleman Street, appointed Deputy of his Ward in 1977 by Lady Donaldson (Alderman and Gardener), and served until his death on 17th June 1984. He was able to show his interest in the environment to full effect during his Chairmanship of the Corporation's Trees, Gardens and Open Spaces Committee, and he managed with great effect to relate the interests of both the Worshipful Company of Gardeners and the Corporation by improving almost beyond recognition the amenities of the Square Mile.

The involvement of the Company in numerous horticultural projects in the City from 1960 onwards owed much to the relentless drive with which Fred Cleary pursued his passion for trees and floral displays. His close association with successive Lord Mayors – and with the Company's Clerk Frank Steiner, who served with Cleary on the Court of Common Council – did much to keep the Gardeners Company in the City limelight.

From 1959, Cleary was closely involved with the conduct of the Church Gardens Competition. The Metropolitan Public Gardens Association, of which he was Chairman from 1954 until his death thirty years later, judged and reported on that competition while it continued, in addition to supplying advice to any place of worship of any denomination which had a garden or churchyard.

On 5th February 1964, Cleary was elected to the Court of Assistants of the Company. He became Master in 1969, and one of his first acts was to divide the Flowers in the City awards into three categories. He also led a delegation to Holland and Belgium in the following year. His book *The Flowering City* (City Press, 1969) has since run into eight editions, the last being published to mark the centenary of the Metropolitan Public Gardens Association in 1982. Copies have been presented to distinguished guests and contacts of the Company, including the Queen on the occasion of a personal presentation of the replica Coronation bouquet.

Cleary, together with Liveryman R.C. Balfour, was instrumental in the planting of the Rose Garden at St. Paul's Cathedral in 1976, to mark the centenary of the Royal National Rose Society, and another product of Cleary's strenuous efforts was the first City of London Flower Show in September 1979.

Fred Cleary received many honours. He was invested with the M.B.E. in 1951, received an Honorary Fellowship from Magdalene College Cambridge in 1975, became an Officer of the Legion of Honour in 1976, and saw his tireless efforts fully recognised in 1979 with the award of the C.B.E. Then on 17th March 1982, the Court of the Worshipful Company of Gardeners was able to congratulate Cleary on the award by the Royal Horticultural Society of the Veitch Memorial Medal for services to gardening in the City.

Shortly afterwards the Metropolitan Public Gardens Association inaugurated the Cleary Garden in Queen Victoria Street, on a site leased by the Corporation of London. The Garden was subsequently maintained by the Corporation under the direction of the Superintendent of Parks and Gardens (Liveryman Peter Stagg) and his successor (Freeman David Jones), and in 1993 the lease was surrendered to the Corporation and remains a memorial to Fred Cleary's service to horticulture in the City.

Such a record of public service prompted a remark by the Lord Mayor, Sir Robin Gillett, in 1977. It was a known fact, he said, that no manhole cover was ever left off during the lunch hour, because the workmen on their return would have found that Fred Cleary had planted a tree in the hole!

And Many Others

There have, of course, been many other people who have given sterling service to the Company. Whether by initiating or organising special projects, or by contributing their time and expertise over many years, they have ensured that the Company has developed a standing in keeping with the motives of that dedicated band who promoted the revival of 1890. In some cases, this devotion to the Company has been shown by many generations of the same family.

While this Chapter has had to be selective, the Appendices abound with the names of long-serving members and officials. The Index, with its numerous references, also draws attention to the many members whose various contributions have been recognised throughout this book.

CHAPTER 7

The Honorary Freedom of the Company

The Court has the power to confer the Honorary Freedom of the Company on persons who have distinguished themselves by public service or individual merit.

The first such Honorary Freedom was conferred on 14th October 1896 on the Hon. Alicia Margaret Tyssen Amherst, in recognition of her work *The History of Gardening in England* (Quaritch, 1895). She was later admitted to the Freedom in open Court by the Master, N.N. Sherwood, and her Freedom Certificate was enclosed in a silver casket subscribed for by members of the Court. At that time it was not customary for ladies to be heard and her father, Lord Amherst of Hackney, returned thanks to the Court on her behalf. Miss Amherst subsequently became Mrs. Evelyn Cecil, and later Lady Rockley.

In October 1907 the Master (Sir Thomas Dewar) raised in Court the question of conferring the Honorary Freedom on a number of Presidents or Chairmen of Societies in the fields of horticulture, botany and agriculture. On 24th March 1908 formal resolutions were submitted and passed to confer the Honorary Freedom on H.S.H. The Duke of Teck, President of the Royal Botanic Society of London, in recognition of his ten years' association with the work of that Society; on the Earl of Meath, Chairman and founder of the Metropolitan Public Gardens Association, in recognition of his twenty-six years' interest in its work and the encouragement he had given to the formation of similar bodies in the Colonies; on Lord Monkswell, Chairman of the Kyrle Society, in recognition of his seventeen years' association with the work of the Society and of his interest in its open spaces branches; on Prof. W.A. Herdman, President of the Linnean Society, in recognition of his twenty-eight years' association with the Society and of his services to science; and on F.S.W. Cornwallis, Trustee and Past President of the Royal Agricultural Society of England, in recognition of fifteen years' work with the Society and of his services to agriculture.

Meath, Herdman and Cornwallis were admitted to the Freedom at a special Court on 19th May 1908 held at Fishmongers Hall; Monkswell on 8th July 1908 at Salters Hall; and the Duke of Teck at a special Court on 26th April 1909.

CHAPTER 7

On 20th June 1913 Lord Grenfell, President of the Royal Horticultural Society, was elected to the Honorary Freedom to mark his twelve years' connection with the Society. This was followed on 14th July 1914 by the admission of Viscountess Wolseley, Principal of the School of Gardening at Glynde in Sussex, "in recognition of her services to horticulture in the training of women as gardeners".

31st May 1917 saw the election of R.E. Prothero (later Lord Ernle), the President of the Board of Agriculture, with whom the Company had been in touch on ways in which it could assist horticulture and agriculture during the war.

There was then a long gap until 8th April 1931, when the first Honorary Freedom was conferred on a foreigner in the person of the Comte de Kerchove de Denterghem, the President of the Royal Horticultural Society of Belgium. His son Jacques, in the same capacity, received the honour in 1955 at a special Court in Ghent during the Company's visit to the Floralies Gantoises. Indeed that worthwhile tradition was maintained when, in 1983, the Honorary Freedom was conferred on the Comte Andre de Kerchove de Denterghem, who had succeeded to the Presidency on the retirement of his uncle Jacques.

The Hon. Henry Duncan McLaren (later Lord Aberconway), as President of the Royal Horticultural Society and the owner of the renowned gardens at Bodnant, was elected on 2nd November 1932. Then followed on 5th May 1933 Princess Mary (the Princess Royal), and on 5th March 1935 the Prince of Wales (Edward, later the Duke of Windsor), details of whose admission ceremony perished in the Blitz.

Three past Clerks have received the Honorary Freedom (though strangely enough not Ebblewhite) – Stephen William Price in 1947, Arnold Francis Steele in 1956 and Frank Nathaniel Steiner in 1969. Steele and Steiner were also elected Honorary Liverymen.

12th September 1951 saw the election of Sir Edward James Salisbury, Director of the Royal Botanic Gardens at Kew; and 17th July 1957 that of Frank Kingdom Ward, the botanist, explorer and author.

In Chapter 10, reference is made to the election of Queen Juliana of the Netherlands in 1950, and King Baudouin of the Belgians in 1962, in connection with visits of the Court abroad. In fact the Company has a proud record of conferring its Honorary Freedom on members of European royal families who have shown great interest in horticulture – continuing this tradition in 1971 with King Gustav VI Adolf of Sweden, and in 1975 with Queen Fabiola of the Belgians.

In the case of our own Royal Family, recent decades have seen the Honorary Freedom conferred upon the Duke of Gloucester, who was also admitted as an Honorary Liveryman (1963), the Duchess of Gloucester (1963) and the Prince of Wales, who was also admitted as an Honorary Liveryman (1987). As mentioned in Chapter 5, the Duchess of Gloucester later became the first lady to be invested with the Livery of the Company, on 28th October 1974.

Meanwhile the Honorary Freedom continued to be conferred on a small but wide-ranging number of people dedicated to horticulture or agriculture, or who had performed special services to the Company. 22nd November 1961 saw the election of the third Lord Aberconway, who had succeeded Sir David Bowes Lyon as President of the Royal Horticultural Society; in 1967 the honour was conferred on Sir George Taylor, Director of the Royal Botanic Gardens at Kew; in 1971 on His Excellency Contra-Almirante Americo Deus Rodrigues Thomaz, President of Portugal; in 1978 on Blanche Henrey, author of the three-volume *British Botanical and Horticultural Literature before 1800* (Oxford University Press, 1975); in 1979 on Sir Giles and Lady Loder, owners of the famous gardens at Leonardslee; in 1982 on Professor William Thomas Stearn, President of the Linnean Society and of the Garden History Society; and in 1990 on Robin Arthur Elidyr Herbert, President of the Royal Horticultural Society.

Mention has already been made of the Company's recognition of those who have performed direct services, by conferring its Honorary Freedom on three successive Clerks. This also happened in the case of Arthur Herbert Hall, Honorary Librarian, on his retirement in 1966.

The Company has always been eager to recognise outstanding services to it, but this has normally taken the form of the gift of Freedom by Presentation without fine, which is not to be confused with the Honorary Freedom. The Freedom by Presentation was given in various cases following the Company's revival, and it is also worth recording that it was given on the retirement of two Honorary Librarians – Bernard Kettle in 1926 and Raymond Smith in 1956. Mention is made elsewhere of the gift of Freedom by Presentation to the Company's scholars from 1894, and these are denoted in Appendix C. The honour was similarly awarded in 1953 to Miss Constance Evelyn Fears, in recognition of her skill and artistry in connection with the Queen's wedding and Coronation bouquets; in 1955 to Arthur Blanchard Booth, who served as Beadle from 1945 to 1967; and to many others before and since.

To summarise the above, only thirty-six Honorary Freedoms have been conferred in almost one hundred years. This surely indicates the importance with which the Court regards its powers in this respect, and the careful selectivity with which the honour is bestowed.

To conclude in humorous vein, however, it may be said that historians sometimes give added prestige to an honour by referring to those who have declined it. In the present case, some examples may be quoted. It is recorded that in 1896 the Honorary Freedom and Livery of the Company were refused by Joseph Chamberlain, who pleaded pressure of state affairs. In 1947 Princess Elizabeth declined the Honorary Freedom on the grounds that she had received so many similar requests, and the same fate met a request to Princess Margaret in 1953, it being pointed out that two other Companies would have priority in the event of her wishing to become a Freesister of one of the Livery Guilds. At about that time it was hoped that David Bowes Lyon, President of the Royal Horticultural Society, would consent to election to the Honorary Freedom, but the regulations of the Clothworkers Company, of which he was already a Liveryman, prevented his acceptance of membership of another Guild. Earlier, in 1943, the Duke of Norfolk had been obliged to refuse the honour on similar grounds, as he was already an Ironmonger.

CHAPTER 8

Royal Occasions

The most interesting and valued privileges of the Company relating to the Royal Family are those of providing the Queen's bouquet for her Coronation and the bridal bouquets of Royal Princesses.

It is impossible to say how these privileges grew up, owing to the loss of all Minute Books from 1605 to 1764 and the virtual absence of records between the mid-1830s and 1890. Furthermore, regarding the privilege of supplying the Queen with her Coronation bouquet, there is no reference in the minutes to this having occurred on the Coronation of King Edward VII and Queen Alexandra in 1901.

On 26th April 1909 the Duke of Teck, brother of Princess May, Princess of Wales, became an Honorary Freeman of the Company, and on 29th November 1910 was presented to the Chamberlain of London to make application for the Freedom of the City which was granted by the Court of Aldermen on 6th December. He took up his Freedom of the City on 16th February 1911, attended by the Master (Charles Bayer), Sir Trevor Lawrence (Past Master, acting as Upper Warden), Sir Horace Brooks Marshall (Renter Warden), Beaumont Shepheard (Past Master) and the Clerk.

As the date for the Coronation of King George V and Queen Mary approached, the Duke of Teck was asked to ascertain Her Majesty's pleasure. He presented to the Company the original letter to him and the envelope, both in Queen Mary's hand, and the letter reads:

"Yes, of course I will accept a bouquet from the Gardeners Company on Coronation Day, but I cannot promise to take it with me as this would be impossible. – Mary."

A resolution of "respectful homage" to Her Majesty was passed, coupled with a request that she would receive a deputation from the Company for the purpose of the presentation. On 10th May 1911 the Queen's Private Secretary wrote to the Clerk:

"I spoke to the Queen this morning. Her Majesty would much like a sort of permanent gilt stand into which growing flowers could be put. This would really be preferable to a bouquet. I believe I am right in saying that the Queen likes carnations and that pink is a colour which is pleasing to Her

Majesty but she would prefer to leave all these details to the donors. The only thing that Her Majesty cannot stand is 'asparagus grasses' as she suffers at times from hay fever."

On 11th May 1911 it was reported that "Lady Hermione", a pink border carnation, had been chosen for the large Coronation bouquet as well as for the smaller one to be carried in the public procession on 23rd June. The offer of Leopold de Rothschild, President of the National Carnation and Picotee Society (Southern Section), to obtain the blooms from growers appointed by them, was gratefully accepted. The flowers were supplied by Charles Blick, of Warren Nurseries, Hayes, Kent, the making of the bouquets being entrusted to Edward Piper, a Freeman of the Company.

It was further reported that "the Queen would much like a permanent silver-gilt flower-stand in the form of the Jacobean basket represented in the Company's crest", which the Master had commissioned from Elkington and Company at his own expense. The Court voted, however, that the cost (estimated at £70) should be shared by the members of the Court, and that the flower stand "should be filled with cut blooms of the white self border carnation 'Mrs. Everard Martin Smith' and a new light pink seedling at present un-named". This choice had been approved by the Queen.

This conflicts with a statement in the note prepared in 1938 for the annual presentation to the Lord Mayor – which was the last of these notes before the Second World War – that "the flower stand was filled with cut blooms of two new border carnation seedlings, a white, named 'King George' in honour of the occasion, and a light pink afterwards known as 'Queen Mary'...On 23rd June 1911, during the Royal Progress, Her Majesty carried another bouquet of Lady Hermione carnations, the gift of the Company."

The Times reported that Queen Mary received at Buckingham Palace on 19th June 1911 a deputation from the Company, together with others from the Fanmakers, Glovers, Needlemakers and Makers of Playing Cards, from whom she received gifts. The officials received on this occasion were the Master (Charles Bayer) and the Clerk (E.A. Ebblewhite). It must be presumed that the Company's gift was the flower stand and the bouquet and that, as the Queen had said in her letter to the Duke of Teck, no bouquet was carried by her at the Coronation itself. But it is clear that she carried a bouquet from the Company on the Royal Progress on the following day, and indeed had asked to see a specimen bouquet beforehand.

A resolution of thanks to Ebblewhite for his "initiative and personal influence" and "the excellent manner in which he has carried out the elaborate arrangements and dealt with the mass of detail" was passed by the Court, and ordered to be emblazoned on vellum and issued to him under the Common Seal.

Curiously enough, the minutes of the next Court after the Coronation – on 3rd July – contain no report of the presentation, although there was a letter of thanks from the Queen's Private Secretary and at the October 1911 Court the Master was congratulated on having received the Coronation Medal.

In February 1912, it was resolved that "such of the Master and Wardens Assistants and Clerk as were members of the Coronation Committee...should bear an emblem on or over the chain loop or ribbon by which their respective badges of office may be suspended". The emblem was described as containing the Queen's crown and a representation of the Lady Hermione carnation, the Coronation flower, with the legend "Coronation 1911". It may still be seen on the badges of office of the Master, Wardens and Clerk and the Past Master's Badge of Sir Robert Tasker, until his death the last surviving member of the Court of that day.

Although it is known that the Company similarly provided the Queen's bouquets for the Coronation of King George VI and Queen Elizabeth on 12th May 1937, and for the subsequent Royal Progress, enemy action in May 1941 resulted in the destruction of the Minute Book covering that event.

Soon after the accession of Queen Elizabeth II in February 1952, enquiries were made from the Remembrancer of the City of London which established that the Company's privilege was a matter of the personal pleasure of the sovereign, and not one for the Court of Claims set up to investigate the rendering of services to the sovereign at his or her Coronation. This is borne out by what took place in 1911 regarding the Coronation of King George V and Queen Mary, the approach to the Queen then being informal. Application was accordingly made for the renewal of the Company's traditional privilege, although on this occasion it concerned the Coronation of a Queen Regnant rather than a Queen Consort.

Her Majesty was graciously pleased to permit the Company to furnish the bouquet to be carried on the Coronation Drive to Westminster Abbey in 1953. It was, however, felt inappropriate to seek leave to make the presentation in person, particularly as the other Companies who had participated in 1911 were not making presentations on this occasion.

The Court entrusted the making of the Coronation bouquet to Martin Longman, the member of the Court who had also made Her Majesty's bouquet on the occasion of her marriage, as Princess Elizabeth, with the Duke of Edinburgh. Longman had the inspired thought that the Coronation bouquet should be composed of flowers from all parts of the British Isles. This symbolism caught the fancy of the press and, as the date of the Coronation approached, newspaper cuttings on the subject poured into the Company's office from throughout the world.

Such was the interest that the Company received cuttings from the *South China Sunday Post*, the *Cape Times*, the *East African Standard*, the *Times of Malta*, the *Barbados Advocate*, the *Western Mail* (of Perth), the *Ottawa Citizen*, the *Trinidad Guardian*, *Dawn Karachi*, the *New Zealand Herald*, the *Toronto Star*, the *Montreal Star*, and *Ekstrabladet* (of Copenhagen). One over-zealous gossip writer allowed his imagination full rein, by drawing a word-picture of Prince Philip treasuring in his pocket book the bill for the bouquet!

The final choice was of white catleya orchids from Crowborough and Tunbridge Wells, odontoglossum orchids from Tunbridge Wells, cyprepedium orchids from Bodnant in North Wales, white roses from Cheshunt in Hertfordshire, stephanotis from Ayr, white carnations from Belfast, and lily of the valley from Honiton in Devon. As a last minute addition, at the request of the Manx Government resulting from the publicity given to the bouquet, lilies of the valley were flown from the Isle of Man, with one spray from the garden of the Master (R.B. Ling). The predominant flowers in the bouquet were the orchids and stephanotis.

The Clerk (Arnold Francis Steele) had been instructed to attend at the Privy Purse door of Buckingham Palace at 9 a.m. on Coronation morning, when he would be escorted to the apartments of the Lady in Waiting to whom he was to hand the bouquet. But this arrangement fell through, as it was found that at that time the Privy Purse entrance would be thronged by those about to take their places in the procession and the Lady in Waiting would be in the Abbey. Finally it was arranged that the Clerk (accompanied by Martin Longman) should be taken to Her Majesty's private apartments, where the bouquet would be handed to her personal page.

Armed with a special police pass and taking a route south of the river, the party had an unexpectedly quick journey from Longman's premises in

Fenchurch Street to the Palace, and they arrived in the corridor outside the Queen's apartments just as the page was serving Her Majesty's breakfast. The bouquet was duly handed to him, and those who saw the Queen carrying it on the drive to the Abbey were unanimous in their approval of its beauty.

Another bouquet was provided by the Company a few days later for the State Drive of the Queen and the Duke of Edinburgh to Guildhall, to be entertained at a Luncheon given by the Corporation of London to celebrate the Coronation.

In view of her inability to receive the Coronation bouquet in person, Her Majesty was graciously pleased to receive the Master and Wardens (F.A.B. Luke, Sir Brunel Cohen and Lord Nathan), with the Clerk in attendance, at Buckingham Palace on 19th May 1954. In a delightfully informal ceremony, they presented a bouquet for the Queen to carry on her State Drive with the Duke of Edinburgh to Mansion House, to be entertained by the Corporation of London on their return from a tour of New Zealand and Australia.

The Presentation of "Replica" Bouquets

Each year, on the anniversary of their respective Coronations, the late Queen Mary and Queen Elizabeth the Queen Mother have consented to accept what has usually been described as a replica of their Coronation bouquets, but in many cases has been in fact a gift of choice flowers.

In July 1916 it was reported that Messrs. Piper and Son had been unable to supply "King George" and "Queen Mary" carnations for the bouquet presented in that year (which was composed of Lady Hermione carnations, as in the original Coronation bouquet – a fact upon which her Private Secretary commented in acknowledging the gift), but that they could supply seedlings. It was decided to ask five members of the Company to grow some of these for the 1917 bouquet, but this appears not to have been successful, for an acknowledgement from the Palace reads:

"Her Majesty understands that several of the members have tried to grow 'King George' and 'Queen Mary' carnations for the Royal Bouquet, but she fully realizes that owing to the effects of the war and the weather their efforts have been unsuccessful. The Queen trusts that, under brighter conditions, difficulties may be overcome. Her Majesty is most grateful to the Gardeners Company for their charming offering and she heartily appreciates the fact that, in the midst of their anxiety and sorrow, the members continue to render this tribute of their loyalty and devotion."

CHAPTER 8

The annual gift to Queen Mary was in the early years usually taken to Buckingham Palace or Windsor Castle by the Master and Clerk and handed to her Private Secretary, but on a number of occasions the presentations were made in person. Thus the Minute Books show that the following personal presentations took place, while others might have been recorded in those Minute Books destroyed by enemy action in 1941.

Queen Mary – presentations at Buckingham Palace
23rd June 1913, by the Master (S.G. Shead) and the Clerk.
    June 1915, by the Master (Benjamin Hansford) and the Clerk.
22nd June 1918, by the Master (Sir Charles Cheers Wakefield) and the Clerk.
22nd June 1922, by the Master-Elect (G.H. Thompson) and the Clerk.
22nd June 1932, by the Master (John Weir) and the Clerk, marking the 21st anniversary of the Coronation.

The 1922 presentation was particularly interesting, as Queen Mary showed the deputation the Company's Coronation gift of the silver-gilt basket, which she said was regularly used for cut flowers. Her Majesty again showed the basket at the 1932 presentation, and honoured the Master by accepting from him an autograph of Queen Victoria at the age of fifteen.

After the Second World War, these personal presentations were revived as follows, but at Marlborough House:

21st June 1947, by the Master (W.F. Bishop), the Wardens and the Acting Clerk.
22nd June 1950, by the Master (C.E. Page Taylor), the Wardens and the Clerk.
22nd June 1951, by the Master (Maj. K.E. Schweder), the Wardens and the Clerk, on the 40th anniversary of the Coronation.

Queen Elizabeth (now the Queen Mother) – presentations at Buckingham Palace
12th May 1938, by the Master (Lt.Col. S.S.G. Cohen), the Wardens and the Clerk.
12th May 1948, by the Master (Seymour Howard), the Upper Warden and the Clerk.
12th May 1951, by the Master (J.W. Whitlock), the Wardens and the Clerk.

Queen Elizabeth, the Queen Mother – presentations at Clarence House
10th May 1957, by the Master (Donald Byford), the Upper Warden and the Clerk.

[97]

12th May 1959, by the Master (G.J. Gollin), the Wardens and the Clerk.

12th May 1967, by the Master (Maj.Gen. K.C. Appleyard), the Wardens and the Clerk.

Queen Elizabeth, the Queen Mother – presentation at the Royal Lodge, Windsor

12th May 1980, by the Master (C.E. Talbot), the Clerk and the Assistant Clerk.

Queen Elizabeth II, by letter from her Private Secretary dated 23rd March 1954, was graciously pleased to consent to an annual presentation of flowers on the anniversary of her Coronation, so this treasured privilege of the Company has continued during her reign. The presentation in person is only made from time to time at Her Majesty's pleasure.

On June 1st 1956 the first such personal presentation was made by the Master (Lord Nathan) and the Wardens (Donald Byford and Martin Longman) at Buckingham Palace, accompanied by the Clerk, and Her Majesty expressed delight that these traditional ceremonies should not be allowed to lapse. There was another personal presentation on 3rd June 1958 in the Mastership of Martin Longman, when Her Majesty consented to sign the Company's Golden Book and presented the Master with an autographed photograph of herself as a reminder that it was he who was responsible for the making of the original bouquet. To commemorate this fact, in February 1958 Longman had been given by the Court a framed copy of Miss Anna Zinkeisen's painting of the bouquet.

Further personal presentations were made as follows, all at Buckingham Palace except 1989 (at the former Royal Mint):

2nd June 1964, by the Master (Rt.Hon. Roger, 2nd Baron Nathan), the Renter Warden and the Clerk.

5th June 1969, by the Master (L.H. Kemp), the Wardens and the Clerk.

2nd June 1976, by the Master (David Longman), the Wardens and the Assistant Clerk.

2nd June 1981, by the Master (L.J. Reddall), the Upper Warden and the Clerk.

1st June 1984, by the Master (R.Adm. M.J. Ross), the Wardens and the Clerk.

2nd June 1989, by the Master (E.G. Chandler), the Wardens and the Clerk.

2nd June 1993, by the Master (D.E. Dowlen), the Wardens and the Clerk.

In 1992, the Company had the privilege of providing the Queen with a basket of British spring flowers on the 40th anniversary of her accession.

Royal Bridal Bouquets

Another traditional privilege, that of providing the bridal bouquet for a Royal wedding, appears not to be as old as was at one time thought. It would seem from the tenor of a minute, when it was decided to seek leave to present the wedding bouquet of Princess Mary on her marriage with Viscount Lascelles in February 1922, that this was the first time the suggestion had been made and it was based on the analogy of the Coronation bouquet. The reply from the Lady in Waiting to the Princess was, however, somewhat negative – "Her Royal Highness will not be carrying a bouquet at all on her wedding day".

A similar application on the marriage in April 1923 of the Duke of York with The Lady Elizabeth Bowes-Lyon (now the Queen Mother) met with greater success. The bouquet was accompanied by a rather flowery letter from the Master (G.H. Thompson) in which he referred to the bride's "happy decision the flowers of 'Scotland and of York to join'. May the white roses typify to you 'Sweet York, sweet Husband' and the white heather voice our own heartfelt wish 'and they shall have good luck'". This brought a reply, addressed from Buckingham Palace and signed by the bride in her own hand: "I very greatly appreciate the gift not only for its intrinsic charm but for the kind and friendly good will to which it bore witness and it was with real and cordial pleasure that I accepted from the Worshipful Company of Gardeners the delightful present emblematic of their delightful occupation."

Bridal bouquets were similarly furnished by the Company on the occasions of the marriage of the Duke of Kent with Princess Marina in November 1934, the Duke of Gloucester with The Lady Alice Montague-Douglas-Scott in November 1935, and on the marriage of our present Queen (as Princess Elizabeth) with the Duke of Edinburgh on 20th November 1947, of Princess Margaret with Mr. Antony Armstrong-Jones on 6th May 1960, and of the Duke of Kent with Miss Katharine Worsley on 8th June 1961.

It was reported to the Court on 13th February 1963 that the household of Princess Marina, Duchess of Kent, had been approached with the request that the Company should be permitted to maintain its privilege of presenting the wedding bouquet on the occasion of the wedding of a Princess of the blood, in this case the marriage of Princess Alexandra with the Hon. Angus

Ogilvy. The request had been granted, and details of the preparation of the bouquet were placed in the hands of Past Master Martin Longman.

Of all these events, the day of the present Queen's wedding, 20th November 1947, must have been particularly memorable – not least for Martin Longman and the Clerk, who delivered the bouquet to Buckingham Palace. They followed a route prescribed for them by the police, which covered the entire length of the route of the bridal procession to and from Westminster Abbey, only an hour or so before the wedding took place. On arrival at the Palace they were taken by the Lady in Waiting into Princess Elizabeth's private sitting room, to admire the wonderful display of flowers sent to her from all parts of the world (including an enormous screen of flowers which had been flown from the U.S.A. the previous day). They looked down on the gaily decorated Mall, crowded with excited sightseers anxious to welcome their beloved Princess.

A letter of thanks to the Master (Seymour Howard), signed by Princess Elizabeth personally and dated 28th November, read:

"I should like the Worshipful Company of Gardeners to know how beautiful I thought the Wedding Bouquet which in accordance with tradition they gave me. I thought it perfect in every way, and so I am sure did the many people who afterwards saw it lying on the Tomb of the Unknown Warrior. Will you please thank all concerned for a present which was of great personal significance to me on my Wedding Day."

Other Royal Bouquets

There have been other occasions when the Company has been granted permission to provide bouquets for royal occasions, notably for the present Queen Mother in 1948 for the State Drive by the King and Her Majesty to St. Paul's for the service to commemorate their Silver Wedding, and in 1953 for her State Drive to Guildhall to receive the Honorary Freedom of the City, on which occasion the Master (F.A.B. Luke) and his lady were invited to be present at the ceremony.

It is also recorded that Queen Elizabeth II accepted bouquets for the christenings of Prince Charles, Prince Andrew and Prince Edward, though at her request these were described as "posies".

The Royal Prefix Declined

In February 1914 the Clerk (E.A. Ebblewhite) reported that he had conducted "a private correspondence and delicate negotiations with the Duke of

Teck, the Home Office, the Queen's Private Secretary and others to ascertain the probabilities of success in connection with a possible application by the Company to use the prefix 'Royal' but had been obliged to advise the Master that any such application would be premature at this stage".

The Master (S.G. Shead), whose knowledge of Palace protocol was evidently less than his enthusiasm for the prestige of the Company, forthwith instructed Ebblewhite to apply to the Queen for the use of Her Majesty's name as Patroness, but this move was no more successful. A reply was received from Buckingham Palace:

"Her Majesty, although fully realising and appreciating the educational and charitable work done by your Guild, regrets that it is not possible to comply with your request. The Queen feels sure that you will readily understand that if Her Majesty were to confer her patronage on the Gardeners Company she would be creating a precedent which would render it difficult to refuse similar applications from the many other Livery Companies."

In both the above cases the Clerk was careful to minute that the approaches were taken by him "at the instigation of" or "at the request of" the Master. One cannot help feeling that his shrewd sense of the right course to adopt in pursuance of their common desire to enhance the prestige of the Company was overborne by his Master, and that advice from his great store of knowledge of protocol had been disregarded.

The Honorary Freedom of Princess Mary

In June 1918 there appears to have been discussion with the Queen's Private Secretary (perhaps at the time when the Coronation bouquet was presented to Her Majesty in person) about the possibility of Princess Mary, the Princess Royal, becoming an Honorary Freeman of the Company, but in a manuscript letter he wrote on 22nd June that on further consideration he thought that it would be best to take no action at the present time.

The matter was successfully revived in 1933, as evidenced by a letter dated 31st January from Princess Mary's Lady in Waiting. Arrangements were made for the ceremony of Admission to take place at a special Court on 5th May 1933 at Grocers Hall, to be followed by a luncheon. The speech of the Princess at the ceremony, and the toast by the Master (John Weir) and her reply at the luncheon, are set out in full in the minutes. In the course of his speech the Master said, referring to Princess Mary's practical knowledge of gardening, that Sir Jeremiah Colman had told him that she had performed for him the delicate operation of fertilising one of his orchids which gained a first prize at the Ghent Floralies, from which the Company's deputation had only recently returned. At Sir Jeremiah's request the Master presented her with a bouquet of orchids from Gatton Park.

In thanking Past Masters Sir Robert Tasker and Lord Marshall for proposing and seconding her, Princess Mary said: "Your new Freeman will always follow your history with interest and be loyal to your traditions. I can assure you that I shall ever bear in mind the terms of my declaration and be proud of belonging to your Company." Shortly afterwards, the Princess wrote to the Master in her own hand:

"I feel I must write to thank you very much for all your kindness to me last Friday. I can assure you that I feel very proud indeed to be admitted an honorary member to the Worshipful Company of Gardeners and shall always remember May 5th 1933. I must admit I felt rather nervous at the ceremony and the luncheon, but thanks to your help I soon got over this. I very much appreciate your taking the flowers from the luncheon table to the London Hospital in person, and for asking me which hospital I wished the flowers sent to. With again many thanks, Believe me, Yours sincerely, Mary."

Some Other Royal Occasions

There was a similar ceremony on 5th March 1935, when the Prince of Wales (subsequently the Duke of Windsor) was admitted to the Honorary Freedom of the Company, but sadly the record of this event perished in the flames of the Blitz.

Princess Mary attended functions of the Company on several other occasions as a "Free Sister", notably the Ladies Banquet at Mansion House in May 1950 and, with the Countess of Harewood, a similar Banquet at Fishmongers Hall in March 1961. She was prevented by illness from being present at a Ladies Banquet at Mansion House in December 1954, in the Mayoralty of Sir Seymour Howard.

In October 1952 the Duke and Duchess of Gloucester honoured the Company with their presence at a Ladies Banquet at Fishmongers Hall, and the Duke, in proposing the toast to the Company, made a graceful reference to the wedding bouquet of the Duchess which had been provided by the Company.

Then in 1955, the opportunity was taken by the Company to declare its loyalty to the Crown on a most significant anniversary. On 18th September of that year, a telegram was despatched to Her Majesty The Queen in the following terms:

"Lord Nathan as Master of the Worshipful Company of Gardeners begs, with humble duty, on his own behalf and on behalf of the Wardens and Court of Assistants and Members of the Livery, to renew this, the 350th anniversary of the grant of the first Royal Charter to the Company, the oath of fealty which every member makes on his admission to the Company, and to wish your Majesty a long and prosperous reign."

The following reply was received:

"The Master of the Worshipful Company of Gardeners – Please convey to the Wardens, Court of Assistants and members of the Worshipful Company of Gardeners the sincere thanks of the Queen for their kind and loyal message."

There have been many other "Royal Occasions", and the interest of members of the Royal Family in gardening has frequently been demonstrated.

In July 1949 Queen Elizabeth (now the Queen Mother) visited the garden of the Goldsmiths Company on a blitzed site in Gresham Street opposite their Hall, and the Master (C.E. Page Taylor) and the Clerk were presented to her. In July 1953 another visit to a City garden was planned – this time on a blitzed site in Moorfields – but the Queen Mother was indisposed and her place was taken by Princess Margaret, who was shown round the garden by the Master (F.A.B. Luke) with the Clerk in attendance.

For many years the Queen Mother, as Patron of the London Gardens Society, has made regular tours of London gardens accompanied by the Master and other representatives of the Company.

At the meeting of the Court on 13th February 1963, it was resolved that the Freedom of the Company be conferred upon the Duchess of Gloucester, and that the Freedom and Livery of the Company be conferred upon the Duke of Gloucester, in both cases at a special meeting of the Court at Mansion House on 13th March 1963 – that being the occasion of the Ladies Banquet, which Their Royal Highnesses, the Lord Mayor and Lady Mayoress, with the Sheriffs and their Ladies, had already agreed to attend. The ceremonies were duly performed in the drawing room at Mansion House, and after the Banquet the Ladies of members of the Court were presented to Their Royal Highnesses.

In May 1970, a gift of flowers was sent to the Duke of Gloucester, Honorary Freeman, on the occasion of his 70th birthday; and on 2nd March 1971, a bouquet was presented to Princess Anne by the Master (J.P. Schweder) and Clerk on the occasion of her accompanying the Prince of Wales on his admission to the Freedom of the City of London.

The Company had the honour of entertaining Queen Elizabeth the Queen Mother to Dinner at Mansion House in February 1972, but a sadder occasion was to follow soon after. On 28th June 1972 the death of one of the Company's Royal Freemen, the Duke of Windsor, was reported to the Court. A wreath had been sent to Windsor Castle and a posy of mixed flowers sent to the Duchess, who had written expressing her thanks and stating how deeply touched she had been that the Company had thought of her at a very sad time.

On the occasion of the marriage of Prince Richard of Gloucester with Miss Brigitte van Deurs in 1972, the Company was informed by its Honorary Freeman, the Duchess of Gloucester, that the wedding bouquet would be made by her with wild flowers grown at Barnwell Manor. Accordingly it was arranged that the Company would present a floral tribute, to form part of the central floral exhibit at the wedding reception held at Barnwell.

On 20th November 1972, the Master (Bishop R.W. Stannard), Wardens and Clerk were received in audience by Her Majesty the Queen at Buckingham Palace, and presented a floral tribute from the Company on the occasion of the 25th anniversary of her marriage. Created by Assistant David Longman, this was an exact replica of her wedding bouquet.

In June 1973, the Master (Bishop R.W. Stannard) and Queen Elizabeth the Queen Mother each planted in the Chelsea Physic Garden trees presented by the Company to commemorate the Tercentenary of the Garden.

The wedding of Princess Anne (now the Princess Royal) with Captain Mark Phillips in 1973 presented the Court with a problem, when it became known that Her Royal Highness had decided to accept her wedding bouquet from a source other than the Company. After representations, the Court was delighted to be advised that Her Royal Highness would be most grateful if the Company would provide a floral set piece for the wedding breakfast. This was duly carried out, with the flowers – roses, carnations, lilies, gerbera, gladioli and dainty foliage – arranged on either side of the wedding cake in the Ball Supper Room at Buckingham Palace. Some years later, on

CHAPTER 8

27th February 1976, a bouquet was presented to Her Royal Highness by the Master (David Longman), Wardens and Assistant Clerk on the occasion of her admission to the Freedom of the City of London.

A major Royal event in the Company's history was the Silver Jubilee of Queen Elizabeth II, not least because the Clerk (Frank Steiner) was the Corporation of London's Chief Commoner and Chairman of its Silver Jubilee Reception Committee. On 7th June 1977, the Master (C.R. Crosse) and the Wardens (John Brunel Cohen and D.A. Huggons), accompanied by the Assistant Clerk, were privileged to present a bouquet to Her Majesty in the garden of St. Paul's Cathedral as she commenced her "walkabout" from St. Paul's to the Luncheon at Guildhall given by the Corporation. The bouquet on this occasion was all white and consisted of orchids, roses, carnations, lilies of the valley and stephanotis, some supplied by Liverymen Peter Black and Paul Bleaney, with the bouquet designed and made by Longmans Limited.

In August 1977 Her Majesty, while on holiday on the Royal Yacht Britannia, visited Truro in its centenary year. With the consent of the Company and at the request of the Mayor of Truro, Treseders' Nurseries produced a replica of the Company's Coronation bouquet, which was given to Her Majesty by the Mayor's grand-daughter. In a letter to the Mayor, the Queen's Private Secretary stated that Her Majesty was touched that such a beautiful replica should have been produced.

There was a further presentation in the Jubilee year of 1977, when on 24th November the Master (John Brunel Cohen), accompanied by the Assistant Clerk, planted a magnolia tree in the Queen Mother's garden at Clarence House.

The next Royal event of great significance was the marriage of the Prince of Wales with Lady Diana Spencer, in St. Paul's Cathedral on 29th July 1981, for which occasion the Company was granted the privilege of providing the bouquet. Past Master David Longman was appointed to prepare the bouquet and, accompanied by the Clerk, he attended a meeting at Buckingham Palace with Lady Diana to discuss her wishes. Early on the wedding day, the bouquet was delivered to St. James's Palace by the Master (R.L. Payton) and David Longman.

The Company also provided the flowers at the Cathedral for the occasion, and the Master's invitation to members of the Company to contribute to the cost had resulted in a sum of £625. The flowers were arranged by the

Ladies Flower Committee of St. Paul's, under the chairmanship of Mrs. Ann Ballard, and Liveryman Tom Gough constructed huge Prince of Wales feathers out of fresh, dried and silk flowers.

The early 1980s saw several occasions when members of the Royal Family attended Court functions. Prominent among these was the attendance on 10th March 1981 of the Queen Mother at a Court Luncheon at Girdlers Hall, when Her Majesty so kindly displayed her relationship with the Company on being informed of the absence through illness of the Father of the Court (Past Master Donald Byford) by signing a menu to be sent to him – and, under her "Elizabeth R.", wrote "Wish you were here".

On 11th February 1985, the Company's Ladies Banquet at Mansion House was attended by Princess Alice, Duchess of Gloucester, who honoured the Company again on 19th December 1985 by attending the Court Luncheon to commemorate Freeman John Tradescant. Her Royal Highness had previously been present at the first of the Tradescant commemorative luncheons, on 18th December 1981, at the Savile Club.

The association of Princess Alice with the Company has been longstanding and warm. As mentioned in other Chapters, Her Royal Highness became the Company's first lady Liveryman in 1974, having since 1963 been an Honorary Freeman. It was therefore a notable occasion when, to celebrate her ninetieth birthday on Christmas Day 1991, Her Royal Highness graciously accepted the offer of the Master (R.C. Balfour) to present some plants of a new rose named "Many Happy Returns". The Master and members of the Company visited the gardens at Barnwell Manor in 1992, and were received by Her Royal Highness.

Turning again to Royal Weddings, on the occasion of the marriage of Prince Andrew (now the Duke of York) with Miss Sarah Ferguson on 23rd July 1986, the Company presented a bouquet in the form of the initial "S".

Then, in the late 1980s, there was a notable addition to the list of the Company's Royal Liverymen. On 12th June 1987, the Honorary Freedom was conferred upon Prince Charles, the Prince of Wales, and His Royal Highness was also admitted as an Honorary Liveryman, at his Gloucestershire home, Highgrove. The Master (A.B. Hurrell) was supported by the Wardens (His Hon. G.F. Leslie and E.G. Chandler) and the Clerk, and accompanied by several Past Masters and Assistants. A London plane was planted by the Prince to commemorate the occasion, and His Royal Highness then conducted the Company's representatives and their Ladies on a tour of the garden which he had personally designed and planned.

CHAPTER 8

Footnote

The minutes record that on 11th November 1986 Past Master David Longman advised the Court that Mrs. Doris Wellham of Longmans Limited had been making the royal bouquets for almost forty years. She had been involved as a junior with the Queen's wedding bouquet in 1947, as a senior assistant with the Coronation bouquet in 1953, and as head florist with the Silver Jubilee bouquet in 1977, as well as many others. It was therefore unanimously agreed that she be granted the Freedom of the Company by Presentation.

There can be few Livery Companies, if any, which can claim such close and happy association with so many members of the Royal Family. Indeed, these "Royal Occasions" have not been confined to our own country – and Chapter 10 records many examples of the Company's warm contacts with other Heads of State.

CHAPTER 9

The Company and the "Craft" or "Mystery" of Gardening

Throughout the history of the Company, one cannot fail to be impressed by the numerous efforts to foster the craft from which it takes its name.

Ambitious proposals were made in the first years of the Company's revival for developing the art of gardening, prepared by Sir Trevor Lawrence (Upper Warden, and President of the Royal Horticultural Society), the Reverend William Wilks (Renter Warden, and Secretary of the Society), and Messrs N.N. Sherwood and Philip Crowley. At this time, the recently reborn Company had only twenty-one members, of whom nineteen were on the Court.

The scheme, first considered by the Court on 6th April 1891, is extensively covered in the minutes for 20th May. It proposed that the Company should establish a Technical School or Institute to enable young men to study gardening, and it was felt that this might result in the establishment of experimental gardens and a fruit farm, with residential accommodation for the students. An approach to the Royal Horticultural Society was suggested, on the basis that the Society would use its existing gardens at Chiswick and the Company would provide the students' house and a warden.

It was further proposed that sufficient fees should be charged to cover all working expenses, but that annual scholarships should be given in the form of reduction of fees to a number of deserving students. Periodical examinations were proposed, open to students and outsiders, with the Society making arrangements for these at the Company's expense and certificates being awarded jointly by the Company and the Society.

The scheme also raised the question of making provision for life assurance, sick funds, retirement pensions for craftsmen, and for the maintenance of orphans on the lines of a mutual assurance society guaranteed by the Company. Understandably at this stage, the Court decided that this "would require longer thought and care" and limited its immediate decision to the obtaining of actuarial statistics.

Less ambitious proposals, designed primarily to benefit the public, were prizes for essays on gardening subjects, lectures on gardening in different centres, and the encouragement of the cultivation of unusual vegetables.

The Committee to which the whole matter was referred became a joint Committee of the Company and the Royal Horticultural Society. Its report was adopted on 6th November 1891, and referred back for examination of the financial aspects. A further report was considered by the Court on 16th December 1891 (by which time the proposed school had been given the name of the British School of Gardening and Small Husbandry), and estimated the annual cost of the school at £2,000 and suggested an annual payment of £40 by each student. It was proposed that an appeal be made to other Livery Companies and the general public, the Gardeners heading the list with a donation of £250, and that the Lord Mayor be asked to allow a meeting to be held at Mansion House to further the objects of the appeal.

In June 1892, however, it was resolved "that the matter remain in abeyance for the present". About that time the more modest question of giving a scholarship to the Royal Horticultural Society arose, and the larger scheme appears to have died a natural death – perhaps not surprising, as it was a highly ambitious undertaking for the Company at that early stage of its revival.

The Company's Scholarships

In December 1892 it was resolved to create an annual scholarship on terms to be agreed by a joint Committee of the Company and the Society, and the Master (Sir Trevor Lawrence) offered a further scholarship. At a Court held on 10th February 1893, a report from the Committee on scholarships was received, which announced the foundation of another scholarship by Baron Schroder. This report, which was unanimously adopted, stated:

"The Committee appointed at the last Court have met and taken into consideration the papers relating to 'Horticultural Education' and 'Examination in Horticulture' laid before them by the Royal Horticultural Society. They unanimously express their approval of the principles contained therein, and of the proposed details for carrying them into effect.

"The Committee take this opportunity of expressing their gratitude to Baron Schroder and Sir Trevor Lawrence for founding additional Scholarships.

"The Committee approve of the proposal that these Scholarships should be awarded at the examination to be held by the Royal Horticultural Society in May, 1893.

"The Committee recommend that Candidates for the Scholarships should be between 18 and 21 years of age, and that successful Candidates should study for the first year of their tenure of a Scholarship in the Gardens of the

Royal Horticultural Society, and for the second year in some public, private or other Garden or Nursery, subject to the approval of the Joint Committee of the Royal Horticultural Society and the Gardeners' Company.

"The Scholarships are of the annual value of £26, and are tenable for two years."

This significant report was signed by Sir Trevor Lawrence, Beaumont Shepheard, Henry Wood and Robert Gofton-Salmond. Baron Schroder (1824-1910), incidentally, had Britain's finest collection of rare orchids at The Dell in Egham, and was closely associated with Sir Trevor Lawrence in the affairs of the Royal Horticultural Society.

The next reference in the minutes appeared on 26th February 1894, when it was resolved "to combine with Sir Trevor Lawrence and Baron Schroder in the presentation of two Scholarships of £39 each" on the conditions recommended by the joint Committee, except that the successful candidates had to be British subjects.

Though the scholarships were presented through the Company, in the early years they were funded by the personal donations of members. In November 1897, it was reported that Lord Amherst (whose daughter Alicia had been awarded the Honorary Freedom of the Company in 1896) wished to give two scholarships of £25 for the years 1899 and 1900. These amounts were duly paid in June 1898, with a further £25 from Assistant Henry Wood. Then in 1899 there is a reference to the receipt of £25 from G.W. Burrows, who became Renter Warden in the same year, as the first payment of the Burrows Scholarship which had been won by Miss Olive Mary Harrison, and this amount was forwarded to the Royal Horticultural Society. In December 1900 Assistant E.A. Strauss paid £100 for a scholarship for four years, and in December 1902 Sir William Farmer promised £25 for the same purpose. Other similar amounts were given from time to time by members, and it was not until some years later that the cost of the scholarship became a charge on the Company's Charitable Fund.

The scholarship scheme led to a certain amount of what, after this lapse of time, seems to have been unnecessary friction between the Company and the Royal Horticultural Society. It was not long after Ebblewhite became Clerk that, after giving his attention to the more pressing matters of the qualification of members for admission to the Court and the irregular admission of Liverymen in the past, he turned to the question of the scholarship. In October 1903 he presented a report setting out the holders of the scholarship to date, and there followed a slightly frosty correspondence with the

Secretary of the Royal Horticultural Society concerning the financial position between the two parties. The Society claimed that £47 18s. 4d. was due from the Company, which only admitted liability for £25. The Company agreed to pay the balance but, overlooking the fact that a two-year scholarship meant that two scholarships were running concurrently, wished to limit its liability to an annual £25.

This led to the appointment of a Committee of the Court to confer with the Society, and ultimately a letter was written by the President of the Society (Sir Trevor Lawrence) to the effect "that no useful purpose can be served by prolonging a futile controversy regarding the scholarship" and accepting the £47 18s. 4d. in full settlement down to 31st December 1903. So ended a storm in a teacup.

A few years earlier, in May 1900, it had been resolved "that a certificate of the Freedom of the Company be given to those who, having won the scholarship given by the Company, have conducted themselves during the two years of their studentship in such a way as to be thought worthy of recommendation for the purpose by the President and Council of the Royal Horticultural Society".

In accordance with this resolution the names of Messrs. G.F. Tinley, H.S. Langford, C.J. Gleed and Bertram Smith were laid before the May 1901 Court, and they were elected to the Freedom. They were admitted in June 1901, but when the industrious Ebblewhite became Clerk in 1903 he discovered that Messrs. Gleed and Smith were not of age at the time of their admission and were therefore ineligible for the Freedom. This was rectified by the fresh admission of Smith (who was then of age) in April 1903, and Gleed in December 1903 when he came of age. Other scholars admitted later were Messrs. L.L. Goffin and G. Fox Wilson in 1920 – then, after a very long break in the practice, Messrs. E.K. Lawrence and J.M.S. Potter in 1953.

Further controversy about the scholarship broke out with the Royal Horticultural Society in October 1908, when it was seen that in the latter's "Book of Arrangements for 1908" the payments for scholarships were not all attributed to the Company. It appears to have been settled by a friendly correspondence between the Clerk and Sir Trevor Lawrence, but this was followed by a letter from the Reverend William Wilks, Secretary of the Society, reporting that his Council had decided that it would be more satisfactory to bring the combined system of scholarships to an end, and the Society would not therefore look to the Company for any further payments to the Scholarship Fund.

This led to the formation of another joint Committee, which poured oil on the troubled waters and devised a formula whereby the scholarship was awarded for two years by the Company and the Society alternately.

Sad to say, Wilks had apparently become antagonistic toward the Company, notwithstanding the fact that he had been Master in 1893-94. In connection with the petition to the King in 1905 for leave for the Company to continue to bear its ancient arms, he had been the only member to write in opposition.

At one time there was a shortage of suitable applicants for the scholarship, but many enquiries were prompted by a letter circulated in 1929 to headmasters of public schools, county secondary schools, secretaries of county and borough education committees, and scholastic agencies.

In November 1926 the scholarship was increased to £50 in alternate years, and was in future to be awarded by examination designed to test the candidate's ability to profit by a course of instruction in horticulture, rather than on the basis of a general examination. A new scheme was mooted in 1932 and brought into effect in 1934, by which was established "The Bursary and Scholarship of the Worshipful Company of Gardeners augmented by the revenues of the Sir James Knott Fund and a contribution from the Royal Horticultural Society". This offered a bursary of £200 for one year to a student gardener of promise who, at the end of his term, on production of a satisfactory report, was granted a travelling scholarship of £250 for a maximum of two years to pursue specialised or research work.

Only two such scholarships were awarded before the outbreak of war in 1939 disrupted the scheme, but in 1947 steps were taken to revive them on slightly different terms. The first year of the scholarship was normally to be spent at Wisley, at the end of which the scholar was expected to submit a satisfactory thesis on an approved subject, and the second and third years were normally to be spent elsewhere at a horticultural centre either in this country or abroad. At the same time the amount of the scholarship was raised to £250 for the first year and £300 for the second and third years, of which the Company's share was £110 and £135 respectively. In 1958 yet another alteration was made, the scholarship being for two years at £300 per annum, and finally, in 1962, the Company undertook the full financial responsibility.

The scholarship was awarded until the 1960s, when it became increasingly difficult to attract suitable candidates, primarily because it was impossible for the Company's charitable funds to provide significant amounts of money. Research in horticultural matters came to be financed by industry, and the Company's scholarship was abandoned after a long and worthwhile history. A list of scholars from 1894 to 1965 appears as Appendix C.

The Royal Horticultural Society has, of course, long been an examining body in its own right. In 1962 the Company agreed to give six prizes of ten pounds, for award in connection with the Society's examinations for the National Diploma in Horticulture (founded in 1913). Later that same year it was decided that, instead of cash, the prizewinners would receive the Society's *Dictionary of Gardening* – a practice which has continued to this day.

The School of Gardening at Glynde

The Company took an interest in the School of Gardening at Glynde in Sussex, founded by Viscountess Wolseley, who was made an Honorary Freeman in July 1914. Lady Wolseley was an author, and donated several of her works to the Company's library – *Gardening for Women* (1908), *In a College Garden, being an account of the work of the College of Gardening for Women at Glynde* (1916), and *Gardens, Their Form and Design* (1919).

In 1914, after a deputation of the Master (S.G. Shead) and Wardens and their ladies had visited Glynde in the previous October, Lady Wolseley sought the Company's official support and patronage in connection with a proposed appeal for an endowment fund for the School. It must be remembered, however, that this was still at a comparatively early stage of the Company's revival, and major funding would have been required for such a project. The Court therefore decided with reluctance that "while they fully appreciated how well she deserves praise and recognition for all she has done for the cause of horticulture, having regard to the fact that the Company has no corporate funds available for the purposes of her appeal, they cannot do more than promise her advice and assistance should she be able to make a public appeal for an Endowment Fund". The Court also felt such an appeal should only be made under the advice and direction of the Royal Horticultural Society.

Then in 1920, it is minuted that in reply to letters from Lady Wolseley asking for the Company's support "the Clerk was instructed to inform her Ladyship that the Company had no funds out of which to make a grant and was not disposed to enter into a profit-sharing business".

The Proposals of Mawson and Prothero

In February 1917, Thomas Mawson of Lancaster was admitted to the Freedom and elected to the Livery. He was a leading landscape architect, one of his commissions being the layout of the grounds of Lord Leverhulme's residence on Hampstead Heath, and he was also a lecturer at the Liverpool University School of Civic Design. In April 1917, Mawson delivered a lecture to the Company on "The Needs of Academic Training for the Profession of Landscape Architecture". He outlined a scheme which the Court promised to consider when it was more clearly defined, and a month later he applied for the Company's patronage for the foundation of a Chair of Landscape Gardening in one of the universities. It was resolved by the Court to recommend such a foundation to the Minister of Education, but there is no later minute to show the result of this.

More information about Thomas Mawson can be found in his autobiography, *The Life and Work of an English Landscape Architect* (privately published in 1927), a copy of which is in the Company's library.

Late in 1917 the Company received a letter from R.E. Prothero (subsequently Lord Ernle), President of the Board of Agriculture, who had recently been elected to the Honorary Freedom of the Company, suggesting two directions in which the Company might materially assist agriculture and horticulture:

(a) by endowing one, two or three scholarships for research in horticultural subjects of economic importance to be held at an approved horticultural establishment; and

(b) by the establishment of a Readership in the economies of distribution in connection with the School of Agriculture and Forestry at Oxford to match a corresponding school at Cambridge, the equipment of which had been financed largely by the Drapers Company.

"This is a very important subject," wrote Prothero, "but one which is sure to come to the front more and more. We are realising now the inadequacy of some of the existing methods of distribution." Although this was years before the establishment of Marketing Boards, it shows how the minds of Ministers and civil servants run in the same groove down the years.

The letter was referred to a special Committee of the Court but, as Prothero rather anticipated, the question of expense proved a stumbling block. The Committee's report stated that the cost of founding a Readership would be at least £12,000, and made no recommendation.

The same Committee considered representations from Hackney Borough Council and the Board of Agriculture on the subject of the development of allotments to further food production, and recommended that, provided the President and representatives of the Food Production Department of the Board would consent to address a public meeting in the City at an early date, the Court would undertake to run an active propaganda campaign in London and that the Lord Mayor (Sir Charles Hanson, an Honorary Member of the Court) be requested to make Mansion House available for such a meeting. This was adopted by the Court, but unfortunately Prothero had been unable to accept the suggestion of a public meeting, and no further action was taken.

Prothero then decided to form a committee "to advise the Board of Agriculture on all questions connected with the promotion of market gardening, fruit-growing and horticulture generally and in particular with regard to the distribution of produce and the organisation of the trades connected with those industries in the situation created by the war", and he invited the Committee to nominate a representative. The Court nominated Assistant Francis Agar, and he was appointed to the Educational and Research Sub-Committee.

In November 1918 Agar reported that he had attended the inauguration of the Chamber of Horticulture, but the Court was recommended to take no action until it had received a full report from the Secretary to the Chamber. In the meantime, he suggested, the Company should not become an ordinary member but if asked might accept the position of Patron of the Chamber. Although there is no record to confirm whether or not a proposal to this effect was made by the Chamber, Agar became the Company's representative, and on his retirement in November 1920 was succeeded by D.C. Haldeman (then Upper Warden).

Agar was subsequently – in June 1921 – appointed to the Council of the Chamber, and in April 1922 was succeeded by Victor Brown, who became Renter Warden of the Company a month later. The part played by the Company in the Chamber's affairs is not recorded in detail, but from time to time Council papers were laid before the Court, and in April 1924 the Court voted a contribution to the cost of entertaining overseas delegates to the International Conference of the Federation Horticole Professionelle Internationale.

Activities in Support of Allotment Holders
The 1920s was a busy decade for the Company. In November 1920 a petition was received from the National Union of Allotment Holders, asking the

Company to identify itself with an exhibition of produce in the City and a scheme of technical training for allotment holders in London. The report of a Committee of the Court, to which the petition was referred, was sympathetic and said it "appeared desirable that the prominent position now held by the Company should be justified, not merely by its historical traditions and interesting associations, but by some scheme of technical training in connection with horticulture which shall prove of far-reaching benefit to the community". The Committee accordingly recommended:

(a) an endeavour to obtain the use of Guildhall for the proposed exhibition;
(b) the gift of a cup for competition;
(c) that the Freedom of the Company free of fine be conferred on the winner of the first prize at the exhibition;
(d) the inauguration of an annual series of fifty lectures in different centres of the metropolitan area, to be prefaced by a brief summary of the history of the Company and to conclude with discussion; and
(e) that a capital sum of £1,200 be raised by the Master from amongst the members to further the Company's work.

The report also proposed the provision of one pension in perpetuity through the Gardeners Royal Benevolent Institution and a maintenance grant in perpetuity for orphans through the Royal Gardeners Orphan Fund, and these recommendations were accepted. Indeed the Master (Francis Agar) was able to report to the Court that he had already received, in anticipation, donations amounting to £725, and by June 1921 the Fund had reached £1,031 which the Master made up to £1,100.

The exhibition was fixed for 10th September 1921, to be opened in Guildhall by Lord Leverhulme. Unfortunately, owing to drought, it had to be postponed and was ultimately held with great success on 2nd September 1922. J.R. Smith, a railway signalman and member of the Watford Allotments Protection Society, was the winner of first prize and was admitted to the Freedom of the Company in Court. The Company's cup was won by the Well Hall Allotment Holders and Amateur Gardeners' Society.

The plans for the lectures went ahead, and at the April 1921 Court the Master was able to report that they had been given already in eight named suburbs "and other places" and had received favourable press notices in *The Times*, the *City Press* and local papers. The scale of lectures never reached the somewhat optimistic total of fifty, and in 1922 the total was only eight. In 1923 it was proposed that they should be extended to societies affiliated to the Vacant Land Cultivation Society within the metropolitan area, as well as to those affiliated to the National Union of Allotment Holders, and ten lectures were reported. During the 1924 season the lectures were not as successful as had been anticipated, owing partly to the fact that the London County Council had instituted similar lectures, and sadly in 1925 the venture was abandoned.

During the war years the Company had been in close touch with the Ministry of Agriculture, and this contact continued into the 1920s. The services of the Master and Wardens were offered to the Ministry as arbitrators in disputes between employers and employees in the horticultural and agricultural industries, though there is no record of how many times they were called upon. At a public meeting to discuss future legislation regarding allotments, held at the Memorial Hall in Farringdon Street in March 1922, the Minister of Agriculture (Sir Arthur Griffith-Boscawen) referred appreciatively to the work being done by the Company to further the movement, and the Master (D.C. Haldeman) "in a felicitous speech" supported a resolution in favour of a proposed Allotment Bill to be introduced into Parliament.

Owing to the loss of the Company's Minute Book from January 1934 to April 1941 there is little recorded of the Company's activities in the 1930s, but the public activities of the Company were renewed during the Second World War.

In April 1942 a sum of £150 was voted to the National Allotments Society to assist in the development of allotments, as a result of a meeting between a Committee set up by the Court and representatives of the Society. It was decided that the gift should be used to start a circulating library of popular and inexpensive books on gardening, which would be lent by the Society for short periods to affiliated allotment associations and by them to their members. By this means it was calculated that 2,400 members would have the opportunity of reading the books and improving their gardening knowledge.

In April 1944 the Society was able to report that the library consisted of over five hundred books, which were in constant circulation, and the demand was such that it had to ration the number sent to each association. It also reported that a number of local officials, some from quite a distance from London, paid personal visits to examine the books in the library and discuss new publications, and that it was "looking forward to the time when it would be possible to extend this valuable service".

A further grant of thirty pounds was made to the Society in 1951.

St. Paul's Garden

One venture in which the Company played a prominent part was in the creation of St. Paul's Garden, immediately to the south-east of the Cathedral. The idea of a Garden of Remembrance originated in 1946 with Lord Nathan who, shortly before his election to the Court, suggested "the establishment of a Garden of Remembrance in the vicinity of St. Paul's, the same to be maintained in perpetuity by the Gardeners Company and to contain a plinth in memory of the Officers and Other Ranks of Troops of the City of London". Lord Nathan's idea was subsequently widened, so that the plinth commemorated "the people of London destroyed in the war".

The proposal was passed to the City Corporation and, in the report of the consultants employed by the Corporation to advise on the reconstruction of the City, provision for such a garden was made. It soon became obvious, however, that the cost of maintenance would be too heavy for the Company to bear, and an approach was made to the Corporation to see in what other manner the Company could be associated with the scheme.

After consultation with Professor (later Sir Albert) Richardson, it was decided that the Company should give three bronze heads of lions for the water supply to the fountains and pool in the garden, and that the gift should be recorded on the stone parapet by a bronze tablet with the Company's arms. This was done at a cost of £500, and the Master (J.W. Whitlock) attended the formal opening of the garden in the spring of 1951. This was the year of the Festival of Britain, which led to the garden becoming known as The Festival Garden.

Window Boxes in the City

A further striking way in which the Company justified its existence as a City Guild was the role it played in popularizing the idea of window boxes in the City. Toward the end of 1948 it was felt that something should be done to brighten the City, much of which was still derelict after the wartime bombing. The Company was able to enlist the support of the Goldsmiths Company, who for several years had maintained an attractive garden on a bombed site in Gresham Street opposite their Hall, and who offered to run a competition among British silversmiths for the design of two cups to be given by the Gardeners Company for perpetual competition for window boxes in the City. The Goldsmiths offered substantial money prizes for the best designs, and their competition attracted a large number of entries which were publicly displayed at Goldsmiths Hall. The design of Miss Joyce Titcomb was adopted for both the Company's cups.

The draft conditions for the window box competition were approved at the March 1949 Court, when it was decided to divide it into two sections – one for window boxes maintained by professional nurserymen, and the other for those looked after by amateur gardeners in the employ of the firms displaying them. The co-operation of the London Gardens Society was enlisted for the judging, and the Society promised to give silver and bronze medals annually to the second and third places in the competition.

In spite of considerable publicity, the entries for 1949 were disappointingly small – only five in the first class and one in the second. It nevertheless proved possible to make the awards, and the Company's cups were presented to the National Provident Institution in Gracechurch Street for the professional class and to Mr. R.V. Cocker for the amateur class. The London Gardens Society's silver and bronze medals were presented respectively to the Union Discount Company of London in Cornhill and to Fester Fothergill and Hartnung, but sadly there could be no second or third places in the amateur class.

The shortage of contenders dismayed neither the Gardeners nor the Goldsmiths, and in September 1949 the latter promised a third cup (subsequently designed by M.E. Gould) for the best garden on a blitzed site. This was first awarded in 1950 to the Goldsmiths Company's own garden in Gresham Street, and silver and bronze medals went to Hodder and Stoughton Limited and I.G. Walker respectively.

It was the Festival of Britain in 1951 which gave the necessary fillip to the competition, although in the meantime the number of window boxes had been slowly increasing. For the Festival celebrations the Master (J.W. Whitlock), at the instance of the City Corporation, prepared a copiously illustrated booklet on "The City Gardens". This included an introduction by Sir Edward Salisbury, Director of the Royal Botanic Gardens at Kew, an article on the new St. Paul's Garden, and a detailed tour of gardens in the City. An appeal by the Master, supported by a letter from the Lord Mayor commending the scheme, was sent by the Company to hundreds of firms in the City asking them to consider installing window boxes in their premises, and this met with a magnificent response. Indeed, the *City Press* reported that there were nearly 2,000 window boxes on the route of the King's drive to St. Paul's for the opening of the Festival.

Efforts were again made in 1953, Coronation year, which resulted in a further increase in window boxes throughout the City. In 1952 the number of entries had increased so much, and the competition became so close, that it was decided to give gold and silver medal certificates to a number of outstanding displays which were not in the top three.

The conditions of the competition were amended from time to time to meet altered circumstances. With the increase in rebuilding on blitzed sites, the class for this type of garden was discontinued after 1954. So too was the class for amateurs, who may well have felt discouraged by the large number and variety of the professional displays.

The Court decided in 1954 to give to each year's winners of the cups an illuminated certificate bearing a photograph of the cup, and the help of the City and Guilds Art School was enlisted. The School held a competition for the design of the certificate, and as a result the Court selected that by Roy Middleton.

In 1959, representations were made to the Company that the judges might be influenced in their awards by the size and complexity of the displays, and it was decided to hold the competition in two classes according to size – the first for a frontage of less than forty feet, and the second for larger displays. This did not prove entirely satisfactory, however, as the number of entries in the class for small displays was very few, and in 1960 a special Committee was appointed to investigate the whole matter.

This Committee reported in 1961, and recommended discontinuing the "competitive" element which had prevailed until then. The reason underlying that decision was that the provision and maintenance of window boxes had become concentrated in the hands of a few professionals, who were most successfully supplying the majority of the displays. It might be thought that the firms concerned were hardly likely to encourage their clients to enter into competition with other clients supplied by them – but, for whatever reason, the number of entrants was falling. Accordingly the Committee recommended that, "in view of our ancient privileges and connections both with the City and gardening", the Company should widen its consideration of what it could do to encourage floral decorations in the City, both in window boxes and in internal arrangements.

The Floral Awards

The Committee suggested that the Window Box Competition be renamed "Window Box Awards" (later to become "Floral Awards", and to include displays in courtyards and gardens). There were to be no entry forms but any floral display, on a date decided annually by the Master and Wardens, would be eligible for an award. On the date concerned, the Master and Wardens were to tour the City and make awards to those displays which met with their approval. The awards were to take the form of metal or plastic plaques, to be affixed to the approved display; these were to be of a different colour each year, and bear the year of the award. It was also recommended that a cup might be presented annually by the Master and Wardens to an outstanding display, with particular emphasis upon new displays.

The report of the Committee paid tribute to the work of the London Gardens Society, which over many years had provided advice and judges for the Window Box Competition.

It was also suggested that there should be a City Flower Show, to assist in making firms and individuals aware of the importance and delights of displaying flowers. Such an exhibition was not in fact held until September 1979, in the Royal Exchange, primarily as a result of action by Past Master F.E. Cleary, and this included a Company stand designed and constructed by Liveryman Tom Gough of Longmans Limited.

The Flower Show has since become an annual event, held in Guildhall in September, and usually includes a Company stand. The Show is the responsibility of the Trees, Gardens and City Open Spaces Sub-Committee of the Corporation of London, with which the Company has always had strong links – in recent years its Chairman was successively Liveryman and Common Councilman Christopher Mitchell and Liveryman and Common Councilman Mrs. Christine Cohen. The management of the Show is in the hands of the Corporation's Superintendent of Parks and Gardens – successively Liveryman Peter Stagg and Freeman David Jones.

Returning to the recommendations of the special Committee concerning the Floral Awards, these were adopted by the Court. The first tour of inspection was undertaken by the Master (Edward Howard), with the Wardens and the Clerk, on 11th June 1961. Sixty-five plaques were awarded, rising to 108 in 1962, when the Lord Mayor agreed to present the Company's cup. A few years later, in 1965, the judging featured in a film on the Livery Companies of the City of London.

In 1963 another special Committee was appointed by the Court, to consider the extension of the awards. In addition to the Master and Wardens, the Committee included Past Master Edward Howard, Past Master Martin Longman, Assistant F.E. Cleary (then a member of the Planning and Streets Committees of the City Corporation), and Assistant Fred Utting (then

Chairman of the Corporation's Planning Committee). The Clerk, Frank Steiner, was an *ex officio* member of the special Committee but was also a member of the Corporation's Planning Committee. It is incidentally worth noting that F.E. Cleary was at that time Chairman of the Metropolitan Public Gardens Association, so it was little wonder that a partnership between the Company and the Association blossomed (to use an appropriate term) into what came to be known as the "Flowers in the City" campaign.

"Flowers in the City"

The idea of approaching the City Corporation for a grant to give publicity to floral displays was suggested in 1965, and for many years such a grant was received by the Company and used to publicise the virtues of using flowers and plants to brighten and enliven City premises. Successive Lord Mayors provided written exhortations to this end, which were included with leaflets distributed throughout the Square Mile.

In 1965, toward the end of his Mayoralty, Sir James Miller presented a shield to the Company to be awarded in accordance with rules laid down by him. The intention was that the Miller Trophy should be awarded to the person, company or organisation responsible for providing the most original and interesting new feature in the City, incorporating such things as fountains, seats, trees, shrubs, flowers and bulbs. The objective was to enhance the amenities for the benefit of those who live or work in the City, and for this reason it was decided that schemes which members of the public could not visit or view would be ineligible.

The Miller Trophy was first presented in 1967 to the British Petroleum Company Limited, for their layout of fountains and flower beds at Britannic House in Moor Lane. Since that time a panel of Company members has adjudicated annually. The highest standards have been maintained in keeping with the original intention of Sir James Miller, and there have been years in which the Trophy has not been awarded.

The "Flowers in the City" campaign proved to be successful. In 1967 the award for the best floral display went to National Mutual Life Assurance of Australasia, and that year also brought significant outside recognition of the Company's efforts. In July the Court was informed that John Smith, Member of Parliament for the Cities of London and Westminster, had presented to the Metropolitan Public Gardens Association a silver spade, for annual award by the Association to the organisation or individual contributing most to the visual amenities of the Cities. The award had been made that year to the Company for its work on the "Flowers in the City" campaign, and on the Church Gardens Competition which is covered later in this Chapter.

The efforts of the Company were recognised by the Court of Common Council in the following resolution passed on 21st September 1967: "That this Court desires to convey to the Worshipful Company of Gardeners and the Metropolitan Public Gardens Association its sincere congratulations upon the success of the 'Flowers in the City' campaign, and welcomes the opportunity of expressing publicly its sincere thanks to the numerous institutions and business firms, and to those officers of the Corporation whose joint contributions to the campaign have culminated in the award to the City of London of the 'Britain in Bloom' trophy."

Among the officers referred to were the City Architect, Liveryman E.G. Chandler (who became Master in 1988), and the Superintendent of Parks and Gardens, Liveryman Peter Stagg.

This was but the first reference to the City's success in "Britain in Bloom", for in February 1972 the Court was advised in a letter from the Town Clerk that the City had been awarded further trophies in that national event. This letter conveyed the thanks of the Court of Common Council to the "Flowers in the City" Committee, and acknowledged that the success of the campaign was in no small way responsible for the award of the City's prestigious trophies. It is also of interest to note that in 1969 the Company had presented a salver for award in "Britain in Bloom".

Early in 1975 the Court agreed to subscribe up to thirty pounds for floral decorations at Mansion House, on the occasion of a reception hosted by the Lord Mayor (Alderman Sir Murray Fox) on 4th March 1975 to launch that year's "Britain in Bloom". This was attended by the Master (A.J. Carton), the Upper Warden (David Longman), Past Master F.E. Cleary and the Clerk (Frank Steiner). By that time, Cleary had become Chairman of the Corporation's Trees, Gardens and Open Spaces Sub-Committee, and Steiner had become Chairman of the Corporation's Planning and Communications Committee. Liveryman Peter Stagg, Superintendent of the Corporation's Parks and Gardens, provided flowers from West Ham Park at the expense of the Company.

The City's success in "Britain in Bloom" continued, and in October 1975 the Town Clerk informed the Company of the award yet again of both the London Regional Trophy and the National Trophy for the city, town or village in which shopkeepers and other commercial interests had made the year's best efforts. The Company's major contribution was acknowledged with thanks, and this was followed by a similar letter in 1976 and further awards to the City for many years afterwards.

Having noted the part played in "Britain in Bloom" by the "Flowers in the City" campaign, it is necessary to go back a little in time in order to complete the picture relating to "Flowers in the City" itself. It proved to be an enduring feature of the Company's calendar, but success brought with it complexities which needed to be overcome. In 1968, for example, it had to be agreed that more judges should be appointed in order to provide smaller divisions of the City for each pair of judges to cover. Then in 1969 the Master (F.E. Cleary) reported on the difficulties that he and the Wardens had experienced in judging gardens as against courtyards or window boxes. They had accordingly decided to make awards in each of these three categories, and the Master and Upper Warden (J.P. Schweder) had each donated a cup for presentation in the gardens and courtyards categories respectively.

Awards for 1969, for the first time in three categories, went to Girdlers Hall (for gardens), Rugarth Property and Management (for courtyards) and National Mutual Life Assurance of Australasia (for window boxes). In September of that year a reception was held in the Livery Suite at Guildhall, when presentations were made by the Lord Mayor to the winners of the various competitions sponsored and promoted by the Company – namely the James Miller Trophy, the "Flowers in the City" awards, and the Church Gardens Competition which is covered below.

In 1973 the Court noted that the winners in each category – Girdlers Hall, National Westminster Bank and National Mutual Life Assurance of Australasia – had won the trophies for several consecutive years. It was therefore decided that, to continue to encourage participation in the scheme, no trophy would be awarded to any competitor for more than three consecutive years.

Then in 1974, in order to improve the efficiency of judging, the City was divided into eight areas (now twelve) with two judges allotted to each. For some twenty years it has been the practice for the Master and the Chairman of the judges to spend the third or fourth Sunday in June deciding the overall winner. Then, on the following Sunday, the judges meet at Cutlers Hall and the Master announces the winner. It is a convivial occasion, on which the Cutlers provide hospitality and the Company entertains the Master Cutler or his representative to lunch.

In 1987 a new trophy was introduced, known as "The Master's Award for General Excellence", which was first awarded to Whitbreads of Chiswell Street, and in 1992 a further new award was added for the best floral street in the City.

From 1975 onwards, the Lord Mayor of the day has been pleased to present the Company's trophies at a short ceremony at Mansion House, thus further setting the Corporation's seal of approval on the Company's efforts to promote floral decoration throughout the Square Mile.

It will be clear from much of the above, and indeed from the many matters already covered in Chapter 4, that there has long been successful cross-fertilisation (to use another appropriate term) between the Company and the City Corporation, which has been of mutual benefit – and, not least, of benefit to the City's environment.

The Hospitals Competitions

The original Window Box Competition, followed by the need to make modifications which in turn resulted in the more extensive "Flowers in the City" campaign, shows clearly how one thing can lead to another. Thus the early success of the Window Box Competition, and the Company's ready involvement in such a venture, led also to the introduction of various other competitions.

In 1953 it was suggested that it would be of benefit to patients in the London Teaching Hospitals if these hospitals were encouraged to brighten them with flowers in gardens, or in window boxes and other displays. The idea was enthusiastically adopted by the Court, the assistance of the London Gardens Society enlisted for the judging, and the competition held for the first time in 1954. The Company had a silver cup designed by J.E. Stapley, one of the entrants for the Goldsmiths Company's competition mentioned earlier, which was awarded in the first year to The Middlesex Hospital. Silver and bronze medals of the London Gardens Society were awarded respectively to The London Hospital and Maudsley Hospital.

There followed a proposal for a separate competition among the London Non-Teaching Hospitals. This was a much larger proposition, even though entries were limited to hospitals within six miles of the City – that being the area laid down in the Company's Royal Charters for the exercise of its exclusive rights. With the support of the secretaries of the four Metropolitan Regional Hospital Boards, however, a scheme was devised and approved by the Court in October 1954. This provided for the entries to be judged firstly in regions, by judges of the London Gardens Society, and then for the regional finalists to be judged to find the overall winner of the event and the Company's cup.

At first the competition was divided into two classes (each with a cup), for hospitals with gardens and for those with only window boxes, roof gardens, or displays in such areas as entrance halls and corridors. In the first year, 1955, the Company's cup (designed by Robert Welch) was awarded in the first class to the South London Hospital for Women, while the Goldsmiths Company's trophy was awarded in the second class to the Medical Rehabilitation Centre in Camden Road.

In 1958 it became necessary to split the classes further, and thereafter there were three classes. These were for window boxes, roof gardens and gardens under a quarter of an acre; gardens between a quarter of an acre and two acres; and gardens exceeding two acres. The Company provided the necessary third cup, designed by K.W. Lessons.

The awards in the three classes in 1958 went to the South London Hospital for Women (the Company's cup), St. Michael's Hospital (the Company's cup) and the Royal Northern Hospital (the Goldsmiths Company's trophy).

Year by year the judges' comments on the entries were most flattering. For instance their report in 1960 reads: "The judging ... has once again proved what can be done by the really keen Committee and gardeners to make their premises a pleasure to both patients and visitors.... They are a most enterprising band of people who work hard and are never beaten by the difficult circumstances under which a great deal of their work is carried out. The quality of the plants is high and there is almost no end to their ingenuity."

Only those who have been in hospital can fully appreciate the comfort given by such displays in convalescence after an operation or serious illness. No doubt the Hospitals Competitions gave a great deal of pleasure throughout their long history until they were discontinued in the late 1980s, following many years during which they were organised by the London Gardens Society with financial support from the Company.

The London Church Gardens Competition
It might be a little unfortunate to turn from hospital gardens to churchyards, but in January 1958 an interesting suggestion was made by the then Bishop

of Woolwich, the Rt. Revd. R.W. Stannard, who was a member of the Court and the Company's Honorary Chaplain. The proposal was that the Company should do something to brighten up the many churchyards in London within six miles of St. Paul's, and this idea was welcomed.

A special sub-committee recommended that initially a competition should be limited to four boroughs north of the Thames (Shoreditch, Bethnal Green, Poplar and Stepney) and four boroughs south of the Thames (Southwark, Bermondsey, Deptford and Greenwich). This was estimated to give a maximum of thirty-one entries, and the prizes were to be vouchers for garden supplies to the value of ten, five and three pounds respectively.

The competition was first held in 1959, and the three prizes were awarded respectively to St. Mark's (Presbyterian) in Greenwich, St. John the Evangelist in Blackheath, and St. Peter's in Deptford. It proved so successful that in 1960 it was extended to include the boroughs of Holborn, Finsbury and Camberwell. Then in 1969 the competition was divided into new sections rather than boroughs, the original London Boroughs in any case having been amalgamated into larger units by legislation in the mid-1960s.

The three new sections from 1969 were for gardens over 4,000 square feet, between 2,000 and 4,000 square feet, and under 2,000 square feet. The first winners under the new arrangements were respectively St. John's Church in S.E.15, Dulwich Congregational Church, and Perry Rise Baptist Church in S.E.23.

There were further rule changes in 1981, but by that time it was proving difficult to maintain the number of competitors and the costs of prizes and judging were becoming disproportionate. Accordingly in July 1983, after a report of most disappointing entries, the competition was discontinued.

Flowers for St. Paul's

The Company has for some years provided floral decorations in St. Paul's Cathedral, at the principal annual services and on special occasions. This arose from a conversation in June 1979 between the then Dean of St. Paul's, the Very Reverend Alan Webster, and Past Master Sir Edward Howard. The Dean referred to his previous experience in Norwich, where ladies in the area had organised displays of flowers in the Cathedral, and he said that he would very much like to have such displays organised for St. Paul's, which attracted some three million visitors each year.

Sir Edward Howard approached Mrs. Ann Ballard, wife of Kenneth Ballard (Sheriff of the City in 1978), whose interest in flower arrangement was well known to him and who agreed to take responsibility for the matter. Although Sir Edward had in mind an approach to the Gardeners Company for funding, his preoccupation with many other City affairs prevented his playing an active part in the scheme. By October 1979, however, Past Master F.E. Cleary had attended a meeting at the Deanery and was able to report the promise of a donation of three hundred pounds from the Company, together with three wrought-iron stands with plaques indicating their origin, and he himself donated a fourth stand.

The first full meeting of the St. Paul's Cathedral Flower Committee was held at the Deanery in November 1979, by which time Cleary had invited Liveryman Janet Owen (daughter of Past Master Martin Longman and sister of Past Master David Longman) to be a member and to help with the purchase of flowers and foliages. The Dean was the first Chairman of the Committee, Ann Ballard acted as Vice-Chairman, Frank Steiner (the Clerk) as Treasurer, and Diana Shears (wife of the then Registrar of St. Paul's) as Secretary. The Master of the day was to be an *ex-officio* member each year, and when L.J. Reddall became Master in 1980 his wife Jill became a permanent member of the Committee.

Most appropriately, the scheme was launched on 25th January 1980 – St. Paul's Day. Fred Cleary gave a lunch on that day at the offices of the City and Metropolitan Building Society in Ludgate Hill, attended by representatives of the Company and the Cathedral. The Master (C.E. Talbot), Wardens and Clerk attended evensong, and a sherry reception at the Deanery following the service. The Master presented to the Cathedral the Company's three stands, together with a pledge of £350 per annum towards the cost of filling them with flowers.

Since that time, the Company has provided funds each year. The scheme has flourished, and now includes flower arrangements in St. Dunstan's Chapel. Many ladies connected with the Company have helped with the scheme, which has done much to enhance the Company's reputation within the City for sponsoring the craft from which it originated.

Company Visits

Apart from these successful efforts to promote the "craft" of gardening, there have been lighter moments when the members of the Court, sometimes accompanied by their ladies and sometimes by members of the Livery and their ladies, have refreshed themselves and given encouragement by paying visits to notable gardens and horticultural establishments. Many such visits have occurred over the years, and just a few examples will suffice to demonstrate their wide range.

A fleeting but interesting connection with the first Garden City of Letchworth took place in 1905, when the Secretary of First Garden City Ltd. wrote to invite the Court to pay a visit and gave particulars of the proposed "experiment" which "admitted of many opportunities for the development of horticulture and gardening and the application of horticultural knowledge to City development". After a preliminary reconnoitre, the Renter Warden (W.T. Crosweller) reported that he was favourably impressed; a number of houses had recently been built, gardens planted, roads marked out, the waterworks finished and a sewerage scheme completed; several manufacturing firms and many private residents had selected sites, and there would be much to interest and instruct the members.

The visit occurred on 31st May 1905, the party being entertained to lunch by the directors, and Past Master C.E. Osman opened Howard Park in the afternoon. On their return to London the Court entertained the directors to dinner at the Albion Tavern in Aldersgate. This seems to have been the end of the matter, however, perhaps because the Court declined to offer a prize for a "cheap cottage competition" later that year, suggesting that more practical good would be done by offering prizes to the residents themselves later on.

In May 1921 a visit was paid to the Chelsea Physic Garden, established in 1673 by the Society of Apothecaries under a lease granted by Charles Cheyne (later Viscount Newhaven), and second in age only to the Botanical Gardens in Oxford (1632). The Physic Garden was superintended successively by one Piggott, Richard Pratt, John Watts, Samuel Doody and James Petiver. In 1722 Sir Hans Sloane (1660-1753), having ten years earlier purchased the Manor of Chelsea which included the Garden, conveyed the site to the Society of Apothecaries in perpetuity on condition that it was always to be a Physic Garden. Philip Miller became perhaps its most eminent superintendent, from 1722 to 1771, and was succeeded by William Forsyth. Miller was also a prolific writer, and his works are well represented in the Company's library – see Appendix F (1741, 1748 and 1771).

Despite the Company's expectation that the Physic Garden would be devoted exclusively to medicinal plants, it was found that it was a general botanical collection arranged for educational purposes. It was minuted that "the house and lecture rooms are conveniently arranged and might be available for a special meeting of the Company". The Curator was subsequently invited to the Company's Fairchild Lecture as one of the "official representatives", but this practice seems to have lapsed.

The Chelsea Physic Garden visit was followed by one to the Royal Horticultural Society's gardens at Wisley, later in the same summer – and naturally, such a key centre in the field has been the subject of other visits since that time.

In July 1950 the Wardens (J.W. Whitlock and Major K.E. Schweder) and the Clerk, in the unavoidable absence of the Master, attended the Annual Commemoration at Wye College near Ashford. This contact with the College, the agricultural and horticultural branch of the University of London, began the close association which is mentioned in Chapter 11 in respect of the Company's charitable activities. A further invitation was extended to the Master and the Clerk to attend the Annual Commemoration in July 1958, which was graced by the presence of Queen Elizabeth the Queen Mother, to whom the guests were individually presented by the Principal of the College.

Then in June 1951, under the leadership of J.W. Whitlock as Master, official visits were paid to Wisley and to Rothamsted Experimental Station; and in July 1952, with R.B. Ling as Master, to East Malling Research Station, where in the 1910s Sir Ronald Hatton's studies had revolutionised fruit-growing.

In May 1954 a more lengthy and elaborate visit was arranged to Spalding, to see the Lincolnshire bulbfields. The Master (F.A.B. Luke), Wardens, members of the Court, and the Clerk and their ladies were entertained to luncheon by the Tulip Time Committee. After touring the bulbfields, they spent the night at the Petwood Hotel in Woodhall Spa, the former home of Sir Archibald and Lady Weigall, where the Court gave a dinner to local dignitaries including the Lord Lieutenant and the High Sheriff of Lincolnshire, the Chairman of the Holland County Council, the Recorder of Lincoln and members of the Tulip Time Committee.

Annual visits have since been made to Spalding at the time of the Tulip Time Parade, and the Company's silver trophy has since 1956 been presented by the Master or his representative. The winner each year is the individual or organisation nominated by the Tulip Time Committee as having done most to contribute to the success of the event. The Master, Wardens and

Clerk, with their ladies, are the guests of the Committee at luncheon before the parade, and in reciprocation officials of the Committee have from time to time attended Company Dinners.

Among other official visits by the Court were those in May 1958 to Leonardslee near Horsham, the home of Sir Giles Loder, to see the magnificent display of rhododendrons and azaleas; and to the Royal Botanic Gardens at Kew in 1960, in which year proposals were made (and subsequently carried out) for visits to Carters Seeds grounds at Raynes Park and to Edmund de Rothschild's home at Exbury in Hampshire, to see his garden in the spring of 1961 when the rhododendrons and azaleas were at their best.

The Company has continued to show its interest in horticultural affairs well beyond the City of London, and the period since 1960 has been marked by a busy programme of visits and events. These have served to ensure that the Company retains a high profile in its field, as well as being highly pleasurable and instructive to the participants. By way of example, the following details demonstrate the Company's lively programme.

For the first of these, representatives of the Company did not have to stray too far from the City. Neither was their destination a garden, nursery or seat of horticultural learning – but a pub in Battersea. In 1962 the Court agreed to a request from Watney Reed & Co. Ltd. to display the Company's arms on a new public house. The Master (J.E. Talbot), on 29th May 1963, was duly accompanied by the Wardens and the Clerk at the re-opening of the reconstructed "Gardeners Arms". A notice in the bar gave acknowledgement to the Company, with a description of the arms. Such an engagement might require ingenuity to justify its inclusion in an account of the Company's sponsorship of the craft or mystery of gardening, although it could be regarded as the encouragement (albeit indirectly) of the cultivation of fine hops!

On 31st July 1962, Past Master Edward Howard and the Clerk (Frank Steiner), accompanied by their ladies, represented the Company at the Anglo-Belgian exhibition of begonias at the Royal Horticultural Hall. Subsequently the Clerk advised the Mayor of Lochristi, who had been responsible for some of the floral arrangements at the exhibition, that on behalf of the Company he would visit the Begonia Show in Lochristi on his way back from a holiday in Germany. He later reported on this impressive event, in which the whole village had been transformed into an exhibition of begonias.

In 1963, members of the Court and the Livery, with their ladies, visited the estate of Honorary Freeman the Lord Aberconway, at Bodnant in the Conway Valley, and the garden of Liveryman Sir Clayton Russon at Glan-y-Mawdach.

On 22nd May 1973, the Company hosted a reception at Brewers Hall for delegates attending the 4th World Congress of the International Federation of Parks and Recreation Administration. This was a most fitting gesture, given the international contacts built up by the Company over many years, and some twenty-four countries were represented.

The Southport Flower Show has long been one of the major events in the British horticultural calendar, and the Company was represented by the Master, Wardens and Clerk in 1973 and 1975.

A further enjoyable event occurred on the weekend of 27th to 29th April 1984, when the Master (R.Adm. M.J. Ross) spent a weekend in Jersey with members of the Company and their ladies, at the invitation of the Lieutenant Governor, General Sir Peter Whiteley. The arrangements for a very full and successful visit had been made by the States of Jersey Tourism Committee. Several fine gardens were visited, including that at Government House, together with nurseries devoted to orchids and carnations.

"Tradescantia"

It is worth drawing attention also to the activities of the Company in the field of "Tradescantia", for in the reigns of James I and Charles I the Tradescants were the most active collectors of foreign plants, some of which were discovered on their own expeditions while others were provided by friends who travelled overseas. The Tradescants were later described by Sir William Jackson Hooker (1785-1865), the first Director of Kew Gardens, as "these first of English gardeners and naturalists". Furthermore Eleanour Sinclair Rohde, in *The Story of the Garden* (Medici Society, 1932; facsimile reprint Medici Society, 1989), asserted that "In the galaxy of great names associated with the history of gardening in early Stuart times, the Tradescants hold a unique place".

Among their many other achievements, it is believed that the Tradescants gave us our first lilac, our first acacia and our first occidental plane. Having said this, it must be recognised that experts have differed on the question of precisely which plants were imported by the Tradescants personally, which plants were raised by them after being imported by others, and indeed which plants have been wrongly attributed to them. It might therefore be that the few examples quoted in these pages are open to question, but at the very least the general statement must stand that the Tradescants introduced countless trees, shrubs, fruits and flowers which today are regarded as the staple stock of the British garden.

John Tradescant the Elder (c.1577-1638) was successively gardener to the first and second Earls of Salisbury at Hatfield House; Edward, Lord Wotton at St. Augustine's Abbey in Canterbury; George Villiers, the Duke of Buckingham at New Hall near Chelmsford; and King Charles I at Oatlands Palace near Weybridge (from 1630 to the rise of Cromwell). He went to live in South Lambeth some time between 1626 and 1628 and, at his house later called "Tradescant's Ark", he created not only the first public museum in Britain but also a most notable garden.

From his extensive travels – which included expeditions to the Low Countries, France, Russia, Algiers and the Mediterranean – he frequently returned with plants new to English gardens. From Russia in 1618, for example, he brought back to Canterbury the first larch tree; and in 1627, from the Island of Rhe off the French coast, he introduced the corn poppy (*Papaver rhoeas*) from which the Shirley strain was developed. His explorations also provided him with innumerable specimens of natural history and artefacts, to swell his "collection of rarities".

There is no evidence that John Tradescant the Elder personally visited Virginia in the United States, but he had several friends who acted as contacts, and there is reason to believe that he had some investment in the development of the colony. Alexander Brown, in *The Genesis of the United States* (1890, re-issued Russell and Russell, 1964), includes him in his "List of Additional Members of the Virginia Companies" from 1606 to 1616, and from this might be attributed the later interest of Tradescant the Younger in Virginia.

The contents of Tradescant's garden are well documented, firstly because he made notes of additions at the end of his own copy of the herbalist John Parkinson's *Paradisus in Sole* (1629), which is in the Bodleian Library. Secondly, four years before his death, he published a list of his plants, *Plantarum in Horto* (1634), of which the only known copy is in the library of Magdalen College Oxford, although it was reprinted with footnotes in R.T. Gunther's *Early British Botanists and Their Gardens* (Oxford University Press, 1922). In fact Gunther suggests that this might be a proof of a work that was never put into general circulation.

John Tradescant the Younger (1608-62) not only assisted his father in his work as a professional gardener, but in 1638 was appointed "keeper of his Majesty's gardens at Oatlands, in the place of his father, deceased". He also enthusiastically pursued the maintenance and enhancement of their own garden and museum at South Lambeth. Much is known about the content of both collections, as fortunately for posterity the younger Tradescant published *Musaeum Tradescantianum: or, A Collection of Rarities. Preserved At South-Lambeth neer London* (1656), of which the final section lists his plants, and which contains fine engravings by Wenceslaus Hollar. A copy of the first edition is in the library of the Worshipful Company of Gardeners, and it was also reprinted in the Tradescant biographies by Allan and Leith-Ross mentioned below.

The garden was occasionally visited by the gardener and diarist John Evelyn, who once commented on one particular plant: "Poplar of Virginia – I conceive it was first brought over by John Tradescant, under the name of tulip-tree (from the likeness of its flowers) . . . I wish we had more of them, but they are difficult to elevate at first."

John Tradescant the Younger followed the family tradition by travelling widely, and his forays included three visits to Virginia (in 1637, in 1642 and for a lengthy period from 1653) which resulted in the introduction of many plants to England. *Liriodendron tulipifera* (the tulip tree) has already been mentioned, but among many others he introduced the Virginia creeper, bergamot (*Monarda fistulosa*), and a columbine (*Aquilegia canadensis*).

There was in fact a third John Tradescant born in 1633, whose sudden death in 1652 cruelly denied him the opportunity to perpetuate the work of his father and grandfather.

John Tradescant the Younger died in 1662, having bequeathed the museum to his wife Hester for her lifetime and thereafter to the University of Oxford or Cambridge. Soon after, however, legal proceedings were instigated by Tradescant's acquaintance of some twelve years, Elias Ashmole (1617-92), who claimed (eventually with success) the existence of an earlier Deed of Gift in his favour which could not be revoked by the will. Both Hester and Ashmole wanted the Tradescants' collection of rarities to go in due course to Oxford University – and so it did after Hester's death, but donated by Ashmole rather than by Hester and thus forming the nucleus of the original Ashmolean Museum (1683).

Admittedly Ashmole had contributed to the collection over the years and had worked with Tradescant on the catalogue of 1656, the publication of which Ashmole financed. Many authorities, however, have shared the view that he could be described as untrustworthy, and that at the very least he took advantage of the Tradescants' gullibility and used his own superior knowledge of the law in extracting the Deed of Gift. This all had the sad result that, with the passing of the Tradescants, less prominence was given to the name of those who had painstakingly developed the collection.

It is equally sad that many of the exhibits in the first Ashmolean Museum were later dispersed to other collections in Oxford, and that this memorial to the Tradescants did not therefore survive intact. For readers wishing to learn more, reference may be made to the book *Tradescant's Rarities: Essays on the Foundation of the Ashmolean Museum 1683 with a Catalogue of the Surviving Early Collections* (Clarendon Press, 1983), edited by Arthur MacGregor.

The remains of the Tradescants' garden at South Lambeth still existed in 1749. Indeed Sir William Watson wrote a paper describing it for the Royal Society, which was published in the Society's *Philosophical Transactions* (Volume 46, 1750). Today the site is marked by Walberswick Street (in memory of the family's Suffolk connections and relatives) and Tradescant Road, following re-development in the late nineteenth century.

The tomb of three generations of Tradescants (John the Elder, John the Younger and the short-lived John the Third), in the churchyard of St. Mary the Virgin at Lambeth, was repaired by public subscription in 1773, and an epitaph was added which had been written by John Aubrey but not used on the original tomb. In 1853 the existing tomb was erected, again by public subscription.

More than a century later, the history of the Tradescants became a subject of keen interest to the Worshipful Company of Gardeners. In February 1964 the Clerk reported to the Court on his interview with Mea Allan, whose book *The Tradescants: Their Plants, Gardens and Museum 1570-1662* (Michael Joseph, 1964) was shortly to be published. This was to contain various references to the Company, of which John Tradescant the Younger had been a Freeman from 19th December 1634 until his death in 1662.

The ingenious epitaph on the family tomb is worth quoting in full. The "Rose and Lily Queen", incidentally, was Henrietta Maria, Queen to King Charles I.

"Know, stranger, ere thou pass, beneath this stone,
Lye John Tradescant, grandsire, father, son.
The last dy'd in his spring, the other two
Liv'd till they had travell'd Orb and Nature through;
As by their choice Collections may appear,
Of what is rare, in land, in sea, in air.
Whilst they (as Homer's Iliad in a nut)
A world of wonders in one closet shut.
These famous Antiquarians that had been
Both Gardiners to the Rose and Lily Queen,
Transplanted now themselves, sleep here, and when
Angels shall with their trumpets waken men
And fire shall purge the world, these three shall rise
And change this Garden then for Paradise."

Perhaps the latter sentiments were somewhat prophetic, as a minute of the Company's Charity Committee in April 1977 records the association of the Company with the Tradescant Garden, which was to be created as an adjunct to the first Museum of Garden History being planned by the newly created Tradescant Trust. The proposal was to use the church of St. Mary the Virgin at Lambeth, redundant since 1972 and scheduled for demolition, and a meeting had been held earlier that year between the Upper Warden (John Brunel Cohen), Mrs. Rosemary Nicholson (Chairman of the Tradescant Trust), Colonel John Innes (one of the trustees, and a descendant of the John Innes of compost fame), and the Clerk.

Immediately after the meeting, the Upper Warden and the Clerk had visited St. Mary's and found it to be boarded up and vandalised. The garden was uncared for, but for the Company its significance lay in the fact that it contained the Tradescant tomb, and it seemed possible to convert it into a garden in the style with which the Tradescants might have been associated in Stuart times.

Progress was slow, but on 28th October 1980 the Charity Committee agreed that the Company must be associated with the garden at St. Mary's, and that the Company's name should be clearly indicated in some way. This association is indeed recorded on a plaque near the entrance to the garden from the Museum, although it was not until 1983 that the garden was formally opened by Queen Elizabeth the Queen Mother. A little later, in 1984, the Freedom of the Company by Presentation was granted to Mrs. Rosemary Nicholson, Chairman of the Tradescant Trust.

On 18th December 1981, at the instigation of the Master (R.L. Payton), a Court Luncheon was held at the Savile Club to celebrate the anniversary of the admission to the Company of John Tradescant the Younger, and this became an annual mid-December event at various venues. As mentioned in the previous Chapter, the Court was honoured by the attendance of Princess Alice, Duchess of Gloucester, on the first such occasion and again on 19th December 1985.

In 1982, as will be seen in Chapter 10, members of the Company followed in the footsteps of Tradescant the Younger in the United States, on a visit sponsored by The Garden Club of Virginia.

Since the foundation of the Museum of Garden History, with its close association with the Tradescants and its adjoining Tradescant Garden, there has been renewed interest in the story of this dedicated family. It is surprising that Mea Allan's book (in 1964) was the first full-length study of the Tradescants for the non-specialist reader, but it is not so surprising that the new enthusiasm of the 1980s gave rise to further research and another book – *The John Tradescants: Gardeners to the Rose and Lily Queen* (Peter Owen, 1984), by Prudence Leith-Ross.

As with Mea Allan's book, Leith-Ross includes reprints of the various Tradescant lists of plants, most notably *Plantarum in Horto* and the *Musaeum Tradescantianum,* but the addition of modern botanical names increases its usefulness for present-day readers. There is also a valuable attempt to distinguish between plants first grown in England by the Tradescants and those introduced by them to England (i.e. collected by their own hands).

The Craft Committee
Finally, it must be recorded that the Company has continued to take very seriously its role in supporting and encouraging the many aspects of the craft of gardening. This was clearly demonstrated in 1990 when, with David Howard as Master, it set up a new Craft Committee.

This was facilitated by the considerable increase in the number of Liverymen and Freemen with experience of horticulture and gardening, both professional and amateur, and the objects of the Committee were to advise the Master and the Court on all matters relating to the craft of gardening and to horticulture in the widest senses, and to recommend ways of broadening the role of the Company and increasing its reputation in the horticultural world.

It was agreed by the Court that in this matter Past Master D.A. Huggons would act as the Master's deputy, and so in effect would provide the necessary continuity by chairing the Craft Committee. At the time of writing, it is expected that the Craft Committee will fulfil an important role in co-ordinating, and taking further, many of the sorts of activities described in this Chapter – as well as initiating new activities.

Among the specific objects proposed at the outset may be mentioned –

Considering and recommending ways of establishing or improving links with amateur and professional horticultural and gardening organisations such as the Royal Horticultural Society, the Botanic Gardens, training establishments, specialist horticultural societies, landscape architects and garden designers, etc;

Providing the Master with any advice he may need about garden visits, etc;

Providing the Charity Committee with any advice they may need about appeals received relating to gardening projects, horticultural therapy, etc., and recommending to that Committee donations to other worthy projects;

Suggesting eminent people in horticulture or gardening, professional or amateur, who might be considered for invitation as the Company's guests at official functions, and/or as candidates to join the Company;

Considering the award of horticultural scholarships, and if agreed selecting the recipients;

Considering the Company's participation in exhibitions, shows, conferences, etc., and organising any agreed exhibit with the exception of the quinquennial Floralies Gantoises (which, as will be seen from Chapter 10, is covered by separate arrangements); and

Organising the floral displays at Company functions, including church services, the provision of bouquets, the annual presentation of produce to the Lord Mayor, etc.

From such a list, which will doubtless be supplemented in scope and in detail as time goes on, it is clear that the Craft Committee has taken on a large and vital role. No doubt it will also be the catalyst or instigator of many special events and projects in the future, given the Company's long-standing aims such as the beautification of London and the enhancement of horticulture nationally.

16. Flowers in the City 1989 — front page of publicity leaflet.

17. Flowers in the City — Middle Temple, the Best Large Garden 1992.

18. Flowers in the City — New Broad Street, the Best Floral Street — 1st Award, 1992.

19. John Tradescant the Younger (1608-1662). Copy of a painting attributed to Emmanuel de Critz with acknowledgement to Ashmolean Museum, Oxford.

20. 'Unconquerable.'

21. The 1990 Ghent Floralies — King Baudouin and Queen Fabiola inspect the Company's exhibit.

22. The 1990 Ghent Floralies — part of the English Spring Garden.

23. Visit to Virginia — planting of a tulip tree in Richmond's Capitol Square (1982).

24. The Master David Howard greets Senior Past Master Geoffrey J. Gollin (1990).

25. Thomas Fairchild Citizen and Gardener 1667-1729.

26. The Company's Golden Book (Appendix E, item 72).

27. The Master's badge and chain of office, the Company's ceremonial spade and chair back with the Company's Arms. (Appendix E, items 30, 37, 59 and 92).

CHAPTER 10

Foreign Relations

Not the least important of the Company's activities have been the visits paid to horticulturalists in foreign countries.

The first of these was to Holland, from 27th April to 1st May 1911. The Master (Charles Bayer) was accompanied by Past Master Beaumont Shepheard (acting as Upper Warden), Past Master N.N. Sherwood (acting as Renter Warden), two Assistants, four members of the Livery, the Clerk (E.A. Ebblewhite) and the Beadle (A.H. Boone). The party also included A.G.L. Rogers, Head of the Intelligence Branch of the Board of Agriculture and Fisheries, as a guest of the Master and Wardens, and throughout the tour the party was accompanied by Heer R.P. Bonthuis (Horticultural Expert to the Board of Agriculture of the Netherlands) and Heer K. Volkersz (Horticultural Expert for the Bulb District).

The object of the tour was "to study, apart from the purely horticultural aspect of bulb-growing, the general economic conditions of that industry and to learn the nature of the work carried on by the Netherlands Government in connection with plant disease and insect pests", and this was reflected in a strenuous itinerary which included visits to Leyden, Katwijk, Wassenaar, Den Haag, Lisse, Hillegom, Haarlem, Aalsmeer (including the Winter School of Agriculture and Horticulture) and Wageningen (including the Phyto-pathological Institute). The total cost of the tour, including the fare to Holland and the expenses of the Beadle and the two Dutch experts, was £119. *Tempora mutantur!*

Belgium, 1913

The success of the Dutch tour was such that a similar visit to Belgium was soon mooted. An invitation to the Clerk in December 1912 to serve on the Jury of the Floralies at Ghent in the following April was accepted, and a Committee of the Court recommended that this should be followed by a Company visit to coincide with the International Congress of Agriculture in June.

On his return from the Floralies, Ebblewhite submitted a report setting out the provisional arrangements for the June visit. The Master (G.R. Blades, later Lord Ebbisham) wrote a short monograph on the history of the Company which was translated into French – *The Worshipful Company of Gardeners of London et Un Chapitre de son Histoire* – and printed for presentation to the Company's hosts. Indeed the booklet was much later updated and reprinted, in connection with the Company's visit to the Ghent Floralies in 1955.

The visit took place from 2nd to 10th June 1913, and the party consisted of the Master, the Wardens, two Past Masters, three Assistants, three Liverymen, a Freeman, the Clerk and the Beadle. On this occasion, there were also six ladies in the party. The itinerary was intensive, and included visits to establishments connected with horticulture at Bruges and Ghent, arboriculture at Tournai, viticulture and pomology at Hoeylaert, horticulture training at Vilvorde, market gardening in the neighbourhood of Malines, as well as the Royal Gardens at Laeken, private gardens at Woluwe St. Pierre, and the orchid houses at Loo Christi (now Lochristi). The party was present at the opening of the International Congress of Agriculture at the Palais des Academies in Brussels, and the Master and Clerk were presented to the King at the Royal Palace by the Minister of Agriculture.

A copy of the Company's report on the tour was subsequently presented to the King of Belgium through the British Embassy in Brussels, and in February 1914 His Majesty conferred on Blades and Ebblewhite the Decoration Speciale Agricole, First Class.

France, 1914

So gratifying had been the success of the Belgian visit that a visit to France was suggested, and Ebblewhite was sent in January 1914 with official introductions from the Foreign Office and the Board of Agriculture to make preliminary arrangements for the tour.

This took place from 7th to 13th June 1914, and the deputation consisted of the Master (S.G. Shead), the Wardens, one Past Master, five Liverymen, the Clerk, the Beadle and two ladies. The itinerary was a happy combination of horticultural studies and sightseeing, with the former including visits to the National School of Agriculture in Versailles, the flower gardens of the City of Paris at Auteuil, the vineyards of Veuve Amiot at St.Hilaire-St.Florent, the Roserie de l'Hay-les-Rosses, and numerous nurseries and public and private gardens in Versailles, Angers, Vendome, Orleans, St.Marceau and Verrieres Le Buisson.

Belgium at War

Within two months of this visit war had broken out, and shortly afterwards a cartoon was published in *Punch* which typified the spirit of Belgium. Bearing the inscription "Unconquerable", it showed the Kaiser in full field uniform, leaning on his sword amid the ruins of war and saying to the King of Belgium, "So you see – you've lost everything"; to which the King, defiant and with sword drawn, replies, "Not my soul."

The original drawing for the cartoon was sold for the benefit of the Belgian Refugee Fund, and was bought by the Company for presentation to the Queen of Belgium. It was framed in oak, with the Royal Arms of Belgium to the left and those of Great Britain to the right, and with the Company's coat of arms at the foot. An inscription was added:

"To Her Majesty The Queen of the Belgians – This original drawing of the cartoon which was published in Punch on the 21st October 1914 and purchased in competition for the benefit of the Belgian Relief Fund is humbly presented by the Worshipful Company of Gardeners of London in the Mastership of Samuel George Shead."

A letter from the Lady in Waiting at Belgian G.H.Q. dated 17th March 1915, accepting the gift, expressed the hope that it might be possible for it to be presented personally when next the Queen was in England, "but at present no date can be indicated".

The Belgian Royal Family was steadfastly reluctant to leave the tiny strip of Belgium round La Panne, which was never occupied by the Germans, so this opportunity never arose. Later in the year, however, the picture was dispatched by diplomatic bag, and was acknowledged by the Queen's Dame d'Honneur in the following terms, dated 19th December 1915:

"I am directed by Her Majesty the Queen of the Belgians to ask you to be so kind as to thank the Master and Worshipful Company of Gardeners for the beautiful and interesting gift they have sent to Her Majesty. The Queen wishes to express her admiration of Mr. Bernard Partridge's wonderful drawing, and of the singularly artistic and emblematic frame in which the Worshipful Company have been good enough to enclose the drawing. Her Majesty will always treasure this mark of appreciation of an ancient and historic body of the efforts of Belgium in the cause of civilisation, the Queen's only regret being her inability to receive the picture in person at the hands of representatives of the Worshipful Company."

The Company was much concerned during the war regarding the fate of its Belgian friends. In June 1915 it had received a petition from the President and Secretary of the Chambre Syndicale des Horticulteurs Belges of Ghent, then in refuge in Rotterdam, complaining that the refusal of the British government to allow the export of Belgian plants to the U.S.A.

would cause the Belgian growers great hardship if the restriction were not removed in time for the autumn trade, and seeking the intervention of the Company with the government. The Master (Benjamin Hansford) reported in September 1915 that much correspondence and many interviews had resulted in special facilities being obtained from the government, which news had been communicated to the Chambre Syndicale and had been received with warm appreciation and gratitude. The press had been informed of the extended facilities granted, and this was a great feather in the Company's cap. To celebrate it the Belgian Minister of Agriculture and Public Works was entertained to dinner on 29th September 1915, and the Belgian Minister in London to lunch on 16th February 1916.

In the meantime the Burgomaster of Malines had been in touch with the Clerk, with a request on behalf of Belgian market gardeners for a large collection of vegetable seeds. It appeared, however, that the Board of Agriculture had been advised by the Foreign Office that a demand had been addressed to the German authorities for the prohibition of the export of seeds from Belgium, and until the result of that demand was known it would not be practicable to take any action to supply vegetable seeds to Belgium. There is no further indication of how the matter developed, beyond a report that seeds to the value of £118 were procured in response to the appeal.

On 14th November 1918 the Court passed the following resolution:

"At our first meeting after the cessation of hostilities we respectfully desire, with feelings of satisfaction and admiration, to offer warm congratulations to His Majesty King Albert and the people of our gallant Ally, the Kingdom of Belgium, on the conclusion of the Armistice with Germany and the beginning of a great and glorious peace: And to express the hope that it may be the proud privilege of this Company to contribute, in however small a degree, to the restoration of the former prosperity of our horticultural confreres in that brave Country."

This resolution was transmitted to King Albert through the Belgian Legation, and brought a reply from his Private Secretary that "His Majesty has attached much value to the desire expressed by your Worshipful Company to contribute to the restoration of our horticultural industry".

As a result, in April 1919, Lt.Col. Joseph Francis (who had been Master in 1916-17 and 1917-18) and the Clerk paid a week's visit to Belgium, to see for themselves what could be done. Their itinerary took them throughout the country, and they were received by the Belgian Minister of Agriculture. In the battle areas they were appalled at the total destruction of all signs of pre-war horticultural activity, and surprised at the measure of damage far behind the line. At Melle, almost three-quarters of the glasshouses had disappeared, the total loss to one nursery alone being estimated at £20,000. At Merelbeke the orchid houses and plants, the product of twenty-five years' work, had been damaged to the extent of £28,000. The country's total horticultural losses had been estimated at over seventy-six million (pre-war) Belgian francs. Its largest pre-war customer, Germany, had been lost; its second largest, the U.S.A., had imposed special quarantine and other restrictions which rendered almost impossible the export of plants to that country; and Great Britain had imposed restrictions requiring a licence for each consignment, however small.

The most practical way in which it was suggested that the Company could help was by the gift of a large number of reed mats, to replace the glass in hothouses – the factory at Charleroi, which previously made the glass, having been destroyed. These mats could be made in Belgium, and therefore had the additional advantage of giving work to Belgian labour at a time when all was confusion in the economy. A recommendation to purchase 250,000 square metres of mats was enthusiastically approved by the Court in June 1919, and Sir Charles Cheers Wakefield (the Master) offered to give £1,000 to start a fund for this purpose. Representations, ultimately successful, were also made to the American and British governments to relax their restrictions on the movement of Belgian horticultural produce.

By November, when the fund was closed, no less than £3,012 had been collected from members of the Company and £2,700 disbursed – a truly remarkable result for a still small Company, with little in the way of capital resources to augment the generosity of its members. This brought official expressions of appreciation from the Belgian Minister of Agriculture and the Chambre Syndicale des Horticulteurs Belges, with the latter writing: "You may be assured, dear Sirs, that our horticulturalists will not fail in their task and that the generosity of our English colleagues will remain stamped in our hearts and the remembrance of it never be wiped out in a future which, we hope, will soon be brighter." There were also letters from individual horticulturalists and later an illuminated address of thanks was presented by Albert de Smet, a member of the Committee of the Chambre Syndicale, on a special visit to London for the purpose.

Francis and Ebblewhite, who had made the original visit and recommendations to the Court, were each awarded the Order of the Crown of Belgium (Chevalier).

France, 1920

In 1920, from 3rd to 9th June, a similar visit was paid to France. The deputation of ten, led by the Master (Maj. Samuel Weil), renewed the contacts made in 1914 and went to many of the establishments which featured on that earlier itinerary. They concluded that there was no need for the sort of assistance that had been given to Belgium.

In 1923, however, an appeal was received by the Lord Mayor of London from the Verdun Horticultural Society for help in restoring its park and fruit gardens. This was referred to the Company, and after receiving a report from the Society's landscape gardener, the Company agreed to bear the cost of restoration to the extent of 5,450 francs (some £72). This brought a warm resolution of thanks, the election of the Company as a "membre bienfaiteur" of the Society, and the gift of the bronze Verdun medal.

Belgium, 1931 and 1933

There was then a lull in official visits abroad until November 1930, when Past Master Francis proposed a further visit to Belgium and Ebblewhite was deputed to make a preliminary reconnaissance. His lengthy report illustrated once more his fondness for historical research, and he stated that he had found records of the Belgian Guilds and Trade Companies at Antwerp, Audenarde, Bruges, Brussels, Courtrai, Ghent, Liege, Louvain, Malines, Tournai and Ypres. He mentioned by name no fewer than thirty-seven such Guilds, most of which had counterparts in the City of London Livery Companies. All Belgian Guilds were suppressed in 1793, but Ebblewhite's report set out some eight respects in which they resembled Livery Companies, including Admission by Servitude, Patrimony, Redemption or Presentation, that membership was no longer restricted to the particular craft, and that members were required to become citizens or burgesses.

The Belgian Gardeners were never incorporated but, like the London Gardeners prior to 1605, formed themselves into Guilds. In Ghent there were 14th century burghers whose seals contained various gardening implements as heraldic emblems, suggesting that they were gardeners. Ebblewhite mentioned Guilds of Gardeners in Ghent (founded 1637), Brussels (16th century) and Antwerp, and he recommended a visit to inspect their records and suggested an itinerary for the purpose.

Ebblewhite's report also proposed that in connection with the visit, or one to the International Floralies at Ghent in 1933 at which the Company would probably be asked to take a prominent part, the Honorary Freedom of the Company should be conferred on the Comte de Kerchove de

Denterghem, Chairman of the Floralies Committee, Senator and former Governor of East Flanders, Ambassador and Minister Plenipotentiary of the King of the Belgians, "a most distinguished public man and horticulturalist". The report was accepted with acclamation, and the visit was arranged to take place from 17th to 22nd May 1931.

The delegation consisted of the Master (J.S. Pearse), the Wardens, one Past Master, six Assistants, thirteen Liverymen, the Clerk and the Beadle. Their itinerary included visits to nurseries and gardens, but was specially marked by the study of relics of Guild life and activities in Bruges, Brussels and Ghent. The Honorary Freedom was duly conferred on the Comte de Kerchove de Denterghem at the Chateau de Beervelde in Ghent.

One amusing item in the report of the delegation was the heraldic description of the arms of the extinct Guild of Gardeners of Bruges, namely "A spade handle upwards and a rake handle downwards, in saltire, enfiled by a coronet, between, in chief, a round parsnip eradicated, on the dexter a long turnip eradicated, on the sinister a carrot eradicated, and in base a melon slipped and leaved pendant".

Then in November 1931, an invitation was received from the Comte de Kerchove de Denterghem for the Company to be represented at the 1933 Ghent Floralies. This mentioned that the King of Belgium had entered his name as the first prospective exhibitor, which gave Ebblewhite the idea of communicating with the Private Secretary to King George V to enquire whether His Majesty would follow this example – but alas without success.

The Company was represented on this occasion by the Master (John Weir), the Upper Warden (P.M. Stewart), the Immediate Past Master (Edward Dean), the Clerk and the Beadle. In the course of the opening ceremony, they were received by the Duke and Duchess of Brabant.

The National Society of Horticulture of France

In June 1932 a deputation of the National Society of Horticulture of France paid a visit to English gardens, and in view of that Society's hospitality to the Court on their visits to France in 1914 and 1920, it was felt that they should be entertained.

The President of the Society, speaking at a dinner held at the Criterion Restaurant, said that they were "endeavouring to follow on their side of the Channel the best traditions of Kent, Brown, Repton and other distinguished masters of garden design, and that whilst the influence of Le Notre had made itself felt throughout Europe in the 17th and 18th centuries, it must be recognised that the work of Blaikie, who designed 'Bagatelle', and other British gardeners led to the development of landscape gardening in France". The leaders of the deputation were subsequently entertained at a Livery Dinner at Merchant Taylors Hall.

Holland, 1950

It was not until some years after the Second World War – in fact in 1950 – that foreign visits were resumed. The first was to Holland, and even then there was difficulty with the Exchange Control over the supply of the necessary Dutch currency to supplement the members' personal travel allowance, although the visit was sponsored by the Foreign Office.

It was hoped that the delegation would be received by Queen Juliana, who had consented to accept the Honorary Freedom of the Company, and the Control was told that if the additional allowance was refused the Master would be under the painful necessity of informing Queen Juliana's Chamberlain that the visit could not take place, and the reason. Half the required amount was then grudgingly conceded.

The visit, from 17th to 20th April 1950, was made by a large party. Under the leadership of the Master (C.E. Page Taylor), the delegation consisted of the Wardens, three Past Masters, four Assistants, the Clerk (by then Arnold Steele) and the Beadle, and eleven ladies. Although visits were made to the bulbfields and to the Flower Auction at Aalsmeer, this particular trip to Holland was largely of a social nature but was highly successful as a gesture of international friendship. Queen Juliana was presented with the Honorary Freedom at Soestdijk Palace, and signed the Company's Golden Book. Another highlight of the trip was the Court Dinner at the Hotel des Indes in The Hague, at which the principal guests were the Dutch Minister of Agriculture and the Chairman of the Royal Netherlands Horticultural Society.

When Queen Juliana was in London on a State Visit in December 1950, the Company was privileged to supply the bouquet which she carried on her State Drive to Guildhall, where she received an Address of Welcome from the Lord Mayor. Then in June 1954 the Master (F.A.B. Luke), attended by the Clerk, was summoned to the private residence of the Dutch Ambassador. After presenting to the Master the insignia of Commander of the House of Orange, Queen Juliana engaged in animated conversation with her visitors.

The Ghent Floralies, 1955

Soon afterwards the long association of the Company with the quinquennial Ghent Floralies was resumed, when the Court decided to pay an official visit sponsored by the Foreign Office from 22nd to 26th April 1955. The Master (Sir Brunel Cohen) and the Renter Warden (Donald Byford) were accompanied by three Past Masters, four Assistants, the Clerk and the Beadle.

The principal object of the visit was to see the Floralies Gantoises, and at the opening the Master, Renter Warden and Clerk were presented to King Baudouin. There were also, however, opportunities to renew contacts with horticultural interests in Belgium, and to this end visits were made to the vineyards of Hoeylaert, the premises of Sander and Sons in Bruges, and the Jardins Botaniques in Brussels. High points of the trip included the admission to the Honorary Freedom of Comte Jacques de Kerchove de Denterghem, and a Court Dinner at which the principal guests were the British Ambassador, the Belgian Ambassador to the Court of St. James, and the Belgian Minister of Agriculture.

France, 1959

The next visit abroad was to France, from 23rd to 26th April 1959, primarily to attend the International Floralies in Paris. The itinerary also included the Orangerie of the Palace of Versailles, the Potager du Roi and the Chateau of Vaux-le-Vicomte.

On this visit the Master (G.J. Gollin) was accompanied by the Wardens, five Assistants, one Liveryman, the Clerk (by then Frank Steiner) and the Beadle, and ten ladies.

The Ghent Floralies from 1960

No sooner was this visit over than an invitation was received to the Ghent Floralies of 1960. This tour, from 21st to 26th April, was on similar lines to that of 1955. The delegation comprised the Master (F.H. Lymbery), the Wardens, three Past Masters, three Assistants, the Clerk, the Dinner Secretary and the Beadle. The itinerary included the Botanical Gardens at Meisse and the orchid nurseries of Messrs. Sander, and opportunities were also taken to renew contacts with the cities of Brussels, Ghent and Bruges. The Master, Wardens and Clerk were presented to King Baudouin at the opening of the Floralies, and the fact that on this occasion His Majesty signed the Company's Golden Book led later to an invitation to him to accept the Honorary Freedom. This visit to Belgium concluded with a Court Dinner at the Hotel Metropole in Brussels, at which the principal guests were the British Ambassador to Belgium and the Belgian Ambassador in London.

At a Court meeting on 24th May 1961, a resolution was passed which began "mindful of the privileges accorded to members of the Court attending last year's Floralies Gantoises and being received by His Majesty the King of the Belgians", and went on to record the great satisfaction with which the Court had learned that His Majesty had been pleased to accept the Honorary Freedom of the Company. Just over a year later, the Minute Book records that the Master (Edward Howard), accompanied by the Wardens (J.E. Talbot and Roger Nathan), Past Masters F.J.B. Gardner and F.H. Lymbery, Assistant John Shearn and the Clerk, had been received at Laeken Palace and had duly conferred on King Baudouin the Honorary Freedom. His Majesty had also graciously arranged for the party to be shown round the spectacular greenhouses of the Palace.

One incident during the visit caused humour at the time, and was later remembered. On the evening before the audience at Laeken, after a dinner in Brussels at which the Chamberlain of the Belgian Court had been the Company's guest, Assistant John Shearn (then President of Interflora) asked the Clerk if he had brought with him the customary posies to be carried by members of the Court. The Clerk had not done so, and Shearn offered to use his local connections to remedy the defect. The next morning, the Clerk received a large box containing the requisite number of posies – but instead of the customary herbs, they consisted of symmetrically arranged radishes, onions and turnips!

Hastily summoned by a rather alarmed Clerk, the Master inspected the posies and decreed that they should be carried by the members of the Court. In due course he explained to the King what had occurred and what the posies should have contained, and fortunately this was greeted with royal amusement. There the incident ended, but only for the time being.

On the afternoon of 14th May 1963, the King and Queen of the Belgians arrived in London on the occasion of a State Visit. The Master (J.E. Talbot), accompanied by the Wardens (Roger Nathan and M.J. Thurston) and the Clerk, was received at Buckingham Palace by Queen Fabiola, to whom he presented a bouquet of red roses, white lilies of the valley and blue delphiniums. After the Queen had expressed her thanks, King Baudouin reminded the deputation of the visit to Laeken and demanded sternly to know why the party had not on this occasion carried vegetables in honour of the Queen.

The visit to the Floralies Gantoises, as will be evident from the above, has long been a regular feature of the Company's calendar. Indeed it would be superfluous to give full details of each quinquennial visit, since the Company has been represented on every occasion from 1955 and the itineraries have had many common features – including the official opening by King Baudouin and presentation of senior representatives of the Company, and the receipt of warm hospitality from the Burgomasters of Ghent and Brussels and the Royal Horticultural Society of Belgium. In particular, however, the strong involvement of the Company in organising a British exhibit in the Floralies since 1975 is worthy of more detailed coverage.

The delegation in 1965, from 23rd to 26th April, was led by the Master (M.J. Thurston). On a visit to the Chateau de Beloeil and its park, a reception was given by Prince Antoine de Ligne; and the party also had the opportunity to study hydroponic techniques in the greenhouses of Jacques Solvay.

In 1970, the visit took place from 21st to 27th April and the party was led by the Master (F.E. Cleary). On this occasion, Queen Fabiola added her signature to that of King Baudouin in the Company's Golden Book. Then the party moved on to Holland, as Queen Juliana had issued an invitation to an audience with her. This duly took place, and while in Holland the delegation visited the Keukenhof Gardens, the Polder works, a fruit farm which five years previously was below the sea, a bulb farm, and the flower auction at Aalsmeer.

There was a particularly happy aspect of the Company's visit to the 1975 Floralies, which took place from 23rd to 28th April. The Master (A.J. Carton) had the additional pleasure of admitting Queen Fabiola to the Honorary Freedom of the Company. This ceremony took place at Laeken Palace on 24th April 1975, and the following day saw the opening of the Floralies at which King Baudouin, Queen Fabiola and Princess Grace of Monaco greeted all members of the party. A further highpoint was that the party returned to London via Holland, where they received an audience with Queen Juliana in the Royal Palace at the Hague and Her Majesty graciously gave a conducted tour of the Palace and its gardens.

There was also a more challenging aspect arising from the 1975 Floralies – that of considering a more significant British presence in 1980. Over the years, there had been an occasional exhibit from Britain which was usually mounted by the Royal Horticultural Society, but at the time of the Company's delegation in 1975 there had not been a British entry for some fifteen years. At a reception in Ghent, this was sadly commented upon by John Evans, one of the British judges and a Liveryman of the Company. It was seized upon by Assistant C.E. Talbot, who suggested that the Company should shoulder this responsibility.

The idea was to put British horticulture squarely on the European map, and when the Company's delegation returned home a preliminary meeting was held. The original idea was that the Company should act as a catalyst in getting all interested parties together, setting the project in motion and then gracefully withdrawing. It was soon evident, however, that if the project was to proceed the Company would have to be the driving force behind the staging of an exhibit.

Plans were launched during the Mastership in 1975 of David Longman, who was one of those fired with enthusiasm at the 1975 Floralies. In addition to Longman, a Committee of the Company included C.E. Talbot, L.J. Reddall and E.M. Upward. They were fortunate enough to secure the interest of the Bailiff of the Royal Parks, Robbie Hare, who introduced them to the Superintendent of Regents Park, Bob Legge. Legge took the whole idea to heart with great energy, and he and Michael Upward organised the design of the exhibit and the supply of plants. He also secured Ministerial approval for the use of resources and personnel from the Royal Parks, while Longman and Reddall were active and successful in the crucial area of commercial sponsorship.

Early in 1980, the Company was well prepared to mount the first serious attempt for some years at staging a major British display at the Ghent Floralies. The theme was to be a woodland garden, with all its softness and pastel shades, as a direct contrast to the harsher colours of the Belgian azaleas. All went according to plan, except that a broken leg sadly precluded the attendance at the Floralies of Past Master David Longman, who had been such a key figure behind the British initiative.

It is not surprising, given the Company's contribution, that the delegation to the Floralies from 17th to 20th April 1980 was particularly large. It comprised the Master (C.E. Talbot), the Wardens, three Past Masters, three Assistants, fifteen Liverymen, the Clerk and Assistant Clerk, and twenty-five ladies (three of whom were Freemen). They witnessed a major contribution by the Company to the craft of gardening, and it was a proud occasion for the delegation when the British entry secured third place among the international exhibits. The exhibit also won awards for groups and specimen plants.

There was a further pleasurable event in connection with the 1980 Floralies. That year marked the 150th anniversary of Belgium's independence, and it had been decided that the Company should present to the Royal Agricultural and Botanical Society of Belgium a suitable prize for competition at each Floralies. This presentation of the Company's plate was made to Comte Andre de Kerchove de Denterghem, who had recently succeeded his uncle as President of the Society. Some three years later, Comte Andre became an Honorary Freeman of the Company.

Much encouraged by their success, the Company immediately started preparations for the 1985 Floralies. Plans were beginning to take shape, then all concerned were stunned by the untimely death of the principal designer and creator, Bob Legge. Arrangements were temporarily put aside, and it was not until 1984 that the Company resumed its consideration of the matter.

Fortunately the new Bailiff of the Royal Parks, Ashley Stephenson, came to the rescue by taking a close interest in organising the British exhibit for the following year. Again Michael Upward, together with Nick Butler of the Royal Parks, set about putting the exhibit together. The team included staff members from the Royal Parks and some "Young Gardeners", that enthusiastic group of Freemen and Liverymen under the age of thirty-five founded in 1979.

This time the emphasis was on a rock garden leading into formal bedding, a copse and water garden. The British entry did not win a major prize, but still received several individual awards. It was seen by the Company's delegation, which visited from 17th to 21st April 1985, led by the Master (P.D. Marriner). During the visit the Master, accompanied by many of the party, toured the Ypres battlefields and cemeteries and laid a wreath on the Company's behalf at the Menin Gate.

Within months of the 1985 event, a Committee chaired by Past Master David Longman was at work to ensure that there would be a British exhibit in 1990. This time it was decided to set up a competition sponsored by the Company, which attracted entries of high quality from colleges of landscape design. The winning design, submitted by the School of Architecture and Landscape Architecture at Thames Polytechnic (now the University of Greenwich), formed the basis of the British garden eventually created in the exhibition hall in Ghent.

The years from 1986 to early 1990 saw the painstaking processes of collecting both plants and money. The former process was greatly assisted by Liverymen Jeffrey Bernhard and Robert Bent, prominent members of the horticultural trade. Fund-raising was particularly important, since the

Company had to rely upon the generosity of private and commercial sources in the absence of government funds – although it must be acknowledged that again there was sterling support in time and expertise from Ashley Stephenson and Nick Butler of the Royal Parks.

Early in the April of 1990, the Company's enthusiastic team travelled to Ghent to mount the exhibit. Led again by Michael Upward, the party also included some "Young Gardeners" and Nick Butler with his staff. Over some ten days they worked with a heap of soil, peat and rocks and two lorry-loads of plants, shrubs and trees. The final result was an undulating English spring garden, with a waterfall and lake and charming vistas from every angle.

The Company's official delegation to the 1990 Floralies, from 18th to 22nd April, was led by the Master (G.H. Denney). Again the British exhibit was a source of considerable national pride and a credit to all concerned, and its quality was recognised by the special award of a cut glass bowl from the Royal Belgian Horticultural Society.

Some Other Significant Visits

Having recognised the great importance placed by the Company on its representation at the Floralies Gantoises, it is necessary to go back a few years in order to record some other significant visits which inspired good relations with colleagues abroad.

Portugal was visited from 23rd February to 2nd March 1971 by a party led by the Master (J.P. Schweder). The highlight of the trip was an audience at the Palace of Belem with the President, H.E. Contra-Almirante Americo Deus Rodrigues Thomaz, for the purpose of admitting His Excellency to the Honorary Freedom of the Company. The itinerary also included visits to the Palace of Queluz and Pena Palace and their gardens.

In September 1973, a small party led by the Master (N.A. Royce) visited the vineyards of the Rhine. The Company's representatives were able to study the replanning of German vineyards, and the modernisation of the wineries to meet increased output – as well as to sample the finest wines of the area!

Holland was once again the host country in 1978, when a party led by the Master (John Brunel Cohen) visited from 11th to 14th May. Queen Juliana, who clearly had a great affection for the Company, had expressed the hope on the occasion of the brief 1975 visit that members of the

Company would spend more time with her. On 12th May 1978 members of the party received an audience with Her Majesty at Soestdijk Palace, and the Master presented a glass vase engraved with the Company's arms. The tour also included visits to the Keukenhof Gardens, the Co-operative Association United Aalsmeer Flower Auction, and the van Roozen nursery specialising in new varieties of tulips.

Mention was made in the previous Chapter of the Company's involvement with the Tradescant Trust and the inception of the annual Tradescant Luncheon. In the late 1970s and early 1980s the Company's interest in Tradescant history became established, largely through the enthusiasm and encouragement of Roger Payton. An opportunity for him to take this further occurred in April 1982, when as Master he led a party to Virginia on a visit sponsored by The Garden Club of Virginia. Generous hospitality was dispensed to the delegation, consisting of the Master, the Upper Warden, four Past Masters, the Clerk and fifteen others, in numerous social occasions and events of horticultural interest in Richmond, Charlottesville, Williamsburg, Jamestown and other parts of Virginia.

It could be said that the party retraced the steps of John Tradescant the Younger (Freeman 1634-62), and indeed one of Tradescant's notable discoveries was commemorated when the Company had the honour of planting a tulip tree in Richmond's Capitol Square. During the visit, the warm relationship between the Company and The Garden Club of Virginia was marked by the award of the Freedom of the Company by Presentation to Jean Printz, the Club's President.

It is also worth mentioning that the Company itself, in the time of John Tradescant the Elder, appears to have been involved with numerous other parties in the foundation of Virginia. In *The Genesis of the United States* (1890, reissued Russell and Russell, 1964) Alexander Brown quotes "The Second Charter to The Treasurer and Company, for Virginia, erecting them into a Corporation and Body Politic, and for the further enlargement and explanation of the privileges of the said Company and first Colony of Virginia". This was dated 23rd May 1609, and Brown lists "The Company of Gardiners" as an investor in (or from) 1616.

Then in 1987, a visit to France was led by the Master (A.B. Hurrell). The itinerary included several noteworthy gardens in the neighbourhood of Rouen, and the party also visited the invasion beaches at Arromanches. Then in 1988, from 13th to 21st May, the Master (His Hon. G.F. Leslie) led a tour of gardens near the Italian Lakes. This provided the opportunity for the party of twenty to see splendid examples of North Italian gardens at their best, as well as to make many new contacts for the Company.

In June 1992, the Master (R.C. Balfour) led a visit to the Floriade in Holland. A number of Liverymen (including Robert Bent as Chairman) were members of the working group for the British Garden at Zoetermeer, which won the premier award for outdoor exhibits.

Floral Tributes

Not surprisingly, the Company has always welcomed the opportunity and privilege of presenting floral tributes to members of royal families from throughout the world on their visits to London. Just a few examples will be sufficient, from which it will be seen that in this way the Company has played its small but worthwhile part in enhancing such occasions.

In February 1965, a bouquet was delivered to Queen Juliana of the Netherlands on her visit to this country to attend the funeral of Sir Winston Churchill. In a letter of thanks, the Netherlands Ambassador referred to the fact that Her Majesty treasured most highly the Honorary Freedom of the Company. Again in November 1970, a bouquet was presented to Queen Juliana on the occasion of a private visit.

J.L. Stevenson's year as Master saw two important occasions in this respect. On 5th October 1971 he presented a bouquet at Buckingham Palace to the Vice Grand Chancellor for the Empress of Japan, on the occasion of the official visit by the Emperor and Empress. Then on 11th April 1972 the Master, with his Wardens (Bishop R.W. Stannard and N.A. Royce) and the Clerk, attended at Windsor Castle and presented to Queen Juliana a bouquet on her State Visit.

In June 1972 a bouquet was presented to the Grand Duchess of Luxembourg on the occasion of the State Visit by the Grand Duke and Grand Duchess; and in June 1974, on the State Visit of Queen Margaretha and The Prince of Denmark, a bouquet was delivered to Her Majesty on the Royal Yacht "Danneborg" moored in the Thames. Also in 1974, the Company presented a bouquet to Her Imperial Highness Princess Chichibou on her visit to London, which was delivered to the Japanese Ambassador's house in Kensington Palace Gardens.

Some years later, on 18th November 1982, the Master (J.G. Keeling) was invited with his wife to a Banquet at Hampton Court given by Queen Beatrix of the Netherlands and Prince Claus, in honour of Her Majesty the

Queen and Prince Philip. On the following morning the Master, attended by his Wardens (R.Adm. M.J. Ross and P.D. Marriner) and the Clerk, presented a bouquet to Queen Beatrix at Buckingham Palace.

The Incorporation of Gardeners of Glasgow

While it is inappropriate to include Scotland under the heading "Foreign Relations", this Chapter presents a convenient opportunity to record the association between the Company and the Incorporation of Gardeners of Glasgow.

This commenced with a report from the Clerk to the Master on 31st December 1926, stating that "as the result of a couple of field days in the British Museum and Society of Antiquaries' Libraries" he was in a position to urge the claims of the Incorporation for consideration by the Court. The report continued:

"As King James the 1st, our founder would incorporate the English arts, crafts or mysteries by special Royal Charters and the grantees would pay the heavy fees; but as King James VI he could not obtain such financial docility from the Scots, so he was constrained to deal with them on 'wholesale' terms by making 'Grants of Livery' to the Burghs and empowering them to issue charters of incorporation to the arts, crafts or mysteries within their jurisdictions. But the legal effect was the same, and the civic status of the incorporations was as high within their boundaries as the companies within the City of London. Thus the Burgh of Glasgow by charter devolved the royal act of incorporation to those carrying on the craft of a gardener in 1625 and, though the document was accidentally destroyed, it was confirmed by Seal of Cause in 1690, which refers to the craft as 'neer these hundred years begone being incorporate as one of the trades of the Burgh'".

Ebblewhite's report goes on to list nine respects in which the history of the Incorporation was similar to the Company, including Admission by Purchase, Patrimony and Servitude. The roll of members of the Incorporation went back to 1616 and the list of Deacons to 1626, and it had some interesting property and emblems. He therefore suggested that he should visit Glasgow and make further enquiries, with a view to establishing some closer association between the two bodies. This was agreed, and as a result Ebblewhite made a further report to the Court in April 1927.

The argument regarding co-operation turned on the powers of the Master Court of the Incorporation as to the application of its funds (which were considerable) to an active association with the art, trade and craft of gardening which had ceased since the middle of the 19th century. A visit by the Master and Wardens to Glasgow was suggested for the following autumn, but this was delayed owing to the difficulty of agreeing a convenient date, and the question does not appear to have been specifically revived.

Nevertheless for many decades it has been the custom for the Company to entertain the Deacon of the Incorporation at its Livery Banquet (or, in more recent years, the Livery and Ladies' Banquet), and for the Master to be invited to the Deacon's "Choosing Dinner" in Glasgow. From 1959 onwards, reciprocal invitations have also been extended to the respective Clerks, and the association between the two Guilds has continued on a most amicable basis – so much so that, during his Clerkship, John Fleming joined the Incorporation.

When members of the Court visited the Glasgow Garden Festival in 1988, they were warmly entertained. That year might also be said to have given rise to a further example of accord between the Guilds, when the Company's Assistant Clerk from 1987 to 1989 (Gillian May Vanderpump) married a member of the Incorporation.

CHAPTER 11

Charitable Activities

A Charitable Fund was formally established by the Court on 17th March 1903, and was one of E.A. Ebblewhite's first steps on his appointment as Clerk to put the Company's affairs on a secure footing. The conditions of the Fund were wide, being "for the relief of indigent members and other charitable objects by voluntary contributions of members of this Company and amounts to be hereafter collected in the Poor Box". Donations to the Fund amounting to £147 were made by five members attending that meeting. By the next Court this had risen to £250, and further contributions came in response to an appeal circulated to members of the Company.

For many years before the first World War and between the wars, it appears to have been the practice for each newly elected Assistant to make donations of twenty-five pounds or twenty-five guineas to the Scholarship Fund (i.e. one year's scholarship) and five guineas to the Charitable Fund, as well as twenty-five pounds or twenty-five guineas to the Common Hall Fund referred to in the next Chapter.

Several years before the establishment of the Charitable Fund, however, the Company had been associated with the Gardeners Royal Benevolent Institution (founded in 1839) and the Royal Gardeners Orphan Fund (founded in 1887). In June 1895 and April 1897 respectively, the Company endowed pensions through these two bodies for a retired gardener and an orphan.

Then in March 1922 the Company paid to the Gardeners Royal Benevolent Institution a capital sum of four hundred pounds to be known as The Gardeners Company Trust Fund, to provide a pension for an "indigent gardener" to be nominated by the Company. The trustees were the trustees of the Institution, namely Lord Rothschild, Baron Bruno Schroder and J.E.N. Sherwood. A similar payment of three hundred pounds was made in June 1922 to the trustees of the Royal Gardeners Orphan Fund, for the benefit of an orphan male child of a gardener to be nominated by the Company, and in November 1929 a further amount of £185 14s. 4d. in 3.5% Conversion Stock was transferred to the trustees in order to increase the provision for the Company's orphan to 7s. 6d. per week.

The Gardeners Royal Benevolent Society

In the post-war years, the support given to the Gardeners Royal Benevolent Institution (since 1960 the Gardeners Royal Benevolent Society) has greatly increased. When in 1952 the Institution established a residential home for retired gardeners, their wives and widows, the Company gave £250 to endow a bed and afterwards made regular payments toward maintenance. A hospital wing was later added, so that if residents fell ill they could be nursed on the premises in appropriate cases, rather than being transferred to a general or geriatric hospital.

On 9th May 1973, the Duchess of Gloucester opened the Society's new home, Red Oaks at Henfield in West Sussex. The Master (Bishop R.W. Stannard) represented the Company, and Past Master F.E. Cleary announced that a £100,000 appeal which he had launched had reached its target. Past Master Sir Edward Howard, Chairman of the Society, described the move from the noise of the old home near Heathrow Airport to the peace and beauty of Red Oaks.

From time to time, the Company has made donations to the Gardeners Royal Benevolent Society for specific purposes as well as recurrent grants. In 1977 the Company provided an Ambulift, and the then Chairman of the Home Committee wrote to the Clerk that "in view of what we all sincerely hope will be a permanent interest by your Company in our Home, I would like to commemorate your support for the sick bay by a bronze plaque to be exhibited in a prominent part of the sick bay area." The Court agreed that it would be appropriate for the Company to take a continuing interest in the Home, and visits by members of the Company occasionally take place. The Ambulift, incidentally, is still in use.

In 1986 the rules of the Gardeners Royal Benevolent Society were amended, giving certain organisations the right to make nominations to the Society's Council. The Worshipful Company of Gardeners is one such organisation, and at the time of writing the representative is Past Master G.H. Denney. Long before that time, however, prominent members of the Company were active in the Society's affairs – Past Master Sir Edward Howard, in particular, served a notable period as the Society's Chairman – and Liveryman P.V. Jeffries and Past Master L.J. Reddall are currently the Chairman and Honorary Treasurer respectively.

The Royal Gardeners Orphan Fund

In the case of the Royal Gardeners Orphan Fund, the Company has continued to make an annual donation and has been represented on the Executive Committee of the Fund for many years by the Almoner, Donald W. Silverton.

Since 1985 the Fund has extended the scope of its activities beyond the care of orphans, and now provides help to the children and relatives of gardeners and horticulturists in such spheres as special education and medical treatment.

The Metropolitan Public Gardens Association

The Metropolitan Public Gardens Association was established in 1882, originally under the title The Metropolitan Public Garden, Boulevard and Playground Association. Its objective was "to supply one of the most pressing wants of the poorer districts within the Metropolitan area, namely breathing and resting-places for the old, and playgrounds for the young, in the midst of densely populated localities, especially in the East and South of London."

The policy of the Association from the outset was not to usurp the responsibilities of local authorities, and still less to relieve them of their obligations, but to assist and encourage them in their duties. Indeed the Association was instrumental in securing the Open Spaces Act of 1890, which increased the powers of local authorities to acquire and maintain open spaces and removed various detrimental legal barriers. Thus the Association prepared many open spaces in accordance with its stated objective, and afterwards conveyed them to local authorities to maintain for posterity. Between 1882 and 1890, the Association completed 218 projects and opened one hundred acres of playing fields to children on Saturdays.

The first connection of the Company with the Association arose from a gift of £52 10s in June 1895 by Herbert Haynes, to commemorate his election to the Court. This was used for the provision of seats at St. Bartholomew's Hospital and St. John's Clerkenwell, each bearing inscriptions with the Company's name. These seats were placed in position in April 1896, by permission of the City Commissioners of Sewers.

This began a long collaboration between the Company and the Association, of which the Company is a group member and to which it makes an annual donation. In the 1960s, when the two bodies began to work together on the "Flowers in the City" campaign (see Chapter 9), one direct and useful link was in the person of F.E. Cleary – Chairman of the Metropolitan Public Gardens Association from 1954 to 1984, and also a most active member of the Company who became Master in 1969.

At the end of 1969, the Association's annual magazine *The London Gardener* contained the following thoughts by Cleary which were equally relevant to his position as Master of the Worshipful Company of Gardeners:

"Surely one of the fundamental duties of a Local Authority . . . is to maintain the physical features of its area to the highest possible standard by the provision of open spaces, large or small, the planting of trees, the provision of seats and playgrounds, and a constant attack on all who despoil the towns and countryside . . . It is no good talking about environment and it is no use writing about conservation. What we want is action, and the lead must come from Central and Local Government . . . Of course it costs money, but money spent on open spaces or trees or seats is money invested for many years – and what better than an investment to keep England a green and pleasant land?"

In more recent years, the Company's invaluable link with the Metropolitan Public Gardens Association has been continued by Past Master R.L. Payton and Assistant E.M. Upward (serving respectively as the Association's Chairman and Secretary). Indeed Michael Upward (Master of the Company in 1993-94) was Secretary of the Association from 1963 to 1987, and for his services he was awarded the Association's "London Spade" at their Annual General Meeting in 1989.

The Gardeners Company's Day

In 1906 a sum of £8 2s. was voted to the Fresh Air Fund (subsequently known as Pearson's Fresh Air Fund) "to enable 200 poor children to spend a day in the country, to be known as The Gardeners' Day". This was renewed annually until the end of the First World War, when the amount was increased to thirteen pounds, and at some time during that period the outing was limited to poor children of the Shoreditch district and the name altered to "The Gardeners Company's Day".

In 1924 the grant was doubled to twenty-six pounds, and the number of Shoreditch children to share in the treat doubled to four hundred. Earlier in that year one thousand bulbs were bought at a cost of thirty-four pounds, and distributed to the children. The minutes of 1925 record the "20th consecutive year of such outing", which appears to have continued until the outbreak of war in 1939 but not thereafter.

The Royal Horticultural Society Exhibition, 1912

A Royal Horticultural Society Exhibition was planned for the summer of 1912, and the Company was glad to be associated with the project. A sum of fifty guineas was voted by the Court for a cup, to be awarded at the discretion of the Schedule Committee of the Exhibition. Subsequently one hundred pounds was guaranteed by the Company in respect of the expenses of the exhibition, with Past Master Charles Bayer undertaking to indemnify the

Company against any liability under its guarantee which, happily, did not have to be implemented.

The Company's prize, designed and made by Elkingtons of Cheapside, took the form of four oval silver gilt fruit dishes joined in the centre by a shield bearing the Company's arms supported by two female figures, carrying cornucopiae on either side and surmounted by a basket of fruit. This was awarded for a group of roses in a space not exceeding 500 square feet (plants in pots or tubs and in flower), and was won by Paul and Son of Cheshunt in Hertfordshire.

The exhibition was opened by King George V. At this ceremony, according to a report in the *City Press*, the Company was "well represented"; among those who received His Majesty were J.G. Fowler, a member of the Court and Treasurer of the Royal Horticultural Society, and Past Masters Sir Trevor Lawrence and N.N. Sherwood.

Charitable Work in the First World War

In November 1917, in response to an appeal by the Director General of Voluntary Services, it was decided to supply tools for a gardening class of wounded soldiers under the direction of the Officer Commanding No.4 General Hospital.

Shortly before this a donation was given to the Prisoners of War Scheme (Educational) inaugurated by the Board of Education, for books relating to gardening, greenhouse work and fruit culture.

At about the same time, Past Master R.I. Tasker sought to associate the Company with a scheme for the provision of gardens at the War Seal Foundation housing settlement at Fulham, towards which he offered to contribute one hundred guineas, but for reasons not stated the scheme does not appear to have commended itself to the Court.

In November 1918 Past Master Sir Horace Brooks Marshall, who had just begun his year as Lord Mayor, made suggestions for starting agricultural allotments for men disabled in the war. He wanted the Company to found and maintain at least one colony of smallholdings for ex-servicemen, and offered to present to the Company sufficient land to form the nucleus of a scheme. Difficulties nevertheless arose over finding suitable land, and with the inauguration of the Belgian Relief Fund the Court's enthusiasm waned. The matter was shelved, partly because the Master (Sir Charles Cheers Wakefield) intimated that if the scheme did not proceed he would give the five hundred pounds he had promised to the scheme to the Belgian Fund, which was forging ahead successfully.

The Almoner

The office of Almoner to the Company was created in June 1921, and now undertakes considerable work in the acquisition and disposition of the Company's charitable funds. The original purpose was to secure advice on the pooling and allocation of the votes of the Company and its members for candidates for the British Home for Incurables, the Royal Hospital for Incurables and other charities, and on nominations for the Gardeners Royal Benevolent Institution pension and the orphan grants of the Royal Gardeners Orphan Fund.

Sir John Smith Young was appointed the first Almoner and, despite serving two years as Master from 1926, held the office continuously from 1921 until his death in 1932. After a very long break, the office was revived in 1975 with the appointment of Donald W. Silverton.

Tax Problems

In 1930, there were difficulties with the Inland Revenue arising from the Company's charitable activities. The allegation was that Section 37 of the Income Tax Act 1918, which granted relief from tax to charities, did not apply to the investment income of a non-charitable body which was not applicable by Deed of Trust or other legal instrument to charitable purposes only.

As a consequence a Trust Deed was prepared and executed on 11th February 1931, of which the Master and Wardens were trustees, setting out the securities held by the Charity Fund and the purposes for which the income therefrom should be applied by direction of the Court, namely:

(1) Relief of poverty and in particular aid to Hospitals, Gardening Charities and other Charitable Institutions;
(2) Encouragement of Children's Welfare movements;
(3) Furtherance of Gardening Guilds and Colonies and Prizes for Horticultural Exhibitions;
(4) Annual and other payments to Pensioners being Freemen, Widows or unmarried Daughters of Freemen of the Company; and
(5) General public purposes as far as they are legally charitable.

Since the last war the tax authorities seem to have been less rigid, and tax is recoverable on all sums paid out of the income of the Charity Fund for charitable purposes.

CHAPTER 11

Support for Local Horticultural Societies

It is natural that the Company should regard it as one of its duties to foster interest in local horticultural societies. It has done this over the years by the gift of cups to such societies within a radius of six miles from St. Paul's (the area of the Company's exclusive privileges as defined in its Royal Charters), coupled usually with a grant towards their prize funds, and by the attendance of the Master or his representative to open local shows or present the prizes.

The following is a list of cups minuted as given to local societies for perpetual competition before the last war, though it is probably not exhaustive:

February 1909	Highgate Horticultural Society.
June 1916 and June 1920	City of London Rose Society, on the dissolution of which in 1922 the 1920 cup was given to the National Rose Society as a prize for a class for roses grown "within a few miles" radius of the City.
November 1930 and April 1931	Ministry of Agriculture and Fisheries Horticultural Society and Southgate Chase Allotment Society.
February 1931	A challenge shield which had been presented earlier (date unrecorded) to the Shoreditch Gardens Guild was returned on the dissolution of the Guild, and presented to the Mayor of Shoreditch for competition among Shoreditch schools.
February 1931	London Allotments and Gardens Show Society.

After the war this method of encouraging local horticultural societies increased considerably. A cup was given in May 1944 to the Shoreditch Allotments Association, to be known as the Fairchild Cup, and in 1950 cups and grants were given as follows:

Central Hornsey and District Horticultural Society; South-Eastern Postal District Horticultural Society; City of London Special Constabulary Horticultural Society; Peoples Palace Horticultural Society; Central Area (L.T.R.) Horticultural Society; Victoria Park and District Allotments Association (afterwards the Bethnal Green Men's Institute Horticultural Society); Rosendale Allotments Association; L.T.R. Headquarters Horticultural Society.

With the exception of the L.T.R. Headquarters silver cup (which was provided by Past Master Sir Robert Tasker), the cups were specially designed and made for the Company by a nominee of the Goldsmiths Company. To save frequent cleaning they were made in carved black walnut with silver gilt mountings, and were striking examples of craftsmanship.

A gift of fifty pounds by Sir Robert Tasker in 1951 provided the funds to purchase a silver cup for the Shoreditch Schools Gardens Competition and small plaques for each year's winner, together with a silver cup for the London Flower Lovers' League. As the Shoreditch school gardens were all on blitzed sites which were subsequently redeveloped, their cup was diverted in 1955 to a competition for gardens on the Borough's housing estates.

These were followed in February 1951 by the gift of further cups to Associated Newspapers Horticultural Society, the Ministry of Supply Horticultural Society, the South West Ham and District Horticultural Society, the City Area (L.T.R.) Horticultural Society and the London Postal Region (Inner Area); and in May 1951 to the Camberwell Gardens Guild and the Westminster Bank Horticultural Society. Representatives of seven of these societies were invited to the Election Court Dinner in May 1951, to receive their cups.

At the same Court it was resolved to present a silver cup to the Association of London Almshouses for competition among the 106 almshouses affiliated to the Association, and this was followed in December 1952 by a second cup for a separate class among almshouses with smaller gardens.

In 1952 cups were given to the Treasury Gardening Club, the Ministry of Education Horticultural Society and the Camberwell and District Allotments Society; in 1953 to the Supreme Court Horticultural Society and the Bellingham Estate Horticultural Society; in 1954 to the North Area (L.T.R.) Horticultural Society and the Warwick Grove Estates Tenants Gardeners Association; in 1955 to the London Gardens Society for its St. Pancras Spring Show; in 1956 to the Wood Green Horticultural Society; and in 1957 to the Civil Service Horticultural Federation and the Post Office Contracts Department Sports and Social Club.

As it was found that many members of these local societies were unaware of the existence and aims of the Company, a simple form of certificate was designed for presentation to the winners of the Company's cups, and this had on the reverse a summary of the Company's history and privileges.

In many cases, instead of providing cups for local societies, the Company made small cash donations over the years to assist with the administration of shows. In 1964, however, it was decided that such small grants should be discontinued, in order to concentrate the Company's charitable activities in a way that was more effective and valuable to the recipients. Nine cups, inscribed with reference to the Company, were given to those societies to whom grants (normally three guineas) had previously been made.

In the same year the Company gave a cup to the Horticultural Society of King Edward's Building of the Post Office, and for many years since the Master and Clerk and their ladies have attended that Society's annual show.

In October 1968 Past Master Sir Edward Howard, Chairman of the Gardeners Royal Benevolent Society, secured the Court's agreement to provide certificates bearing the Company's arms for award by local horticultural associations. Under the scheme, certificates were to be issued by the Gardeners Royal Benevolent Society on request, and the cost met by means of the Company making charitable donations to the Society. The Company has continued to fund this scheme, and for many years it has been administered by the Gardeners Royal Benevolent Society on behalf of that Society and the Royal Gardeners Orphan Fund. Three quarters of the income from the scheme is allocated to the Society and one quarter to the Fund, and some idea of the useful value of this may be seen from the fact that the total income in 1991 was over £5,500.

There is no doubt that the Company's interest and support has not only been of great help to many horticultural societies, but has been much appreciated by their members. It has also given much pleasure and encouragement to successive Masters to be asked to open shows or present prizes.

In addition to those given by the Company over the years, cups were presented by Past Master Edward Dean to the St. Paul's Cathedral Horticultural Society and by Past Master J.W. Whitlock to the City of London Special Constabulary Horticultural Society.

In June 1968 a letter from the acting Vicar of All Hallows by the Tower, seeking judges for their floral displays in the church during the City Festival, resulted in Past Master Lord Gainsborough and the Wardens (F.E. Cleary and J.P. Schweder) being asked to attend and judge. Ten years later, after successive Masters had acted as judges, the Court decided to present prizes and certificates on an annual basis. Thus began an association with All Hallows that led to the appointment in 1984 of its Vicar, the Reverend Peter Delaney, as the Company's Chaplain.

Some Other Charitable Activities

In July 1948, in response to an appeal by the Joint Gardens Committee of the National Trust and the Royal Horticultural Society, the Company offered to subscribe fifty guineas annually for five years to the fund set up for the maintenance of gardens of national interest and importance. This was renewed for a further five years on expiry of the first period, the amount in this case being earmarked for the upkeep of the gardens at Sheffield Park, Sussex. Then in the same year, in response to another appeal, the Company gave three teak seats to the Trust's gardens at Stourhead Park, Wiltshire.

A new departure was made in 1952, when the Company voted twenty guineas to help establish a gardening section of the library of Queen Elizabeth's Training College for the Disabled at Leatherhead, which included gardening in its courses for the rehabilitation of spastic and other disabled trainees. This proved to be the beginning of the Company's continuing support for this valuable institution, now Queen Elizabeth's Foundation for the Disabled.

Then in 1956 a member of the Court entered into a seven year covenant with the Company to pay the annual sum of three hundred pounds, in order to found "The Worshipful Company of Gardeners Fund". This was to be used for the upkeep of the gardens of the North London Collegiate School for Girls, "so as to inculcate in the scholars attending the school a love of gardens, flowers and beautiful things as part of their education". The gift was in memory of his only child, who had died at the age of fifteen while a pupil at the school.

Wye College

After the visit of the Wardens to Wye College in 1950, the Court agreed to give an annual prize of five guineas. By October 1955, however, the financial position of the Charitable Fund had improved to such an extent that the Company was able to give a scholarship to Wye College of one hundred pounds per annum for a trial period of three years. On the advice of the Principal that scholarships for first degrees only resulted in the saving by the scholar's local authority of the whole or part of its mandatory award, and that the real need was for help to scholars to pursue their studies after the first degree, it was decided that the Company's scholarship should be postgraduate and the terms were approved by the Court in February 1956.

The scholarship was to be tenable at Wye and given on the recommendation of the Principal, advised by the College Academic Board, to a suitably qualified graduate not receiving full grant aid from other sources, to carry out research and investigative work in the general field of horticulture or closely related fields. The holder would be expected either to register for a higher degree or submit a thesis on the work carried out during tenure of the scholarship.

In July 1958, because of the difficulty of finding suitable applicants – no award had been made in the previous year – the Court agreed that the grant should accumulate for a further year and that the College would add two grants of £150 (£50 for the first year and £250 for the second year). It would thus be possible to offer two annual payments of £350 each, towards which the Company would have contributed £400 at the rate of £300 for the first year (including two years' accumulations) and £100 for the second year.

In October 1960 further proposals were advanced by the Principal and approved by the Court. These were for a grant by the Company of a revolving fund of one hundred pounds annually for a trial period of five years, to enable undergraduates or post-graduate students, junior research workers and junior teaching staff to make visits to university departments of horticulture and research institutes overseas. The conditions of the awards, to be made by the Principal advised by the Academic Board of the College, were purposely left very wide; it was not intended, however, that awards should be made merely for attendance at conferences, but to bring the College and young British horticulturalists and scientists into closer contact with developments in the work of institutions overseas, and particularly in western Europe.

In 1964, an annual grant of two hundred pounds for three years was made by the Company to assist in the establishment at Wye College of a research unit in the field of horticultural marketing.

The London Gardens Society

For many years the Company has made an annual donation toward the work of the London Gardens Society, which was originally set up to encourage the growing of flowers in order to provide a "healthy and civilizing influence" on the many Londoners who otherwise had scant opportunities for self-expression. In the pre-war years many parts of London, in contrast to the rapidly developing suburbia, were areas hardly conducive to gardening, and the Society aimed to encourage "the humblest citizen" to improve his surroundings and thus do a civic duty.

In those days of smoke and smog, it can not have been easy for the Society to inspire enthusiasm in the poorest areas of London. Yet, with

Queen Mary as Patron, the Society held competitions for the best-kept gardens and awarded prizes, and it is almost unbelievable today that in 1938 there were 65,000 entries, with 1,611 finalists in the All London Garden Championships. Queen Mary herself undertook an annual tour of inspection of many of the gardens.

Reference has already been made to the close collaboration between the Gardeners Company and the London Gardens Society in joint activities to beautify the City in more recent decades. Indeed this connection has been typified by the long service given to the Society by Company members – with Past Masters Sir Edward Howard and D.A. Huggons serving for many years as Chairman and Treasurer respectively. Office-holders as Treasurer have included Past Master F.J.B. Gardner, and the Society's Secretaries have included Liverymen Mrs. H.G.P. Crosse and Mrs. Vicky Gooding.

Queen Elizabeth the Queen Mother succeeded Queen Mary as Patron of the Society, and for over thirty years has toured gardens in London at the Society's invitation. On these occasions, the Company always makes a point of inviting respective Masters to accompany Her Majesty.

The London Children's Flower Society

Another longstanding institution supported by the Company is the London Children's Flower Society, formerly the London Flower Lovers' League.

The League was founded shortly after the Second World War as an offshoot of the London Gardens Society, when Mrs. Alice Street drew attention to the lack of opportunities for many London children to engage in any form of gardening. Like so many brilliant ideas, it began with a simple suggestion – to organise a competition, open to all school children in London, for pot-grown daffodils to be judged by volunteers from the public parks and horticultural societies. It was proposed that the bulbs should be given to the children free of charge, together with instructions for growing them, and that the winners should receive medallions and certificates as evidence of their achievements. The schools were to be recognised also, by awarding them points based upon the success of their pupils and prizes for the best school efforts.

Thus the London Flower Lovers' League was born, and was chaired from her own home by Alice Street with Helen Nussey as organiser. Following Alice Street's death in 1966 accommodation had to be provided for the administration of the scheme, and it also required the services of more volunteers, as the original idea had developed into something far more extensive. Not only were as many as 100,000 daffodil bulbs required each autumn by several hundred schools, but a summer competition had been introduced under which the children were provided with the seeds of easily-grown annuals – at first restricted to nasturtiums and candy tufts, then supplemented with alyssum and godetia.

Later the scheme was further expanded by the introduction of a competition for school gardens, which also encouraged the cultivation of waste land by schools and the growing of plants in tubs and other containers.

In 1975 the League became the London Children's Flower Society, and since that time there has been sustained enthusiasm on the part of the schools, the part-time staff of the Society, and the volunteers who assist in its work. Such enthusiasm has doubtless been encouraged by the warm attention of Her Majesty Queen Elizabeth the Queen Mother, Patron of the Society, who annually visits one of the school gardens and who has given her name to the Cup which is the Society's highest award.

In 1990 the abolition of the Inner London Education Authority, which had been one of the Society's major sources of finance, caused great concern and made it necessary for alternative sources of funding to be found. While the services of a large number of judges are given free of charge, the administration of the Society's work and the supply of bulbs and seeds requires the sponsorship of commercial and charitable organisations, together with London local authorities. Happily the Worshipful Company of Gardeners has been able to play its part in securing the continued existence of the Society, as it has done for many years, with its annual financial contribution.

The Company has also been very much involved in the Society's management. Currently, Past Master R.L.Payton is a Trustee, and Past Master David Longman is the Society's Honorary Treasurer. In 1993, Past Master David Longman presented to the Society the Longman Cup for the School Rose Competition. At the time of writing, the Company is heavily represented on the Council of the Society, which includes Past Masters R.C. Balfour, G.H. Denney, D.E. Dowlen and W.P. Maclagan, Liveryman Mrs. P.M. Gould and the Company's Clerk, Col. N.G.S. Gray.

Non-Recurring Grants

There have also been many worthwhile examples of specific, non-recurring grants given by the Company for special projects. In this respect, 1977 was a particularly significant year. It saw, firstly, the Company's agreement to pay the expenses of the Disabled Living Foundation in publishing the book *The Garden and the Handicapped Child* by Patricia Elliott (Disabled Living Foundation, 1978). The book was launched at a press conference on 13th June 1978 by the Master (John Brunel Cohen) at the Institute of Child Health.

Again in 1977, the Company provided a greenhouse in the roof garden of the Salvation Army hostel known as Rawson Home in Whitechapel. The idea for this, and for some other subsequent donations for the benefit of senior citizens in and around the City, came largely from Iris Chandler, wife of City Architect and Liveryman George Chandler and herself an active member of the Corporation's Social Services Committee.

On 5th May 1977 the Master (C.R. Crosse), the Wardens and the Clerk, at the invitation of the President and Council of the Royal Horticultural Society, were present in Wisley Gardens at the opening of a garden for the disabled by Lady Hamilton, Chairman of the Disabled Living Foundation. The Company had donated two Batricar wheelchairs for the use of disabled visitors to Wisley, and in his opening address Lord Aberconway (President of the Society and an Honorary Freeman of the Company) expressed warm gratitude. A third wheelchair was donated a few years later.

In more recent years the Company has made donations toward the creation of gardens for various charities, such as the new nursing home for Bristol Age Care, the Children's Hospice at Milton near Cambridge, and Mildmay Hospital.

In other Chapters there has been mention of other charitable activities of the Company, such as The Festival Garden at St. Paul's, various window box and garden competitions and the Royal Horticultural Scholarship, and it might be wondered how all these activities have been financed. For many years it was the custom to transfer to the new Charitable Fund Capital Account a part of the fines paid by new members on election to the Freedom and Livery, but even so the investment income of the Fund in 1960 was only £225. Increasingly the money has come from the annual subscriptions of members, many of whom pay under deed of covenant which enables the Company to recover tax. The total available income from all sources for the year 1960-61 was approximately one thousand pounds, and it was this which enabled the Court to commit itself to the scheme for the award of travel grants at Wye College.

It is not surprising that there have been changes in the charitable activities of the Company since the 1960s. First and foremost, the increased generosity of members has produced far larger sums for the support of worthy causes. In 1986-87, to take one year at random as an example, the income of the Charitable Fund was almost £12,000 – of which the tax reclaimed on covenants produced over £6,000, donations £1,000, gross investment income over £4,000, and the Poor Box (circulated at the conclusion of every Court Meeting) produced £82.

The following list shows recipients of grants in 1987-88. It is not exhaustive, but gives a flavour of the range of causes supported by the Company. This was a particularly interesting (though sad) year, as some of the grants arose from the enormous damage to trees and gardens inflicted by the storms of October 1987. The item relating to the Ironbridge Gorge Museum represented the first instalment of a grant totalling £6,000 towards the redevelopment of their garden at Rosehill, the Company having been associated with the Museum since 1984 by providing trees, shrubs and furniture for its formal gardens.

> Cassette Library for Blind Gardeners
> Chelsea Physic Garden – storm damage
> City Parks Department – storm damage
> Flowers for St. Paul's
> Flowers in the City Campaign
> Gardeners Royal Benevolent Society
> Ironbridge Gorge Museum Development Trust
> London Children's Flower Society
> London Gardens Society
> Lord Mayor's Appeal
> Metropolitan Public Gardens Association
> National Trust – storm damage
> Queen Elizabeth's Foundation for the Disabled
> Royal Gardeners Orphan Fund
> Royal Horticultural Society prizes
> Salvation Army (Rawson Home)
> Vauxhall Centre

A further list for 1990-91, again not exhaustive, shows the Company's continuing support for various projects and organisations as well as its willingness to respond to specific appeals:

> "Come Gardening" (Blind Gardeners)
> Flowers for St. Paul's
> Flowers in the City Campaign

Gardeners Royal Benevolent Society – annual grant
Gardeners Royal Benevolent Society – specific project
Gardening for the Disabled
Horticultural Therapy Society
Lewis W. Hammerson Memorial House for the Elderly
London Children's Flower Society
London Gardens Society
Lord Mayor's Appeal
Metropolitan Public Gardens Association
Queen Elizabeth's Foundation for the Disabled
Royal Gardeners Orphan Fund
Royal Horticultural Society prizes
Royal National Rose Society – specific project
Tower Hamlets Garden Project

CHAPTER 12

The Common Hall

It is the aspiration of every Livery Company to have its own Hall, although for many years this has been an unlikely accomplishment in view of the costs of site, construction and maintenance. Indeed it is ironical that the financial circumstances of many Companies were much improved by the fact that their Halls were "blitzed" in the Second World War, but only the more wealthy were able to rebuild.

The first mention in the minutes of any plans by the Company for a Hall or the use of a Hall was in October 1911, when Charles Bayer (Immediate Past Master) made a gift of one hundred pounds toward that object. The matter was referred to a Committee, which reported that no further steps should be taken until the Court had met and dined in several Halls. This included Bakers Hall, which in the event was adopted in 1913 as the meeting place or "Common Hall" of the Company at an annual rent of forty-five pounds. The agreement provided for five (but not exceeding seven) Court Meetings per annum, with lunches or dinners before or after the meetings, and storage space provided for papers, records and plate.

In April 1913 a Common Hall Fund was set up (to which the investment representing Bayer's gift was subsequently transferred), and the Master (G.R. Blades) paid to the Fund £903 which he had collected from members and former members of the Court. The setting up of the Fund was commemorated by a brass tablet erected in Bakers Hall in 1919 with the inscription

The Worshipful Company of Gardeners of London

During the Mastership of Mr. (afterwards Sir) George
Rowland Blades 1912-1913 was first established a
Common Hall Fund the income from which enables the
Company to hold its meetings in this Hall

followed by a list of forty-one members who had contributed.

The Company continued to meet at Bakers Hall until it was destroyed by bombing. Fortunately the Company's plate had been evacuated for safety, but all its pictures perished on the night of 28th-29th December 1940, when the City of London was devastated by the worst air-raid of the war – a strange coincidence this, as it was precisely the fiftieth anniversary of the Special Meeting held to revive the Company on 29th December 1890. It was feared that the memorial tablet had also been destroyed, but many years later it was found among the ruins, damaged but still legible, and restored to the Company in the 1950s.

Various attempts have been made by the minor Companies to have a joint Common Hall. The Loriners, Weavers and Clockmakers Companies went into the question in April 1921, but nothing resulted from their deliberations. The matter was raised again in April 1932 and the Upper Warden attended at Guildhall to discuss a scheme, particulars of which had been circulated, but it met with no success.

It was clear after the Second World War that the problem of Companies without Halls had become more acute. William Kent, in *The Lost Treasures of London* (Phoenix House, 1947), records that of thirty-four Halls at the outbreak of war, sixteen were completely destroyed and only three – the Apothecaries, Ironmongers and Vintners – were undamaged.

In July 1943 the question of a meeting place for the Company after the war was discussed by the Court, and a Committee was appointed to consider the question of acquiring a Hall for the Company in conjunction with no more than five other Livery Companies. The minutes do not record the result, but the project doubtless foundered on the rocks of finance.

Shortly after this, in November 1944, the Company was asked to support a petition of the Basketmakers Company to the City Corporation. This referred to the rebuilding of Guildhall, and asked for provision to be made of a room for the Court meetings of Companies without Halls. Many years later the Common Council went further and provided not only the Livery Suite, consisting of a Court Room with a small dining-room and ante-room, but also the Livery Hall which is now used for the functions of various Companies as well as for Corporation purposes.

In 1949 the developer of the site of the former Salters Hall, destroyed in the Blitz, had offered to provide on generous terms a Hall in the building that became St. Swithin's House, Walbrook. The offer was carefully considered by a meeting of representatives of the minor Companies, held under the aegis of the Fellowship of Clerks of Livery Companies, and a committee was appointed to go into the scheme in detail; but in this case also the committee had to recommend against the scheme, on the grounds of expense and the difficulty of managing a Hall common to a large number of Companies.

CHAPTER 12

In 1952 there was even a proposal that it might be possible for the Company to buy an old ship in co-operation with the Fruiterers Company and convert it into a floating Livery Hall, as had been done by the Master Mariners with H.Q.S. Wellington, but this also came to nothing.

For some years immediately after the war the Company held its Court Dinners at Tallow Chandlers Hall, which had only suffered relatively minor war damage, but the numbers attending soon outgrew the accommodation. A move was therefore made to the Apothecaries Hall, but the number of dining members continued to rise and that also became too small.

In the 1960s, arrangements were made with the Carpenters Company for the occasional use of their new Hall in Throgmorton Avenue, and for the storage there of the Company's plate and some of its records. It was to the old Carpenters Hall that the Company had moved after Bakers Hall had been blitzed in 1940, but after only a few weeks Carpenters Hall had suffered the same fate.

In recent decades, the Company's functions such as Court Dinners have been held in various Halls – ranging from the old (such as Fishmongers) to the more recently reconstructed (such as Plaisterers).

CHAPTER 13

Hospitality

At an early stage in the Company's revival, the need was felt for an Entertainment Fund to provide for Court Dinners, and in December 1892 an annual contribution of five guineas by members of the Court was fixed.

In 1893 a Ladies' Dinner was given at the Whitehall Rooms in the Mastership of the Revd. William Wilks, in 1894 the Lord Mayor and Lady Mayoress were present at the Ladies' Banquet in the Grafton Galleries, and in 1895 the Company met the ladies at a *conversazione* in the Grafton Galleries. In 1897 the Installation Banquet was held in Vintners Hall, where the Rt. Hon. R.J. Seddon, Premier of New Zealand, was one of the guests. Then in 1898 the Company and their ladies were entertained at a garden party at Ascot Place by the Master, Sir William Farmer.

Philip Crowley, Master in 1899 and 1900, was Treasurer of the Royal Horticultural Society from 1890 to 1900. In July 1899 he gave a garden party at Croydon to meet the President and Council of that Society, together with the foreign delegates to the Conference on Hybrids. He also gave a Ladies' Dinner at the Prince's Restaurant in June 1900 to meet the Lord Mayor and the Sheriffs, the Rt. Hon. C.T. Ritchie M.P., Sir William MacCormac and others, but sadly Crowley died in December 1900 during the second year of his Mastership.

G.W. Burrows, the Master, gave a garden party in July 1903 at Orpington to meet Sheriff Sir Thomas Brooke-Hitching, the Masters of thirty-one Livery Companies and their ladies.

In 1903 a committee was appointed to consider the finances of the Entertainment Fund and provide for its future management, and in accordance with the recommendations of the committee it was decided to hold an annual Livery Dinner free of cost to Liverymen and that at all future entertainments any subscriber to the fund should be entitled to invite guests on payment for them.

The Company is believed to be one of the first to institute a system of dining membership whereby Liverymen could attend Court Dinners on payment of an annual subscription, the purpose and effect of which was to bring the members of the Livery into closer touch with the Court. In April 1920 the Court decided that this plan should start on 1st April 1921 and the annual "voluntary" subscription, which was then £7 17s. 6d. and compulsory in the case of members of the Court, was fixed at five guineas for members of the Livery. In February 1921 the first twenty-one Liverymen were elected as dining members, and in April 1924 the privilege of inviting guests to Court Dinners was extended to dining members on the same basis as members of the Court.

The worthwhile practice of inviting Liverymen to attend the three Court Dinners each year has continued to this day, but the escalating costs of functions at Livery Halls necessitated a revision of the arrangements for dining membership. The full cost is now charged to all attending, and the "subscription" has been abolished.

In 1905, the 300th anniversary of the Company was celebrated at the Albion Tavern in Aldersgate Street, with the Master (George Corble) in the chair. In May 1906, Corble gave a Ladies' Dinner at the Whitehall Rooms. Then in 1907, the Master and Mrs. W.T. Crosweller celebrated their Silver Wedding by giving a Ladies' Dinner at Grocers Hall.

Turning to the question of special hospitality for guests from outside the Company, however, it is worth recording a few examples to demonstrate the great variety of this area of the Company's activities.

The year 1911 was a busy one in the Company's history. It included not only all the arrangements for the Queen's Coronation bouquet, the visit to Holland, the petition for an increase in the Livery and the counter-petition of the Fruiterers Company, the proposal for restoring the Fairchild Lecture and the Company's participation in the International Horticultural Exhibition, all of which are mentioned elsewhere, but also the arrangements for a unique Banquet. This was given by the Company to the Ministers of Agriculture of all the twenty-two Colonial Governments who were visiting this country for the meeting of the Royal Agricultural Society at Norwich, and to meet the Colonial Secretary and the President of the Board of Agriculture and their chief officers. It was minuted that Sir Thomas Elliott, Secretary to the Board of Agriculture, had emphasised to the Clerk that "a visit to one of the old London Guilds would probably prove to be one of the most pleasant recollections of the Government's guests". The dinner was held on 3rd July 1911 at Goldsmiths Hall.

Sundry items of interesting hospitality to and by the Company not mentioned elsewhere, and picked up in perusing the minutes, are: 29th December 1913 – The Master (S.G.Shead) entertained the apprentices and candidates for the Freedom by Patrimony to tea and an entertainment at Bakers Hall.

26th February 1914 – The Duke and Duchess of Teck accepted invitations to attend the Ladies' Dinner at Grocers Hall, but unfortunately the Duchess was unable to be present.

24th February 1916 – The Lord Mayor (Sir Charles Cheers Wakefield, Renter Warden of the Company) entertained the Court to dinner at Mansion House.

21st July 1919 – The Company (in conjunction with the Bakers Company) entertained at Bakers Hall eighty petty officers and men selected from the crews of destroyers and submarines of the Royal Navy, and the Master and Wardens visited the Grand Fleet at Southend on the following day as guests of the Corporation of London.

30th September 1919 – The Lord Mayor (Sir Horace Brooks Marshall, Past Master of the Company) entertained the Courts of the Stationers, Spectacle Makers and Gardeners Companies with their ladies to luncheon at Mansion House.

In the inter-war years, and sometimes earlier, it was the practice for the Lord Mayor and the Lady Mayoress and the Sheriffs and their ladies to be invited to the annual Ladies Banquet. Later, the Lord Mayor and Sheriffs attended the annual Livery Dinner, as was the case with most Livery Companies. This was, however, an all-male function, and more recent years have seen a further agreeable change – the annual opportunity to entertain the full civic party has become known as "The Livery and Ladies Banquet", being a combination of the two previous functions. This change had become well established, even before the admission of ladies to the Livery.

In April 1942 it was proposed to give a Court lunch to the Air Chief Marshal, Sir Philip Joubert, and Officers of Coastal Command of the R.A.F., but this was abandoned at the request of the Minister of Food on account of wartime food rationing.

In October 1948 there was held in London an International Conference on Control of the Colorado Beetle, and the Company welcomed the principal delegates at a Court Dinner at Tallow Chandlers Hall to which ladies were invited. Then in September 1952 a large number of distinguished delegates to the International Horticultural Congress was entertained to a Court Dinner, again at Tallow Chandlers Hall, with some of them coming from as far afield as Asia and Australia. The guests also included six members of the Council of the Royal Horticultural Society.

CHAPTER 13

September 1958 saw a similar dinner for delegates to the International Rose Conference in London. Earlier in the day, Lord Nathan (Past Master) had lectured to the Conference on "The Histories of some ancient London Companies, in particular that of the Worshipful Company of Gardeners".

It would be repetitious to record the many other occasions in more recent years, on which the Company has readily taken the opportunity to provide hospitality to distinguished guests from throughout virtually every field of endeavour. It is unfortunate that, except for the post-war period, there is no complete list of those entertained by the Company. Even from existing records, however, it can be seen that such hospitality has been spread very widely indeed. Guests have included Ambassadors and High Commissioners, church leaders, numerous representatives of the arts and sciences, sports personalities, members of the Houses of Parliament, senior civil servants, judges, members of the armed forces, representatives of City institutions, businessmen and industrialists – and of course a virtual "Who's Who" of horticulture and agriculture.

In recent decades, the conviviality of the Company's occasions has been much enhanced by two worthwhile practices. Firstly, it has been usual for the Clerk to detail members of the Court to look after the guests of the Company during the reception period. That this practice is appreciated is clear from remarks made by many guests, who have thanked the Clerk for ensuring that they feel welcome.

The second practice dates from February 1967, when the Master (Maj.Gen. K.C. Appleyard) told the Court that throughout his term as Warden and Master he had experienced difficulties in caring for his personal guests. He asked the Court to consider appointing three Stewards, to be known respectively as the Master's Steward, the Upper Warden's Steward and the Renter Warden's Steward. They would be distinguished by wands of office, differently coloured for purposes of identification and surmounted by the Company's crest. This was agreed, as was the proposal that the appointment of the Stewards should be in the hands of the Master and Wardens and should be for one year only.

From that time onwards the three Stewards have been included as Officers of the Company, and have made a considerable contribution to Company ceremonial. More particularly, they have added greatly to the enjoyment of the guests of the Master and Wardens. In addition, the Court has accepted that service as a Steward should generally be regarded as a pre-condition of election to membership of the Court.

Finally, it is appropriate to draw attention to two curiosities – in the most agreeable sense of the word.

An item on the menu at many dinners, Gardeners' Pride, often attracts the puzzled attention of guests. This originates from 1936, when Devon farmer A.N. Pitts was Master and complained that the vegetables served at dinners were not fresh and were badly cooked. At the next dinner, therefore, he brought up from Devon a large variety of vegetables and watched them being cooked under his supervision. They were attractively served on silver salvers, and the dish became known as Gardeners' Pride.

The second curiosity arose in 1978. Liveryman Eric Ruddlesden, who had for many years played the piano at Company Dinners for the procession in, the Grace, the Loyal Toasts and the withdrawal of the Master's party, composed the Gardeners' March for the entry of the Master's Procession. A copy was included in the Minute Book dated 22nd February 1978.

CHAPTER 14

Thomas Fairchild and the Fairchild Lecture

On 28th February 1911 the Clerk, E.A. Ebblewhite, presented to the Court a report setting out the facts regarding the will of Thomas Fairchild, which had founded a trust for an annual lecture. He recommended that he be instructed to get in touch with the Bishop of London and the Vicar of Shoreditch, "with the object of reviving an interest in the Lecture and associating this Company with the annual service at which it is delivered".

Thomas Fairchild, Citizen and Gardener and Clothworker of London, was the son of John Fairchild of Alwine or Allane in Wiltshire, and was born in 1667 in Cripplegate, London. On 6th June 1682 he was apprenticed to Jeremiah Seamer or Seamere, Citizen and Clothworker, for seven years, and on coming of age would have been entitled to the Freedom of the Clothworkers Company by Servitude. Instead he devoted his whole time to gardening and eventually, on 13th June 1704, took up the Freedom of the Gardeners Company by Redemption.

Blanche Henrey, in *British Botanical and Horticultural Literature before 1800* (3 vols, Oxford University Press, 1975), stated that Fairchild "possessed a great love of scientific research, and he is the first person known to have raised a hybrid scientifically . . . *Dianthus caryophyllus x barbatus*." In fact Fairchild's experiments in hybridisation, in particular with the carnation and sweet william, were revolutionary. The earliest cultivation of many species is attributed to him, including the flowering dogwood (*Cornus florida*) and red buckeye (*Aesculus pavia*).

Often called "the Father of British Horticulture", Fairchild started work in Hoxton in 1690 and became one of the biggest European market gardeners, introducing many new plants and owning a horticultural collection believed to be the largest in the country. Among his many skills, he was a noted pomologist and a celebrated cultivator of the vine, and was also much involved in planting squares and other public open spaces. His fine collection of North American exotic plants owed much to the botanist Mark Catesby (1683-1749), who worked at Hoxton and was one of the witnesses of Fairchild's will, and who sent to Fairchild plants and seeds from Virginia and the Carolinas.

Fairchild's business occupied land at Hoxton formerly known as "Selby's Gardens", extending from the west end of Ivy Street to the New

North Road, to the north of the present-day Old Street underground station. Hoxton was at that time a popular location for nurseries, and Fairchild worked with others to raise and distribute the tulip tree in large quantities for the first time, some years after its introduction from Virginia by John Tradescant the Younger. Fairchild and his Hoxton colleagues also brought into cultivation other North American plants, such as the catalpa.

The year 1722 saw the publication of Fairchild's *The City Gardener*, described in its subtitle as "Containing the most experienced method of cultivating and ordering such ever-greens, fruit-trees, flowering shrubs, flowers, exotick plants, &c. as will be ornamental, and thrive best in the London gardens". It was the first book to refer to the specific problems of town gardens, such as smoke pollution, but it also sought to provide the experienced advice of one who had experimented successfully with numerous plants in an urban environment.

Fairchild wrote: "I have upwards of thirty Years been placed near London, on a Spot of Ground, where I have raised several thousand Plants, both from foreign Countries, and of the English Growth; and in that Time, and from the Observations I have made in the London Practice of Gardening, I find that every thing will not prosper in London; either because the Smoke of the Sea-Coal does hurt to some Plants, or else because those People, who have little Gardens in London, do not know how to manage their Plants when they have got them."

Even to the present-day reader, Fairchild's little book provides seventy pages of sheer delight, and his coverage may be seen from his chapter headings with his original quaint capitalisation: "Of Squares, and large open Places in London and Westminster: The Plants proper to adorn them . . . Of making and adorning Squares; and how to dispose the several Plants in them . . . Of the Part of London next the River Thames; how far we may promise ourselves Success in Gardening there . . . Of Court-Yards, and close Places in the City . . . Ornaments and Decorations for Balconies, and the Outsides of Windows in large Streets."

Within his discourse, Fairchild made certain comments with which the Worshipful Company of Gardeners, at various stages of its history, would surely have agreed: "Most of those People who sell the Trees and Plants in Stocks and other Markets, are Fruiterers, who understand no more of Gardening than a Gardener does the making up the Compound Medicines of an Apothecary. They often tell us the Plants will prosper, when there is no Reason or Hopes of their growing at all; for I and others have seen Plants that were to be sold in the Markets, that were as uncertain of Growth as a Piece of Noah's Ark would be, had we it here to plant; but when such Plants are bought at the Gardens where they were raised, there can be no Deceit, without the Gardener who sold them loses his Character."

Indeed Fairchild continued by referring specifically to the Company, stating that "this Mischief is no new Thing among us, as we find plainly in the Preamble to the Charter granted by King James the First, for establishing a Corporation and Company of London Gardeners, which then had a good Effect; but afterwards being somewhat neglected, King Charles, by Proclamation, order'd the said Charter to be put in Force in order to suppress those Dealers in Plants, which imposed upon his Subjects, by selling them unwarrantable Goods."

Fairchild's garden at Hoxton was the scene of many experiments, and in 1724 he wrote *An account of some new experiments, relating to the different, and sometimes contrary motion of the sap in plants and trees,* which he read to the Royal Society, and which was published in the *Philosophical Transactions* (volume 33, no.384).

Richard Bradley, a prolific writer in the fields of natural history and gardening who in 1724 became the first Professor of Botany at Cambridge, was particularly impressed with Fairchild's work on the growth of plants, the movements of sap and fertilisation. He also regarded Fairchild as one of the most skilful gardeners of his wide acquaintance, and there is evidence in Bradley's correspondence that it was he who persuaded Fairchild to share his experience by writing *The City Gardener.* When Bradley travelled abroad, Fairchild was one of the people to whom he sent plants – for instance, on his visit to Holland in 1714 his despatches included aloes.

In his *Philosophical account of the works of nature* (1721) Bradley referred to "that curious garden of Mr. Thomas Fairchild at Hoxton, where I find the greatest collection of fruits that I have yet seen, and so regularly disposed, both for order in time of ripening and good pruning of the several kinds, that I do not know any person in Europe to excel him in that particular." For two other works by Bradley, see Appendix F (1724).

It is important to appreciate also that Fairchild was far from solitary in his pursuits, as he was a leading member of the Society of Gardeners – a group consisting largely of nurserymen, all from London and the suburbs, including at least two neighbours (Benjamin Whitmill and Stephen Bacon) in Hoxton. Every month, for at least five years, the Society met at Newhall's

Coffee-house in Chelsea or some other convenient place, and discussed the plants which each member had brought along from his own growing.

Clearly it was desirable to disseminate to a wider audience the names and descriptions of plants so scrupulously registered by the Society of Gardeners, for reasons of commercial enterprise as well as in the interests of scholarship, and the members further decided to commission drawings and paintings of their catalogued plants by Jacob van Huysun. This resulted in the publication, in 1730, of their *Catalogus Plantarum. A catalogue of Trees, Shrubs, &c: for sale in the Gardens near London, by a Society of Gardeners*, of which the following gardeners were the joint authors:

Thomas Fairchild (Hoxton), Robert Furber (Kensington), John Alston (Chelsea), Obadiah Lowe (Battersea), Philip Miller (Curator of the Chelsea Physic Garden from 1722), John Thompson (Chelsea), Christopher Gray (Fulham), Francis Hunt (Putney), Samuel Driver (Lambeth), Moses James (Lambeth), George Singleton (Chelsea), Thomas Bickerstaff, William Hood (Hyde Park Corner), Richard Cole (Battersea), William Welstead, Benjamin Whitmill (Hoxton), Samuel Hunt (Putney), John James, Stephen Bacon (Hoxton – Fairchild's nephew and executor, to whom he bequeathed his estate, but who did not long survive him), and William Spencer.

Sadly only the first volume of the proposed catalogue, on trees and shrubs, was published. Fairchild's name heads the list at the end of the preface, and the British Museum copy is catalogued under his name, so it is tempting to assume that his death in the previous year was the principal reason for the demise of both the publishing project and the Society of Gardeners itself. Philip Miller, however, was secretary or "clerk" of the Society of Gardeners and there is some evidence that he was much involved in the preparation of the *Catalogus*.

Fairchild died on 10th October 1729, and at his own request was buried in the furthest corner of the churchyard of the Parish of St. Leonard in Shoreditch, where the poor were usually buried – some two hundred yards from the church, and later forming the public recreation ground on the west side of Hackney Road. His tomb was restored in 1846 and 1891, and again by the Gardeners Company in 1949.

At some time before 1722 Fairchild was elected to the Livery of the Company, and in that year he claimed to vote as a Liveryman at the City elections in Common Hall. His claim was rejected, however, owing to the refusal of the Court of Aldermen to recognise the Company's Livery granted by its first Royal Charter of James I.

By his will dated 21st February 1728(?9), which was duly proved on 23rd October 1729, he bequeathed to the Trustees of the Charity Children of Hoxton and their successors, and the Churchwardens of the Parish of St. Leonard in Shoreditch and their successors, the sum of twenty-five pounds to be invested. This was to provide one pound annually for ever, for the preaching of a sermon in that church in the afternoon of the Tuesday in every Whitsun week. In case of default, the legacy was to be forfeited to the Churchwardens of St. Giles Cripplegate for a similar purpose.

The first Fairchild Lecture was given at St. Leonard's on 19th May 1730 by the Revd. John Denne, Archdeacon of Rochester and Vicar of St. Leonard's. It was printed, and a copy is in the Company's library.

Some sixteen years after Fairchild's death the legacy was augmented by public subscription, and South Sea Annuities to the nominal value of one hundred pounds were bought. On 11th June 1742 the Trust and the right to appoint the lecturer were transferred to the Royal Society, which regularly appointed the lecturer until 1873. The Trust was then transferred to the Churchwardens of St. Leonards again.

At the time of Ebblewhite's report in 1911 the lecture was still regularly being held, the appointment of the lecturer being made by the Bishop of London. Not surprisingly, given the facts recounted above concerning the major contribution Fairchild had made to the history of gardening in London, the Court took a considerable interest in the matter.

A letter from Ebblewhite to all members of the Company on 29th May 1911 stated that: "The Master and Wardens, being desirous of reviving our ancient connection with the lecture, have made arrangements for the attendance of the Company in state to hear the lecture delivered by the Lord Bishop of Stepney, on Tuesday, the 6th June proximo . . ."

In 1913 it appears that the Charity Commissioners were considering altering the date of the lecture, the Tuesday in Whit week being considered inconvenient, and in June the Commissioners made an order leaving the fixing of the date to the discretion of the Trustees.

The church of St. Leonard in Shoreditch was badly damaged in the Second World War, and for a time the service had to be held elsewhere, but after later restoration work the long connection between the Company and the church was resumed. This connection was also commemorated in a stained-glass east window, by a figure of the Master in his robes of office amongst the crowd in the lower part of the window.

For many years, before the lecture, a wreath was laid on Fairchild's grave. A procession was formed by the Master, Wardens and members of the Court, all gowned and preceded by the Beadle, the Master being preceded by the Company's ceremonial spade. The Honorary Chaplain said a prayer at the tomb, and the Master laid the wreath. The first mention of this ceremony in the minutes was in 1921, on which occasion the wreath was handed by the Master to the Mayor of Shoreditch who placed it on the tomb.

The inscription on the tomb reads:
"Sacred to the memory of Mr. Thomas Fairchild of Hoxton, (Gardener), who departed this life the 10th day of October 1729 in the 63rd year of his age. Mr. Fairchild was a benefactor to the Parochial Schools and Founder of a Lecture annually preached in Shoreditch Church on Whit Tuesday on the subject of 'the Wonderful Works of God in the Creation' or on 'the Certainty of the Resurrection of the Dead proved by certain changes in the animal and vegetable parts of the Creation'. The stone originally placed over his remains having gone to decay the present memorial was erected in the year 1846 being 117 years after his decease in admiration of his benevolence. John Bewley, Jeremiah Long, Churchwardens. This stone was restored August 1891. Thomas Martindill, Alfred Molloy, Churchwardens."

The association between the Company and St. Leonards continued for many years after the Second World War. Indeed in February 1967 the Master, Maj.Gen. K.C. Appleyard, reported to the Court that the Company had donated to St. Leonards a new Bible to replace that which had been in use for over seventy years, and that it had been his privilege to read the lesson from it when it was used for the first time. Soon after, however, a series of difficulties arose.

In February 1968 the Honorary Chaplain (Bishop R.W. Stannard) informed the Court that, through the good offices of the Master (Lord Gainsborough, a prominent Roman Catholic), the Fairchild Lecture would be given by Bishop Butler, Auxiliary Bishop of Westminster and former Abbot of Downside. Sadly the incumbent of St. Leonards was not prepared to permit a non-Anglican to participate in any religious ceremony at his church, which included the traditional reading of the lesson by the Master. This was in spite of the fact that Appleyard, who had read from the new Bible the previous year, was himself a Roman Catholic!

Arrangements had accordingly been made, through the good offices of Past Master Sir Edward Howard, to hold the lecture in 1968 at St. Michaels Cornhill, where the Master duly read the lesson and Bishop Butler gave the lecture. The Court agreed that it be left to the Master, Wardens, Chaplain and Clerk for the time being to make the necessary arrangements for future years, possibly at St. Giles Cripplegate. In fact, the service was held there from 1969 to 1975 inclusive and from 1981 onwards.

All of this resulted in a far looser connection between the Company and St. Leonards – and indeed with the London Borough of Hackney, into which the Borough of Shoreditch had been absorbed in 1964. It had been the custom to hold the Election Court in Shoreditch Town Hall early in the afternoon, followed by the wreath-laying ceremony, but this did not occur in 1968 nor in any subsequent year until 1976. Then in 1976 the Master, David Longman, arranged for the service once again to be held at St. Leonards, with the preceding Court Meeting taking place in the new church hall. This practice continued until 1980.

A list of the Fairchild Lecturers from 1911, the year in which Ebblewhite provoked the Company's direct involvement, appears as Appendix D.

The wreath-laying ceremony gradually fell into abeyance – partly because of the apathy of the councillors of Hackney, whose Mayor was traditionally invited to participate, and to attend the service and subsequent reception. Hackney Council at that time was vociferously opposed to the City of London and its customs, and the Company's ceremony failed to provide a much-needed bridge with the Borough. There was the additional difficulty that traffic congestion was beginning to make a dignified procession virtually impossible, and also the fact that passers-by tended to ridicule the proceedings. In 1968 the Clerk personally laid the wreath, and in 1969 the Master, Wardens, Honorary Chaplain and Assistant Clerk attended the tomb for this purpose. Thereafter the ceremony ceased, at least in respect of the full procession that had been such a feature of the earlier years.

There was a possibility in the late 1970s that a somewhat happier link would be forged, but sadly it came to nought. Discussions took place with a view to the Company accepting responsibility for the landscaping of an area of garden surrounding St. Leonards as a memorial to Thomas Fairchild. Officers of the London Borough of Hackney went so far as to prepare plans and organise site meetings with the Company, but early in 1981 the Chief Executive of the Borough informed the Clerk that the project was to be abandoned.

CHAPTER 15

The Company's Collection

The Company's valuable collection of plate and other items is listed in Appendix E, and the following details of some of the items demonstrate not only their interesting history but a record of generosity toward the Company.

Items 30 and 37: The Master's Badge and Chain
The Court on 20th May 1891 decided to provide a badge of office for the Master, and on 16th December 1891 a design by George Edwards was approved at a cost of seventy-five pounds. The Master's chain of office was presented in April 1902 by the then Master, C.E. Osman. It bore his own coat of arms and those of Past Masters, with blank links for those of subsequent Masters which were added at Osman's expense. In 1907 it was altered by the substitution of the Company's crest for that of the donor as the central link, the arms of five Past Masters which were not registered at Heralds College were replaced with small shields with monogrammed initials, and the arms of several others were corrected.

By 1924 the chain was in need of repair, and could not accommodate the shields or initials of all successive Masters since 1891. Messrs. Spencer and Company were therefore asked to reconstruct it, and to form a smaller chain or chaplet of the rose links connecting the shield links which could not be incorporated in the new design. The cost of this remodelling was thirty pounds. The smaller chain (Item 43) was originally intended to be used by the wife of the Master for the time being, or other lady acting as hostess, whenever ladies were present at the Company's entertainments.

Further alterations were required in 1950 to accommodate the shields of later Masters, and in the course of years the chain has become an elaborate decoration for the Master on ceremonial occasions.

The badges of office of the two Wardens and the Clerk (Items 33-35) were presented at a Court meeting on 6th July 1897 by Assistant W.T. Crosweller, as a memento of the Diamond Jubilee of Queen Victoria. In 1903 the Company's industrious Clerk, E.A. Ebblewhite, reported to the Court that the badges of the Master, Wardens and Clerk differed from the Arms tricked (i.e. sketched) in the second Charter of James I, and it was agreed to have this put right.

It has long been the custom to present a Past Master's badge to each Master at the end of his year of office. In 1905, Past Master Sir Marcus

[188]

Samuel raised the question of the Past Masters' badges, which he felt were unworthy of the Company, and offered to bear the expense of sketches and dies for a new badge. This he did, the design by Allan Wyon F.S.A. being approved, and all Past Masters were asked to wear badges of the new type.

At the same time it was proposed to change the ribbons of all the Company's badges to a green and white check pattern in half-inch squares, and a supply of the new ribbon was presented by Renter Warden W.T. Crosweller. The new ribbon did not meet with unanimous approval, however, and in 1911 it was decided to change it again, with Sir Marcus Samuel offering to defray the cost.

The Court seems in 1905 to have been in iconoclastic mood, as attention was drawn to the fact that there were various inaccuracies in the Common Seal, notepaper and dies, and these were amended, the new Seal being the gift of W.T. Crosweller, then Upper Warden. After he had been installed as Master in 1906, he presented the old Seal and a wax impression of it in a case, bearing an inscription signifying that this was the Seal in use from 1900 to 1906. Unfortunately these seem to be no longer in existence. Sir Marcus Samuel similarly presented the dies for the new Past Masters' badges, in an oak box recording the gift.

Assistants' badges of the present design were instituted in February 1912, and at the same time the "Coronation emblem" for the officers and members of the Coronation Committee was approved as mentioned in Chapter 8.

Item 1: James I Silver Seal Top Spoon
The letter from Liveryman John Lewis accompanying this gift, which was made by him as a mark of appreciation of his election to the Livery, gives the following description of it. "The seal-headed spoon has a pear shaped bowl with the touch or standard-mark of a crowned lion's face affronte and a baluster shaped stile or shaft stamped on the back with the alphabetical mark K for the year 1607; the assay or quality mark of a lion passant guardant, and the marks of a pair of extended compasses, points downwards. The seal, which is pounced with the stippled initials LS WN, is supported by a beaded circle and a Knob incised with four heraldic roses slipped and leaved."

Item 6: Charles II Silver Tankard (1670)
This was a gift by Maj. Samuel Weil on Armistice Day 1920, to commemorate his year as Master. It was made in 1670 by "I.L.", a London silversmith at the time when Richard Staples was Master of the Company. It weighs 31 oz. 10 dwt., and is marked on the bottom with the letters T.S. The arms of

the Company and of the donor were later engraved on the tankard, together with an inscription round the edge of the lid: "Let us so act that the dead may not have died in vain nor the living striven in vain. Haig of Bemersyde Armistice Day 1920".

Item 7: Persian Silver Casket (1752)
This casket, weighing 18 oz. 10 dwt., has an interesting history. It is in the form of a gourd embossed with fruit and flowers, and is inscribed "In the sweat of thy browes shalt thou eate thy bread" and "The gift of Sir Crisp Gascoyne 1752". It appears that in the time of the Commonwealth, Thomas Abraham, a Freeman of the Company, gave financial help to his friend John Gascoyne, Parish Clerk of Chiswick from 1649 to 1682. When the latter's great-grandson, Sir Crisp Gascoyne, Lord Mayor of London, gave the casket to the Company in 1752, he was probably remembering with gratitude the help given by one of its members to his ancestor.

It is assumed that the casket must have gone out of the Company's possession when most of its property was dispersed after 1815. There is no record of how it was found by Sir John Smith Young, who gave it to the Company as a memento of his period of office as Master, adding to it a further inscription: "Recovered by the Gardeners Company, repaired, and given by Colonel Sir John Smith Young C.V.O. Master 1927."

Item 8: Pierced Cake Basket (1759)
In presenting this piece to the Company in 1932, the Master (John Weir) provided particulars of its history. A former owner, Joseph Phillimore (1775-1855), the grandfather of Lord Justice Phillimore, had caused the crest he used to be engraved at the bottom of the basket – On a wreath of the colours or and sable and alighting thereon a falcon with wings all proper.

Item 17: Silver mounted Ostrich-egg Cup with Cover (1809)
This cup is referred to in a report of the Clerk, set out in the minutes of the Court at which it was presented by Assistant Cecil Cronk in June 1924.

"In 1809," wrote Ebblewhite, "we had almost ceased to hold meetings, and that was the year of the incorporation of the Royal Horticultural Society which probably took away a number of our members. The funds had been depleted and quite shortly afterwards . . . the small cash balance disappeared as had all our other property with the exception of the Charters and the then current Minute Book which until about 1880 had been handed down to us. . . . That is the extent of the property we hold which existed prior to 1815. There must have been some plate and other things, but I have never been able to trace the property.

"Yesterday at an auction sale I discovered a very fine George III silver mounted ostrich egg cup of 1809 with a cover crowned with a fine representation of our crest. It has been purchased by Mr. Cecil Cronk, a member of our Court ... and I am sure you will be delighted to hear of the presentation and restoration of this link with our past history."

Item 24: Mull, mounted in silver and with cairn gorm (1826)
This bears an inscription "Presented by the Caledonian Gardeners to Mr. John Young, Gardener, for the best six tulips 1826", and was bought from a dealer in Brussels by Hugh McConnach Reid, who presented it in 1924 after attending one of the Company's dinners as the guest of Col. Sir John Smith Young, then Renter Warden.

Items 26 and 41: Silver Candelabrum Centrepiece (1851) and silver gilt Octagonal Cup and Cover (1911)
These were bequeathed to the Company by Sir Harry Veitch. The cup, made by Carrington & Co. at a cost of eighty-three pounds, was given to the Royal International Horticultural Exhibition at Chelsea in 1912 by its President the Duke of Portland, and had been won by Sir Harry's firm, James Veitch & Son, for the best exhibit in the show. The candelabrum was presented to him and his wife on their silver wedding in 1892 by their gardening friends. It stands about two feet nine inches in height, and was in the form of a growing and fructed vine with three double branches fitted with sconces and a hollow basket at the top for fruit. Later it was adapted as a fruit stand, cut-glass dishes being added to the sconces, and a basket of 1847 silver inserted into the hollow and fitted with a cut glass dish. Both gifts were subsequently inscribed "Bequeathed to the Worshipful Company of Gardeners of London by the Will of Sir Harry James Veitch", as a record of the testator's generosity.

Item 29: Mace Head on Ebony Staff
The original Beadle's staff was lost in Brussels on the visit to Belgium in 1913, and compensation of £3 18s. 8d. was received from the management of the Palace Hotel! It was replaced by a new ebony and silver staff, at a cost not exceeding eight guineas.

Item 54: Bronze Medal of the Confrerie of St. Michael of Ghent
This medal, presented on the 1931 Belgian visit, was struck from the original dies of the Confrerie of 1637.

Item 59: Silver Ceremonial Spade
E.A. Ebblewhite, in presenting this at a Court Meeting on 27th July 1943, congratulated the Master on six hundred years of the Company as a Guild.

"In the old days," said Ebblewhite, "the Livery Companies in all processions, whether public, ecclesiastical, civic or domestic, had each a prominent emblem carried before the Master to indicate the trade or craft which his Company represented, and this was also figured in the Armorial Bearings. For example, the Ironmongers exhibited a gad of steel and a swivel, the Framework Knitters a model of a stocking frame, the Tin Plate Workers a butcher's lamp, and the Gardeners a spade."

Ebblewhite said that for nearly fifty years he had tried to find a suitable spade, and had at last succeeded in finding a fine specimen in silver and carved wood made by craftsmen of his university city of Sheffield in 1901. This was evidently designed for a Royal Personage to perform the ceremony of planting a tree or cutting the first sod in the dedication of a public park or recreation ground, but from the absence of any inscription he judged that it was never so used and remained part of the craftsman's stock. He suggested that following the precedent of the Cinque Ports and certain other seaports (where silver oars are carried before their mayors) the spade be borne by a junior member of the Court on all suitable occasions. This has ever since been faithfully carried out.

It was not until 1979 that a case and rest for the spade was acquired, to be used on ceremonial occasions. This was made, at the instigation of D.A. Huggons, by the Craft Training School of the Worshipful Company of Carpenters, and presented by him to mark his year as Master (Item 138).

In May 1914 F.G. Ivey (Master in 1904-05) presented to the Company a Sheffield plate soup tureen and two wine coolers, which had been given to him on his sixtieth birthday in 1905 by a number of friends through the Company. He had intended, having no son, to leave them by will "to our dear old Guild". Nevertheless, in a rather sad letter he wrote, "Life is short and I am far from well, so it has occurred to me that the Company might like to have them at once in order that many of my friends may derive some little benefit and pleasure out of what I have always admired. It is nice to share one's pleasures with those with whom one is in complete sympathy." Alas, he only survived the gift for four months. Most unfortunately the gifts were lost after the outbreak of war in 1939, when the Company's plate was moved from place to place for safety, and the gift no longer appears in the Company's inventory. This gift was accompanied by eight pictures and an old Boer masonic snuff box, which perished in the Blitz on Bakers Hall in December 1940.

Item 72: Golden Book and Casket
This book, beautifully executed by Sangorski and Sutcliffe in green leather

embossed on the front with the Company's coat of arms in gold, was the gift in 1948 of John Weir, Master in 1932-33.

An inscription in the book reads: "This Golden Book replaces a former one donated by John Weir at the end of his Mastership in 1933 & which was destroyed by enemy action on the 10th of May, 1941. It contained among others, the signatures and painted Coats of Arms of their Majesties King George V and Queen Mary, The Prince of Wales, The Princess Royal, The Duke & Duchess of York, The Duke & Duchess of Kent, The Princess Helena Victoria, Prince Leopold and Princess Astrid of Belgium."

The inscription further refers to the fact that the idea of the "Livre d'Or" was taken from the old Belgian custom followed by the Trade Guilds of Ghent, Bruges, Brussels and Antwerp. Such a book was signed by representatives of the Company on the visit to those ancient cities in 1931 mentioned in Chapter 10, and on the subsequent visit to the Floralies Gantoises in 1933.

The Company's new book was signed in 1948-49 by King George VI and Queen Elizabeth (now the Queen Mother), Queen Mary, the Duke of Windsor, Princess Marina Duchess of Kent and the Princess Royal. The signatures are on separate pages at the beginning of the book, and above each is the coat of arms of the signatory beautifully emblazoned in full colour by the leading heraldic artists of the City.

The original letter of thanks from the present Queen for her wedding bouquet was inserted in the book in 1948, and the Queen signed the book itself in 1958 on the occasion of the personal presentation at Buckingham Palace of the annual gift of flowers to commemorate the Coronation. The Duke and Duchess of Gloucester added their signatures in October 1952, when they attended the Ladies Banquet held at Fishmongers Hall.

Queen Juliana signed in 1950, when she was elected to the Honorary Freedom and received a deputation at Soestdijk Palace, and King Baudouin signed in Ghent in 1960, when a delegation from the Company was presented after he had opened the Floralies Gantoises – as did Queen Fabiola in 1970, on a similar occasion.

The book contains separate sections for the signatures of distinguished men and women who have been entertained by the Company – Lord Mayors; Ambassadors; Diplomatic Representatives other than Ambassadors; Members of the Government in office; Members of the Armed Forces of the Crown; Members of the House of Lords; Members of the House of

Commons; Judges; Representatives of the Church of England; Representatives of the Arts and Science; and Distinguished Horticulturalists.

The Court regards the Golden Book as a priceless possession. At the first Court Meeting after it was presented to the Company, it was resolved that it "should be reserved for the signatures of those persons who have rendered outstanding service to the nation or who are recognised as distinctive national or international characters, and that the Court should decide from time to time who should be asked to sign the book".

At a subsequent Court Meeting it was decided that "only those persons who were the guests of the Company, or were closely connected with it, should be asked to sign, and that the use of the book should not be retrospective, save that former living Lord Mayors should be asked to sign". The practice has grown up of requiring a unanimous vote before anyone is asked to sign the book, and this has sometimes led to amusing discussion before the vote is taken. At one time some members felt that High Court Judges did not qualify!

The gift of the Golden Book led C.E. Page Taylor to mark his year as Master by presenting to the Company a casket in which it could be placed on ceremonial occasions. He was fortunate in being able to obtain a piece of the ancient oak hammer-beam roof of Guildhall, which had been hit by bombs in one of the heaviest air-raids on London, and out of this a skilled craftsman was able to make a casket of outstanding merit, worthy of the book it was to hold. It is of semi-polished oak and on the front are carved the arms of the Company set in a square, round the four sides of which are carved the words "The Worshipful Company of Gardeners Golden Book". The interior is of light green velvet, and inside the lid is a small silver plate with the inscription: "This Casket, made of oak from Guildhall, London (severely damaged by enemy action 29th December 1940), was presented by C.E. Page Taylor Esq. D.L., J.P. to commemorate his year of office as Master of the Company 1949-50".

Having mentioned the Golden Book and its casket, and having earlier dealt with the badges of office, this presents a convenient point at which to draw attention to another historic ceremonial feature.

The Company has at various times been presented with banners to be carried in processions – in 1895, bearing the Company's Arms, from Maj. George Lambert, then Master; in 1896 by N.N. Sherwood, then Master, with his arms; in 1902 by G.W. Burrows, then Upper Warden, with his arms; and in 1905 by Sir Thomas Dewar, then Renter Warden Elect, with his arms. The passage of time has unfortunately left these banners in a somewhat tattered condition, although the Lambert banner was used to decorate the car carrying the Master, Wardens and Clerk in Seymour Howard's procession as Lord Mayor in 1954.

Item 102: Five replicas in silver of Charles I Wine Cups
Since the early 1930s the Master, Wardens and members of the Court of Assistants have been privileged to drink their wine at Company Dinners from silver cups (Items 48 and 49). The growth in size of the Court over the years gave rise to the generous gift of five additional cups in 1964, by Past Masters G.J. Gollin and Edward Howard.

Item 113: Two cut glass Decanters
These, together with twenty-four sherry glasses engraved with the Company's Arms (Item 114), were intended for serving sherry to members of the Court at the conclusion of business. They were presented in 1969 by Past Master L.H. Kemp.

Item 123: Silver Cigarette Box engraved with scenes of London
Following the presentation to the Corporation of London of the stained glass window referred to in Chapter 4, the Lord Mayor (Alderman Sir Edward Howard) presented to the Company this cigarette box with an inscription inside the lid: "The gift of Alderman Sir Edward Howard Bt., G.B.E., D.Sc., Master 1961-62, to mark the many courtesies received from his Mother Company during his Mayoralty. The scene on the lid was specially drawn for the front cover of the menu of his Banquet on Lord Mayor's Day. Edward Howard, Lord Mayor 1971-72."

Item 142: Tradescant Glass Goblet
The first Tradescant Luncheon held on 18th December 1981, in the presence of Princess Alice, Duchess of Gloucester, is referred to in Chapter 9. On that occasion Past Master G.J. Gollin presented to the Company a cut-glass beaker or goblet, engraved by Miss Josephine Harris with the Arms of the Company and of John Tradescant, the latter taken from a newel post on the main stairway at Hatfield House. A rose bowl, engraved by the same artist, was presented by the Company to The Garden Club of Virginia when a party visited that State in the following year.

Item 145: Necklace and Brooch for the Master's Lady
This gift comprises the central portion of the Company's Arms in enamel set in gold, designed to be hung on either the necklace or brooch, and to be suitable for formal or informal occasions.

CHAPTER 16

The Company's Library

One of the earliest acts following the Company's revival was to vote, on 6th April 1891, the sum of five guineas and an annual sum of three guineas for the purchase of books relating to gardening. The intention was to form the nucleus of a Company library within the Corporation of London's Guildhall Library, and in December 1892 Liveryman A.G. Williams presented five more books.

Early in his Clerkship, E.A. Ebblewhite sought to put the position regarding the library on a proper footing – as he did in so many other areas of the Company's work! He was supplied by the Guildhall Librarian with a list of books in hand, and the Court decided that while it did not "at present intend to withdraw any part of the collection of books it feels that the Gardeners Company's property in such collection should be recognised as heretofore". There followed some correspondence with the Town Clerk, and ultimately the Court decided in March 1905 that, without prejudice to the Company's contention, it was willing to present the books then in the library to the Corporation of London.

In 1913 the design of an engraved heraldic bookplate for the Company's library was approved, and this is still in use.

In June 1918 R.P. Hughes, a friend of the Clerk, gave a collection of engravings of flowers with culture notes (1794) believed to have been printed from the plates used for *The Compleat Florist* (1749). These were bound and deposited in the library.

The question of the ownership of the library was raised again in 1921, and discussion took place with the Chairman of the Library Committee of the Corporation. This resulted in April 1922 in a formal agreement between the Corporation and the Company which acknowledged the ownership of the Company, but provided that the collection should be under the control of the Library Committee and placed in such a position as might be approved by the Committee, which was to take reasonable care to preserve it but without liability for loss. At that time there were some 150 books and eighteen pamphlets.

In November 1923 the Master (Victor Brown) opened a fund for the purchase of books, and by February 1924 this had reached £142 and in addition twenty books had been donated by members.

CHAPTER 16

March 1926 saw an exhibition of the most interesting and valuable books from the Company's library, at the Ladies Banquet at Carpenters Hall.

A list of books of antiquarian interest forms Appendix F. Many of these came from the collection of a Mr. Cranfield, which was purchased from his executors in 1948 for the sum of £362 10s, mainly through the good offices of Past Master F.J.B. Gardner. The purchase was reported to the Court on 15th October 1948, but the minute is tantalisingly uninformative for anyone who is interested to know something of the man who collected what was to become a significant proportion of the Company's library.

Recent research in non-Company sources now reveals that he was William Bathgate Cranfield of the City auctioneers Foster and Cranfield, a long established firm with premises at No. 6 Poultry from 1885 and (since 1988) at 20 Britton Street in Clerkenwell. Cranfield lived at East Lodge in Enfield Chase, and held shares in (and died at) the White Hart in Windsor. His will of 27th August 1945 makes no specific mention of the books, but this would not be surprising if they were to be sold rather than bequeathed. Nevertheless the date of his death, 29th May 1948, corresponds perfectly with the fact that a few months later a deal was struck between the Company and the executors of "a Mr. Cranfield". It is also of note that William Bathgate Cranfield's business was situated at the very heart of the City, and it is therefore not too fanciful to suggest that the existence of his book collection was known to acquaintances in the Gardeners Company. Furthermore Cranfield was active in the British Pteridological Society, which presumably accounts for the fact that the Company's library is particularly rich in nineteenth century works relating to ferns.

A copy of Thomas Fairchild's *The City Gardener* (1722) was the gift of Past Master W.T. Crosweller, and that of J. Reid's *The Scots Gard'ner* (1683) was the gift of the Master (John Weir) to commemorate the conferment of the Honorary Freedom of the Company upon Princess Mary (the Princess Royal) in 1933. Maj. K.E. Schweder presented Ellen Willmott's *Genus Rosa* (1914) in 1952, to commemorate his year of office as Master. These are but a few examples, for the collection has benefitted greatly over the years from the generosity of members of the Company.

For many years it was the practice for the Company to purchase, as well as antiquarian volumes, a selection of modern popular works on horticulture. The Public Libraries and Museums Act of 1964 resulted in the rapid development of lending libraries in the City of London, however, and this in turn led to the reasonable assumption that many newly-published books in the field would be acquired by the Corporation for its own libraries. Accordingly the Company decided, on 27th March 1968, to concentrate its resources upon strengthening the existing collection of antiquarian works, together with other notable books on horticulture which the Corporation might consider too expensive or specialised for its general collections.

In 1970 a printed catalogue of the Company's library was produced. Extending to twenty-eight pages, this gave ample testimony to the excellent coverage of the library in its field.

The stock has continued to be enhanced in accordance with the policy of 1968, with each acquisition being subject to the recommendation of the Guildhall Librarian. It has been customary from the outset for the Guildhall Librarian to serve also as the Company's Honorary Librarian, and a list of appointees appears in Appendix B.

Additions to the collection in recent years – whether by purchase from Company funds, by donation or by transfer from general library stock – have maintained its standards as an impressive library of horticultural history and practice which remains invaluable to researchers.

The stock now totals some 600 volumes and fifty pamphlets, all of which are available for consultation at Guildhall Library by any member of the public free of charge.

APPENDIX A

MASTERS OF THE COMPANY

(Pre-1890 records are incomplete)

1605	Thomas Young	1772	Abraham Dalton
1606	Thomas Young	1773	Abraham Dalton
1607	John Markham	1774	Henry Manley
1616	William Wood	1775	Henry Manley
1622	John Grene	1776	Richard Wortley
1623	James Burley	1777	Richard Wortley
1624	James Burley	1778	William Redhead
1632	John Hinch	1779	William Redhead
1633	John Hinch	1780	John England
1634	John Hinch	1781	John England
1635	John Hinch	1782	Charles Hunt
1636	John Hinch	1783	Charles Hunt
1637	John Hinch	1784	Moses Marshall
1638	George Bayly	1785	Moses Marshall
1641	Samuel Hurley	1786	Thomas Heath
1650	Samuel Hurley	1787	Thomas Heath
1666	John Goodspeed	1788	Richard Hughes
1667	John Goodspeed	1789	Richard Hughes
1669	Edward Curtis	1790	John Bowes
1670	Richard Staples	1791	John Bowes
1686	Humphrey Goodspeed	1792	Thomas Good
1688	Robert Chandler	1793	Thomas Good
1690	John Hurles	1794	Benjamin Kennett
1691	Thomas Cooke	1795	Benjamin Kennett
1692	Hugh Berry	1796	Benjamin Kennett
1693	John Cadman	1797	William Burnes
1694	John Cadman	1798	William Burnes
1695	Joseph Arthur	1799	Thomas Shearley Bagley
1696	Joseph Arthur	1800	Thomas Shearley Bagley
1699	Francis Ballard	1801	George Stubbs
1764	Aaron James	1802	George Stubbs
1765	Aaron James	1803	James Field
1766	Joseph Knight	1804	James Field
1767	Joseph Knight	1805	Robert Bagley
1768	John Shelmerdine	1806	Robert Bagley
1769	John Shelmerdine	1807	Robert Bagley
1770	Richard Edwards	1816	Robert Bagley
1771	Richard Edwards	1817	Robert Bagley

Year	Name	Year	Name
1818	George Ives	1922	George Herbert Thompson
1819	John Gaywood	1923	Victor Brown, J.P.
1820	Warwick Bagley	1924	James Henry Solomon
1821	Thomas Nash	1925	William Thomas Roberts
1833	Thomas Nash	1926	Col. Sir John Smith Young, C.V.O.
1834	William Bagley		
1891	Rt. Hon. Sir Joseph Savory, Bt. (Lord Mayor)	1927	Col. Sir John Smith Young, C.V.O.
1892	Sir Trevor Lawrence, Bt., K.C.V.O.	1928	George Ernest Wendover Beeson
1893	Revd. William Wilks, M.A.	1929	John Edward Newman Sherwood, J.P.
1894	Beaumont Shepheard, J.P.		
1895	Maj. George Lambert, V.D., F.S.A.	1930	John Slocombe Pearse
		1931	Edward Dean
1896	Nathaniel Newman Sherwood	1932	John Weir
		1933	Alexander Henry Dence
1897	Nathaniel Newman Sherwood	1934	Sir George Thomas Broadbridge
1898	Sir William Farmer		
1899	Philip Crowley, F.L.S.	1935	Albert Edward Cressall
1900	Philip Crowley, F.L.S. (died)	1936	Arthur Northcott Pitts
1901	Constant Edward Osman	1937	Lt.Col. Stanley Samuel Gilbert Cohen
1902	Rt. Hon. Sir Marcus Samuel, Bt. (Lord Mayor)	1938	Ernest Thornton Thornton-Smith
1903	George William Burrows		
1904	Frederick George Ivey	1939	S.H. Baker (died) Sir Robert Inigo Tasker, D.L., J.P., M.P.
1905	George Corble		
1906	William Thomas Crosweller	1940	Frederick John Baucher Gardner, M.C., F.C.A.
1907	Sir Thomas Robert Dewar, J.P.		
		1941	Frederick John Baucher Gardner, M.C., F.C.A.
1908	Robert Inigo Tasker, J.P.		
1909	Charles Bayer	1942	Marcel Porn
1910	Charles Bayer	1943	Frederick Charles Thomas Lane, F.C.A.
1911	Sir Horace Brooks Marshall, LL.D.		
		1944	Robert Emmanuel Hirch
1912	George Rowland Blades, J.P.	1945	Col. Sir John Dalton
1913	Samuel George Shead	1946	Walter Frederick Bishop, C.B.E.
1914	Samuel George Shead		
1915	Benjamin Hansford, C.B.	1947	Harold Walter Seymour Howard, J.P.
1916	Joseph Francis, J.P.		
1917	Joseph Francis, O.B.E., J.P.	1948	Leonard Arthur Reddall, F.C.A.
1918	Sir Charles Cheers Wakefield, Bt.	1949	Clement Edward Page Taylor, O.B.E., D.L., J.P.
1919	Maj. Samuel Weil	1950	John Wilson Whitlock, J.P., M.A., LL.B.
1920	Francis Agar		
1921	Donald Carmichael Haldeman, J.P.	1951	Maj. Kenneth Ernest Schweder

APPENDIX A

1952	Richard Bertram Ling	1973	Norman Alexander Royce, F.R.I.B.A., P.P.C.I.Arb.
1953	Frederick Alan Balkwill Luke	1974	Arthur Joseph Carton
1954	Maj. Sir Brunel Cohen, K.B.E.	1975	David Martin Hulbert Longman
1955	Rt. Hon. Harry Louis, Baron Nathan, P.C., T.D., F.B.A.	1976	Clive Raymond Crosse
1956	Donald Byford	1977	John Brunel Cohen, O.B.E.
1957	Martin Hulbert Longman	1978	Denis Arthur Huggons, F.C.A.
1958	Geoffrey Joseph Gollin, M.A.	1979	Charles Ellis Talbot, M.A.
1959	Francis Henry Lymbery	1980	Leonard Jack Reddall, F.C.A.
1960	Isidore Kerman	1981	Roger Louis Payton, LL.B.
1961	Hamilton Edward de Coucey Howard	1982	John Godfrey Keeling, O.B.E.
1962	John Ellis Talbot, M.P.	1983	Rear Admiral Maurice James Ross, C.B., D.S.C.
1963	Rt. Hon. Roger Carol Michael, 2nd. Baron Nathan	1984	Peter Duncan Marriner
1964	Maurice James Thurston	1985	William Patrick Maclagan
1965	Arthur James Dale Robinson	1986	Alan Bruce Hurrell
1966	Maj.Gen. Kenelm Charles Appleyard, C.B.E., D.L., J.P.	1987	His Hon. Gilbert Frank Leslie
1967	Rt. Hon. Anthony Gerard Edward Noel, Earl of Gainsborough	1988	Edwin George Chandler, C.B.E.
		1989	Gordon Herbert Denney
1968	Leslie Haggar Kemp, F.R.I.B.A.	1990	David Howarth Seymour Howard, M.A.
1969	Frederick Ernest Cleary, M.B.E., F.R.I.C.S.	1991	Richard Creighton Balfour, M.B.E.
1970	John Paul Schweder	1992	David Edward Dowlen
1971	John Louis Stevenson, F.C.A., A.C.I.S.	1993	Ernest Michael Upward
1972	Rt. Revd. Bishop Robert William Stannard, M.A.		

APPENDIX B

CLERKS, BEADLES, HONORARY CHAPLAINS AND HONORARY LIBRARIANS

CLERKS

1691	William Herbert (No record of when elected and retired or died).
1764-1795	George Stubbs (the Elder) Died in office 1795.
1795-1815	George Stubbs (the Younger) Elected Master 1801 and 1802. Died in office 1815.
1816-1832	Francis Bligh Hookey Resigned 1832.
1833-1853	John Finch (No record of whether retired or died).
1853-1872	Charles Shepheard Resigned 1872.
1872-1890	Beaumont Shepheard, son of the above Resigned 1890. Elected Master 1894. Resigned from the Court 1923. Died June 1930.
1890-1894	James Curtis, F.S.A. Elected Clerk and Solicitor 29th December 1890. Resigned with effect from 31st January 1894. Elected Honorary Assistant 10th January 1894, and resigned 1928.
1894-1902	Robert Gofton-Salmond Elected Clerk 26th February 1894 and resigned his seat on the Court. Died September 1902.
1903-1937	Ernest Arthur Ebblewhite, J.P., LL.D., F.S.A. Elected Clerk 2nd January 1903. Resigned 1937.
1937-1946	Stephen William Price, M.C., D.L. Appointed Deputy Clerk 1925. Elected Clerk 1937. Resigned with effect from 31st December 1946. Honorary Freedom conferred 4th March 1947.

APPENDIX B

1947-1958	Arnold Francis Steele, M.B.E., C.C. Elected Clerk with effect from 1st January 1947. Resigned with effect from 30th June 1958. Honorary Freedom conferred, and elected an Honorary Liveryman, 23rd November 1956.
1958-1969	Frank Nathaniel Steiner, M.A., C.C. Elected Clerk with effect from 1st July 1958. Resigned with effect from 30th June 1969. Honorary Freedom conferred, and elected an Honorary Liveryman, 5th February 1969.
1969-1973	John Grierson Fleming, M.A., LL.B. Elected Clerk with effect from 1st July 1969. Resigned with effect from 1st April 1973.
1973-1984	Frank Nathaniel Steiner, M.A., C.C. Re-elected Clerk with effect from 2nd April 1973. Resigned with effect from 30th June 1984.
1984-1985	Peter de Villiers Rudolph Appointed Assistant Clerk 19th October 1983. Elected Clerk with effect from 1st July 1984. Died 25th August 1985.
1985-1990	Alistair Laird McGeachy, W.S., LL.B. Elected Clerk 13th November 1985. Resigned with effect from 12th December 1990. Admitted Freeman 4th December 1990 and elected Liveryman 13th December 1990.
1990-	Colonel Nicholas George Steel Gray Appointed Assistant Clerk 20th February 1989. Elected Clerk with effect from 13th December 1990.

BEADLES

1605	John Bixon (appointed by the first Royal Charter).
1616	Peter West (appointed by the second Royal Charter).
1763-1764	John Taylor (died 1764).
1764-1772	Charles Wainhouse (died 1772).
1772-	William Tarrant (no record of period of office).
1834-	James Gorsuch (no record of period of office).
1891-1903	Thomas Lovell (retired 1903; died 1909).

1903-1945   Arthur Henry Boone (retired 1945).

1945-1967   Arthur Blanchard Booth (retired 1967).

1967-1976   Frank Hewett (retired 1976).

1976-1981   Frank Carter (retired 1981).

1981-1984   Roy Brooks (resigned 1984).

1984-   Frederick Walter Witch, B.E.M.

HONORARY CHAPLAINS

1890-1903   The Ven. Frederick William Farrar, D.D., M.A.
             (Archdeacon of Westminster, later Dean of
             Canterbury, died 22nd March 1903).

1903-1928   Revd. Hubert Curtis, M.A.
             (Canon of Rochester, resigned 28th May 1928).

1929-1930   Revd. Arthur Stanley Vaughan Blunt, O.B.E., M.A.
             (Vicar of St. John's, Southwick Crescent, died February 1930).

1930-1942   Revd. Tom Wellard, B.A., B.D.
             (Rector of St. Olave, Hart Street, Prebendary 1931,
             died 14th November 1942).

1943-1951   Revd. Frederick Wilson Baggallay, M.A.
             (Rector of St. Swithun, London Stone with St. Mary
             Bothaw, his death was reported to the Court on 16th May 1951).

1951-1971   Rt. Revd. Robert William Stannard, M.A.
             (Bishop Suffragan of Woolwich, subsequently Dean of Rochester,
             resigned on 2nd June 1971 on election as Upper Warden).

1971-1984   Revd. Alfred Basil Carver, T.D., M.A.
             (Vicar of Holy Trinity, Sloane Street, S.W.1.).

1984-   Revd. Canon Peter Delaney, F.S.C., A.K.C.
             (Vicar of All Hallows by the Tower).

APPENDIX B

HONORARY LIBRARIANS

(As the Company's Library is situated in the Corporation of London's Guildhall Library, it has been customary for the Guildhall Librarian to act as Honorary Librarian to the Company)

1892-1904   Charles Welch, F.S.A.
(Elected to the Freedom and Livery of the Company and the Court, 29th December 1890; resigned from the Court on appointment as Hon. Librarian, 28th November 1892; elected an Honorary Assistant, 17th March 1903; resigned both offices, 11th January 1904).

1904-1910   (No record of an appointment as Honorary Librarian to the Company. Welch resigned as Guildhall Librarian in 1906, and Edward Borrajo served as Guildhall Librarian from 1907 until his death in 1909).

1910-1926   Bernard Kettle
(Elected to the Freedom of the Company without fine on his retirement, 14th April 1926).

1926-1943   James Lungley Douthwaite
(Retired as Guildhall Librarian, 25th March 1943).

1943-1956   Raymond Smith, F.L.A., F.S.A.
(Elected to the Freedom of the Company without fine on his retirement, 11th July 1956).

1956-1966   Arthur Herbert Hall, F.L.A.
(Honorary Freedom conferred on his retirement, 6th July 1966).

1966-1983   William Godfrey Thompson, M.A., F.L.A., F.S.A., F.R.S.A.
(Retired as Guildhall Librarian, 31st August 1983).

1984-   Melvyn Peter Keith Barnes, O.B.E., D.M.A., A.L.A., F.B.I.M., F.R.S.A.

APPENDIX C

THE COMPANY'S SCHOLARS

1894-95	William Norman Sands
1895-96	George Frederick Tinley*
1897-98	Henry Stewart Langford*
1898-99	Miss Olive Mary Harrison*
1899-1900	Charles John Gleed*
1900-01	Bertram Smith*
1901-02	Charles Houghton Buck
1902-03	Lawrence Laver Goffin*
1903-04	William Robertson Brown
1906-07	George Sidney Damsell
1908-09	Bertram Paul Perry
1909	J.W. McCaig
1911-12	Isaac George Briggs
1913-14	John Selkirk
1914-16	William Moyse and George Fox Wilson*
1921	Alexander Ernest Sims
1928	Stanley George Smith
1930	Edward Kelvin Lawrence*
1935-36	John Meiklejohn Saunders Potter*
1938-40	J. Bultitude
1948-50	F.H. Allen
1951-54	D.W. Way
1955-58	John E. Bryan
1958-60	M.L. Dixon
1960-62	R.H. Dungay
1962-65	C.D. Sayers

*The Scholars so marked were given the Freedom of the Company by Presentation without fine

Note also that there is in the Company's library *A Report of the travels of Mr. C.D. Sayers undertaken during the period September 1962 to September 1965*. This bound typescript, with photographs, is the record of work carried out under the Scholarship in Ceylon, Nepal, Australia and New Guinea.

APPENDIX D
FAIRCHILD LECTURERS

1911	Rt. Revd. H.L. Paget, Bishop of Stepney
1912	Ven. E.E. Holmes, Archdeacon of London
1913	Revd. Prebendary E.A.B. Sanders, Vicar of Edmonton
1914	Very Revd. H.M. Hackett, Vicar of St. Peter's, Belsize Park
1915	Revd. E.H. Pearce, Canon of Westminster
1916	Revd. Canon J.H.B. Masterman, Rector of St. Mary le Bow
1917	Revd. W.H. Thompson, Vicar of St.Stephen, Ealing, and Gresham Lecturer
1918	Revd. C.L. Drawbridge, Licensed Preacher, Diocese of London and Diocese of Southwark
1919	Ven. E.E. Holmes, Archdeacon of London
1920	Revd. Joseph Jacob, Rector of Whitewell, Shropshire
1921	Very Revd. W.R. Inge, Dean of St. Paul's
1922	Revd. H.R. Meyer, Rector of Watton, Hertfordshire, and Rural Dean of Welwyn
1923	Revd. E.W. Barnes, Canon of Westminster
1924	Revd. W.R. Matthews, Dean of Kings College London
1925	Revd. H.M. Relton, Professor of Dogmatic Theology, Kings College London, and Vicar of Isleworth
1926	Revd. Claude Jenkins, Professor of Ecclesiastical History, Kings College London
1927	Revd. Richard Hanson, Lecturer in Dogmatic Theology, Kings College London, and Vicar of St. Botolph Without Aldersgate
1928	Revd. W.H. Thompson, Vicar of Winkfield, Windsor, and Gresham Lecturer
1929	Revd. Tom Wellard, Rector of St. Olave, Hart Street
1930	Revd. H.V.S. Eck, Prebendary of St. Paul's
1931	Very Revd. W.R. Inge, Dean of St. Paul's
1932	Revd. H.M. Relton, Professor of Historical and Biblical Theology, Kings College London, and Vicar of All Saints, Ennismore Gardens
1933	Rt. Revd. C.E. Curzon, Bishop of Stepney
1934	Revd. W.K. Firminger, Chaplain to the King at Hampton Court Palace
1935	Revd. Prebendary Tom Wellard, Rector of St. Olave, Hart Street, and Hon. Chaplain to the Company
1936	No surviving record
1937	Revd. Prebendary Tom Wellard, Rector of St. Olave, Hart Street, and Hon. Chaplain to the Company
1938	Revd. Prebendary Tom Wellard, Rector of St. Olave, Hart Street, and Hon. Chaplain to the Company
1939	Revd. F.W. Baggallay, Rector of St. Swithun, London Stone

(Note: In the absence of surviving records, it is uncertain which of the three lecturers gave the Lecture in 1940, 1941 and 1942, but the order given is believed to be correct)

1940	Revd. Prebendary Tom Wellard, Rector of St. Olave, Hart Street, and Hon. Chaplain to the Company
1941	Rt. Revd. R.H. Moberly, Bishop of Stepney
1942	Sqdn. Ldr. Revd. T.W.D. Wright, Chaplain to the R.A.F.
1943	Revd. F.W. Baggallay, Rector of St. Swithun, London Stone, and Hon. Chaplain to the Company
1944	Revd. M.C. Petitpierre, Chaplain, Toc.H.
1945	Revd. P.B. Clayton, Vicar of All Hallows, Barking-by-the-Tower, and Founder of Toc.H.
1946	Revd. V.A. Demant, Canon and Chancellor of St. Paul's
1947	Ven. R.W. Stannard, Archdeacon of Doncaster
1948	Rt. Revd. C.K. Bardsley, Bishop of Croydon
1949	Revd. A.St.G. Colthurst, Vicar of Aldenham, St. Albans
1950	Rt. Revd. B.F. Simpson, Bishop of Southwark
1951	Revd. A.C. Raby, Vicar of St. Marks, Purley
1952	Rt. Revd. R.W. Stannard, Bishop of Woolwich and Hon. Chaplain to the Company
1953	Rt. Revd. W.P. Gilpin, Bishop of Kingston
1954	Revd. Leslie Wright, Vicar of Wimbledon and formerly Chaplain in Chief to the R.A.F.
1955	Rt. Revd. Joost de Blank, Bishop of Stepney
1956	Revd. G.E. Parsons, Rector of Ardingly, Sussex
1957	Rt. Revd. R.R. Williams, Bishop of Leicester
1958	Revd. R.M. La Porte Payne, Rector of St. Mary Abchurch
1959	Rt. Revd. R.W. Stannard, Bishop of Woolwich and Hon. Chaplain to the Company
1960	Very Revd. E.N. Porter Goff, Provost of Portsmouth
1961	Rt. Revd. K.E.N. Lamplugh, Bishop of Southampton
1962	Rt. Revd. F.E. Lunt, Bishop of Stepney
1963	Rt. Revd. R.D. Say, Bishop of Rochester
1964	Rt. Revd. G.E. Reindorp, Bishop of Guildford
1965	Revd. Canon R.S. Hook, Precentor of Rochester
1966	Revd. Meredith Davies, Vicar of St. Botolph Without Aldersgate
1967	Rt. Revd. A.P. Tremlett, Bishop of Dover
1968	Rt. Revd. B.C. Butler, Auxiliary Bishop of Westminster
1969	Revd. G.R. Holley, Vicar of Great Burstead, Essex
1970	Very Revd. M.G. Sullivan, Dean of St. Paul's
1971	Revd. Canon C.G. Earwaker, Vicar of Lynchmere, Surrey
1972	Rt. Revd. G.E. Reindorp, Bishop of Guildford
1973	Ven. Dr. E.F. Carpenter, Archdeacon of Westminster
1974	Rt. Revd. F.W. Cocks, Bishop of Shrewsbury

APPENDIX D

1975	Revd. Canon Richard Tydeman, Rector of St. Sepulchre with Christ Church, Greyfriars
1976	Revd. E.L. Rogers, Vicar of St. Giles Cripplegate
1977	Rt. Revd. M.E. Marshall, Bishop of Woolwich
1978	Revd. A.B. Carver, Rector of Holy Trinity, Chelsea, and Hon. Chaplain to the Company
1979	Very Revd. A.B. Webster, Dean of St. Paul's
1980	Rt. Revd. A.P. Tremlett, Bishop of Dover
1981	Revd. M.A. Moxon, Sacrist of St. Paul's
1982	Very Revd. Dr. E.F. Carpenter, Dean of Westminster
1983	Very Revd. The Hon. O.W. Fiennes, Dean of Lincoln
1984	Revd. Canon W.J.D. Down, General Secretary of Missions to Seamen
1985	Revd. Canon D.P. Maurice, Priest-in-Charge, Blakeney, Norfolk
1986	Ven. F.V. Weston, Archdeacon of Oxford
1987	Revd. Canon K.G. Routledge, Treasurer of St. Paul's
1988	Revd. David Rhodes, Rector of St. Giles Cripplegate
1989	Revd. The Lord Soper
1990	Revd. W.D. Platt, Chaplain to the Community of St. Mary the Virgin, Wantage
1991	Revd. I.L. Robson, Vicar of St. Mary Abbots, Kensington, and Freeman of the Company
1992	Revd. Canon R.J. Halliburton, Chancellor of St. Paul's
1993	Revd. Canon C.E. Johnson, Provost of Seaford College

APPENDIX E

INVENTORY OF SILVER, MEDALS AND OTHER GIFTS

Note: The following list quotes inventory number, a brief description of the item, the donor, and the year donated. In many cases the donor was the Master or the Immediate Past Master in commemoration of his year of office, and in such cases the abbreviation (M) is used as the precise date of the gift is uncertain.

Items donated to the Company's Library are not listed in this inventory, but in the catalogue of Guildhall Library. It should also be noted that all the pictures belonging to the Company were lost when Bakers Hall was destroyed by enemy action on 28th/29th December 1940.

Abbreviations: (M) Master   (PM) Past Master   (UW) Upper Warden
(RW) Renter Warden   (A) Assistant   (L) Liveryman
(HF) Honorary Freeman   (F) Freeman.

1.	James I seal-top spoon (1607)	John Lewis (L)	1929
2.	James I seal-top spoon (1616)	Maj. K.E. Schweder (A)	1935
3.	Charles I goblet (1631)	Viscount Wakefield (PM)	1936
4.	Commonwealth beaker (1659)	A.N. Pitts (M)	1936
5.	Charles II tankard and cover (1664)	Lt.Col. J. Francis (PM)	1919
6.	Charles II tankard and cover (1670)	Maj. S. Weil (M)	1920
7.	Persian casket (1752)	Col. Sir John SmithYoung (M)	1927
8.	Pierced cake basket by Edward Aldridge & John Stamper (1759)	John Weir (M)	1932
9.	Pear-shaped coffee pot with chasing (1764)	A.E. Cressall (M)	1935
10.	Silver gilt cup and cover by Andrew Fogelberg (1775)	J.H. Solomon (PM)	1935
11.	C18th Sheffield plate centre-piece with cut glass bowl	Sir William Farmer (PM)	1906
15.	Oval epergne with cut glass fittings by Joseph Preedy (1799)	Francis Agar (PM)	1922
16.	Thistle-shaped cup and cover by Rebecca Emes & Edward Barnard (1809)	Col. Sir John Smith Young (M)	1928
17.	Mounted ostrich-egg cup and cover (1809)	Cecil Cronk (A)	1924
18.	Oval salver engraved with the names of successive Masters by William Bennett (1809)	Benjamin Hansford (M)	1916
19. 20.	Pair of pear-shaped ewers chased with foliage, by Samuel Hennell (1816 & 1817)	S.G. Asher (L)	1916

APPENDIX E

21.⎫	Pair of goblets to match, by	S.G. Asher (L)	1916
22.⎭	Samuel Hennell (1814)		
23.	Silver gilt rose water dish (1820)	N.N. Sherwood (M)	1896
24.	Scottish snuff mull formed from ram's horn (1826)	Hugh McConnach Reid (a guest)	1924
25.	Two circular salvers by Rebecca Emes & Edward Barnard (1828)	Sir Trevor Lawrence (PM)	1907
26.	Candelabrum centrepiece (1851)	Bequest of Sir Harry James Veitch, d.1924	1924
27.	Silver gilt tulip-shaped cup and cover (1881)	Maj. George Lambert (M)	1895
28.	Silver gilt loving cup (1887)	Maj. George Lambert (M)	1896
29.	Silver gilt mace head (1891) on silver mounted ebony staff (1914)	Purchased	1914
30.	Master's badge in gold and enamel (1891)	Purchased – repaired, Lord Gainsborough (M)	1891 / 1968
31.	Silver gilt loving cup (1894)	Beaumont Shepheard (M)	1894
32.	Loving cup and cover (1897)	Sir Thomas Dewar (A?)	1898
33.	Upper Warden's badge in silver gilt and enamel	W.T. Crosweller (A)	1897
34.	Renter Warden's badge in silver gilt and enamel	W.T. Crosweller (A)	1897
35.	Clerk's badge in silver gilt and enamel	W.T. Crosweller (A)	1897
36.	Oblong snuff box (1848)	W.L. Seyfang (A)	1900
37.	Master's chain of office in silver gilt, composed of shields enamelled with arms or monograms of the Masters	C.E. Osman (M)	1902
38.	Loving cup and cover (1903)	Sir Marcus Samuel (M)	1903
39.	Oblong cigar box lined with cedar (1904)	G.W. Burrows (M)	1904
40.	Bronze Medal of Verdun (1916)	Societe d'Horticulture de la Meuse	1923
41.	Silver gilt octagonal vase-shaped cup and cover (1911)	Bequest of Sir Harry James Veitch, d.1924	1924
42.	Beadle's shoulder badge (1921) enamel, adapted in 1924 from item 37.	Purchased	1921
44.	Beaker and cover inset with jewels (1894)	W.T. Roberts (M) and Jane Peak Roberts (F)	1926
45.	Shaped oval dessert bowl	Lady Dron, widow of Sir Thomas Dron (L)	1926
46.	Circular two-handled lobed bowl	Viscountess Wolseley (HF)	1933
47.	Replica of the Silver Jubilee silver gilt casket given by the Company to H.M. Queen Mary	Sir Jeremiah Colman (L)	1935

48.	Replicas in silver of Charles I wine cups, one (gilt) for the Master, one for the Upper Warden and one for the Renter Warden	Edward Dean (M)	1931
49.	Twenty replicas in silver of Charles I wine cups for Assistants	A.H. Dence (M)	1934
50.	Signet of triple cable-link form, engraved with the Company's armorial bearings	Robert John Stannard (A)	1936
51.	Bronze Medal of the City of Ghent (1931)		1931
52.	Silver Medal of the City of Bruges (1931)		1931
53.	Silver Medal of the Royal Society of Agriculture and Botany of Ghent (1931)		1931
54.	Bronze Medal of the Chef-Confrerie Royale et Chevaliere de St. Michel of Ghent (1931)		1931
55.	Bronze Medal of the Art of Gardening Committee of the National Society of Horticulture of France (1932) (Duplicates of this and item 57 were presented by the executors of E.A. Ebblewhite)	John Weir (M)	1933
56.	Silver Jubilee Medal (1935)	Royal Horticultural Society	1935
57.	Bronze Medal of the Societe Royale l'Avenir Horticole of Ghent (1936)		1936
58.	Danish guest cup by Conrad Ludoff of Copenhagen (c.1750)	Marcel Porn (M)	1942
59.	Ceremonial spade (1901)	E.A. Ebblewhite (Past Clerk) Anglo-Danish Society	1943
61.	Circular Copenhagen porcelain ashtray		
62.	Oblong black lacquer snuff box with Masonic emblems		
63.	Gold and enamel brooch, formed as a spray of orchids, former property of Viscountess Wolseley (HF)		
64.	Small German silver gilt tankard and cover, Nuremburg (1599)	Lt.Col. S.S.G. Cohen (M)	1937
65.	George II circular salver by William Peaston (1751)	Sir Robert Inigo Tasker (PM)	1940
66.	Circular sugar basin, part fluted, by Samuel Hennell (1801)	Bequest of Viscountess Wolseley (HF)	1937

APPENDIX E

67.	Old English glass goblet, replica of one made for Lord Nelson		
68.	Oblong poor box, oak, plated mounts	Richard Clout (A)	1893
72.	Golden Book (the original, given by Weir in 1933, was destroyed by enemy action)	John Weir (PM)	1948
	Casket for the Golden Book, from Guildhall timbers	C.E. Page Taylor (M)	1950
73.	Circular salver	J.W. Whitlock (M)	1951
74.	Ballot box	J.W. Whitlock (M)	1950
75.	Two cups (City Window Box Competition)	Purchased	1949
78.	Cup (London Teaching Hospitals Competition)	Purchased	1954
79.	Oblong inkstand	W.J. Done (A)	1953
80.	Oblong cigar and cigarette box	F.A.B. Luke (M)	1954
81.	Order of the Crown of Belgium, awarded to Lt.Col. Joseph Francis (PM) in 1919	F.A. Francis (L)	1954
82.	Silver gilt ewer (1871) and silver gilt rose-water bowl by Stephen Smith (1883)	Sir Seymour Howard (PM and Lord Mayor)	1954
83.	Oval hand-worked bread platter	Mrs. A. Ling (F)	1955
84.	Two-handled vase-shaped cup and cover by Andrew Fogelberg (1779)	Sir Brunel Cohen (M)	1955
85.	Cup (London Non-Teaching Hospitals Competition)	Purchased	1955
86.	Four circular salts by Rebecca Emes & Edward Barnard (1826) and two mustard pots by A.K. (1823)	Lord Nathan (M)	1956
87.	Glass flower bowl	Donald Byford (M)	1957
88.	Ballot box	Martin Longman (M)	1958
89.	Gavel and block	Martin Longman (M)	1958
90.	Cup (London Non-Teaching Hospitals Competition)	Purchased	1958
91.	Master's gown and Toast Master's sash in the Company's colours	F.H. Lymbery (M)	1959
92.	Chair back in silk embroidered with the Company's arms	G.J. Gollin (M)	1959
93.	Film of visit to the International Floralies in Paris in 1959	G.J. Gollin (M)	1959
94.	Continental flagon (c.1850)	E.T. Thornton-Smith (PM)	1959
95.	Bronze Medallion of the Floralies Internationales in Paris (1959)		

96.	Wardens' gowns in the Company's colours	Isidore Kerman (M)	1961
97.	Silver gilt vase-shaped cup and cover	Edward Howard (M)	1962
98.	Portrait in oils of Viscountess Wolseley (HF) by Clyde Christy	Bequest of Mrs M.I. Musgrave	1963
99.	George III silver gilt loving cup and cover	J.E. Talbot (M)	1963
100.	Silver loving cup and cover by Omar Ramsden (1934), set with coloured agates	2nd. Baron Nathan (M)	1964
101.	Silver loving cup and cover	J.B. Shearn (A)	1964
102.	Five replicas in silver of Charles I wine cups for Assistants	G.J. Gollin (PM) and Edward Howard (PM)	1964
103.	Silver bell by Omar Ramsden (1932)	2nd. Baron Nathan (M)	1963
104.	Silver replica of snuff box presented to the City by Thomas Farncomb, Lord Mayor 1849/50	Sir Dudley Bowater (L)	1964
105.	Three cut glass decanters with silver-covered stoppers with the Company's arms embossed	L.H. Kemp (A) and A.L. Kemp (F)	1964
106.	Silver replica of the Rye Bowl made in 1725 by Thomas Farrer	M.J. Thurston (PM)	1966
107.	Silver ink stand and pen	A.J.D. Robinson (PM)	1967
108.	Cigarette box from roof timber of Guildhall	L.A. Reddall (PM)	1967
109.	Three-handled silver loving cup (1892)	Maj.Gen. K.C. Appleyard (M)	1967
110.	Replica in silver of Elizabethan banqueting dish taken from the Spanish Armada	Maj.Gen. K.C. Appleyard (M)	1967
111.	Three Stewards' Wands	E.T. Thornton-Smith (PM) and Maj.Gen. K.C. Appleyard (PM)	1967
112.	The James Miller Trophy	Sir James Miller (Lord Mayor, 1964/65)	1967
	F.E. Cleary Charitable Fund	F.E. Cleary (PM)	1970-82
	Hostess's chain (item 43) re-enamelled and re-gilded	J.L. Stevenson (M)	1971
113.	Two cut glass decanters	L.H. Kemp (M)	1969
114.	Twenty-four sherry glasses engraved with the Company's arms	L.H. Kemp (M)	1969
115.	Gilt pendant – attached to Hostess's chain (item 43)	L.H. Kemp (M)	1969
116.	Cup (London Church Gardens Competition)	F.E. Cleary (M)	1969

APPENDIX E

117.	Cup (London Church Gardens Competition)	F.E. Cleary (M)	1969
118.	Goblet (Floral Awards Campaign)	F.E. Cleary (M)	1969
119.	Goblet (Floral Awards Campaign)	J.P. Schweder (UW)	1969
120.	Hand-painted crest of the Company on mahogany	N.A. Royce (RW)	1971
121.	Hand-painted crest of the Company on mahogany	Anonymous	1971
122.	Flora de la Real Expedicion Britanica del Noevo Reino de Granada 1954 (three volumes)	J.L. Stevenson (M)	1972
123.	Silver cigarette box engraved with scenes of London	Sir Edward Howard (PM and Lord Mayor)	1972
124.	Two coloured photographs of floral decorations at Barnwell Manor on the occasion of the Wedding of Prince Richard of Gloucester	David Longman (A)	1972
125.	Furniture for the roof garden at Mansion House, including engraving the glass top of the coffee table with the crest of the Company	L.H. Kemp (PM)	1972
	Five teak flower tubs for the roof garden at Mansion House	J.L. Stevenson (M)	1972
126.	Six links for the Master's chain	Bishop R.W. Stannard (M)	1973
127.	Silver loving cup	K.G. Higgins (L)	1973
128.	The Lord Mayor of London's Gilt-bronze Medal (one of only 645)	Lord Mais (Lord Mayor)	1973
	Pewter table mats	J.P. Schweder (PM) and N.A. Royce (M)	1974
129.	Gold fountain pen and chain	L.H. Kemp (PM) and A.L. Kemp (L)	1974
	King Charles I Royal Proclamation 1634	A.J. Carton (M)	1975
130.	Reproductions of C17th coloured prints of Ghent	Burgomaster and Aldermen of Ghent	1975
131.	Pair of silver spoons, made for Viscount Wakefield when Master	J.A. Vanderpump (A)	1974
132.	Two silver goblets for "Honoured Guests"	David Longman (M)	1976
133.	The Worshipful Company of Gardeners' Science Prize – City of London Freemen's School (awarded annually)	G.J. Gollin (PM), Sir Edward Howard (PM) and J.L. Stevenson (PM)	1976
134.	Spadebearer's gown in the Company's colours	C.R. Crosse (M)	1976

[215]

135.	Assistant Clerk's gown	C.R. Crosse (M)	1976
136.	Reproductions of prints of six views of Hackney in the 19th century	London Borough of Hackney	1977
137.	Silver and wooden portable lectern	John Brunel Cohen (M)	1978
138.	Case and rest for Ceremonial Spade	D.A. Huggons (M)	1979
139.	The Worshipful Company of Gardeners' Prize – City of London School for Girls	J.L. Stevenson (PM)	1979
140.	Silver gilt loving cup and cover (replica of item 99)	C.E. Talbot (M)	1980
141.	Poor box of selected English woods	L.J. Reddall (M)	1981
142.	Tradescant glass goblet	G.J. Gollin (PM)	1981
143.	Endowment for the provision of carnations at dinners	R.L. Payton (M)	1982
144.	Endowment for the provision of flowers for the Byford Bowl (item 87)	J.G. Keeling (M)	1983
145.	Necklace and brooch for the Master's Lady	R.Adm. M.J. Ross (M)	1984
146.	Chaplain's Assistant's badge and scarf	P.D. Marriner (M)	1985
147.	Embossed Court Minute Book	W.P. Maclagan (M)	1986
148.	Embossed Declaration Book Tudor Hats for the Master, Wardens and Clerk	A.B. Hurrell (M)	1987
149.	Gavel and block	His Hon. G.F. Leslie (M)	1988
150.	Crystal Glass Vase, Prize Ghent Floralies 1990	Royal Belgian Horticultural Society	
151.	Embossed Court Minute Book	G.H. Denney (PM)	1991
152.	Word Processor	David Howard (PM)	1993
153.	Spade Bearer's Badge	His Hon. G. F. Leslie (PM)	1993
154.	Past Masters' Ladies Badges	D. E. Dowlen (M)	1993

APPENDIX F

THE COMPANY'S LIBRARY

Items of antiquarian interest – publication dates to 1900

1576	R. Scot	A Perfite platforme of a hoppe garden, and necessarie instructions for the making and mayntenaunce thereof . . . nowe newly corrected and augmented
1608	D. Mountain (i.e. T. Hill)	The Gardener's labyrinth. Containing a discourse of the gardener's life. . . (Reprint of the 1594 ed)
1629	J. Parkinson	Paradisi in sole, paradisus terrestris; or a garden of . . . flowers . . . with a kitchen garden . . . and an orchard . . . with the right orderinge planting & preserving of them and their uses & vertues
1633	J. Gerard	The Herball or generall historie of plantes . . . enlarged and amended by Thomas Johnson. . .
1634	Charles I, King	A Proclamation for reformation of the many abuses committed against the Corporation of Gardners
1638	W. Lawson	A New orchard and garden. . . (4th ed)
1656	J. Tradescant	Musaeum Tradescantianum: or, a collection of rarities. Preserved at South-Lambeth neer London
1665	J. Rea	Flora: seu, de florum cultura. Or, a complete florilege. . .
1677	A. Lawrence and J. Beale	Nurseries, orchards, profitable gardens, and vineyards encouraged . . . in several letters . . . to Henry Oldenburg. . .
1677	J. Worlidge	Systema horti-culturae: or, the art of gardening. . .
1683	J. Reid	The Scots gard'ner. . .
1685	N. Venette	The Art of pruning fruit-trees. . .
1691	J. Evelyn	Kalendarium Hortense: or the gard'ners almanac. . . (8th ed)

1693	J. de La Quintinye	The Compleat gard'ner; or, directions for cultivating and right ordering of fruit-gardens and kitchen-gardens . . . made English by John Evelyn Esquire. . .
1706	G. London and H. Wise	The Retir'd gard'ner . . . being a translation of *Le jardinier solitaire* (F. Gentil). . . (2 vols)
1717	S. Collins	Paradise retriev'd: plainly . . . demonstrating the most . . . beneficial method of managing . . . fruit-trees. . . together with a treatise on mellons and cucumbers
1717	C. Evelyn	The Lady's recreation: or, the third and last part of the Art of gardening improv'd. . .
1721?	R. Rapin	Of gardens. A Latin poem . . . English'd by Mr. Gardiner (2nd ed)
1722	T. Fairchild	The City gardener. Containing the most experienced method of cultivating . . . such ever-greens, fruit-trees . . . flowers . . . as will . . . thrive best in the London gardens
1723	F. Gentil	Le Jardinier solitaire, ou dialogues entre un curieux & un jardinier solitaire. . . (5th ed)
1724	J. Beale	Herefordshire orchards, a pattern for all England. . . (see note below)
1724	R. Bradley	The Gentleman and gardener's kalendar. . . (4th ed) (see note below)
1724	R. Bradley	New improvements of planting and gardening. . . (4th ed) (Bound with the previous two items)
1730	J. Denne	The Wisdom of God in the vegetable creation. . . (The first Fairchild Lecture)
1733	J. Denne	The Wisdom and goodness of God in the vegetable creation. Further consider'd in a sermon . . . May 15. 1733. . . (Fairchild Lecture)
1741	P. Miller	The Gardeners dictionary. . . (2nd ed, 2 vols)
1748	P. Miller	The Gardeners kalendar. . . (8th ed)

[218]

APPENDIX F

1750	J. Vaniere	Jacobi Vanierii . . . Praedium rusticum (New ed)
1757	T. Hitt	A Treatise of fruit-trees (2nd ed)
1759	T. Perfect (i.e. J. Hill)	The Practice of gardening explained. . .
1769	J. Garton	The Practical gardener, and gentleman's directory. . .
1770	W. Ockenden (i.e. T. Whately)	Observations on modern gardening. . .
1771	J. Dicks	The New gardener's dictionary. . .
1771	T. Hitt	The Modern gardener; or, universal kalendar. . .
1771	P. Miller	The Abridgement of the Gardeners Dictionary. . . (6th ed)
1773	J. Hill	A Decade of curious insects. . .
1776	J. Evelyn	Silva: or, a discourse of forest-trees. . .
1776	W. Withering	A Botanical arrangement of all the vegetables naturally growing in Great Britain. . . (2 vols)
1782	J. Abercrombie, T. Mawe et al	Every man his own gardener. . . (9th ed)
1783	W. Mason	The English garden: a poem. . . (New ed)
1785-1790	J. Bolton	Filices Britannicae: an history of the British proper ferns. . . (2 vols in one)
1785	H. Walpole	Essay on modern gardening
1786	D. Solander	The Natural history of many curious and uncommon zoophytes, collected . . . by . . . John Ellis. . .
1787-1888		Curtis's botanical magazine. . . (vols 1 to 114) – General indexes to vols. 1-70 (2 vols, 1828-1844?)
1789	W. Aiton	Hortus Kewensis; or, a catalogue of the plants cultivated in the Royal Botanic Garden at Kew (3 vols)
1790	W. Speechly	A Treatise on the culture of the vine. . .

[219]

1794		The Compleat florist (2nd ed) (100 plates with letter-press descriptions)
1799	W. Curtis	Directions for cultivating the crambe maritima, or sea kale...
1799	J. Hull	The British flora, or a Linnean arrangement of British plants... (Part II)
1800-1804	J. E. Smith	Flora Britannica (3 vols)
1803	Baron Carrington	The speech... delivered at the Board of Agriculture... March 15, 1803
1803	H. Repton	Observations on the theory and practice of landscape gardening...
1805	H. C. Andrews	Geraniums...
1805	N. Culpeper	Culpeper's English physician; and complete herbal... (Edited by E. Sibly)
1806	W. Pontey	Rural recreations; or, the gardener's instructor... (2 vols in one)
1807	A. McDonald (i.e. R. W. Dickson)	A Complete dictionary of practical gardening... (2 vols)
1807	P. Miller	The Gardener's and botanist's dictionary... (4 vols)
1814	N. Culpeper	Culpeper's English physician and British herbal; to which is added, The Family physician...
1816	G. Sinclair	Hortus gramineus Woburnensis: or, an account of the results of experiments on... grasses... used as... the food of... domestic animals...
1818-1833	C. Loddiges and Sons	The Botanical cabinet: consisting of coloured delineations of plants from all countries... (20 vols)
1818	R. Sweet	Hortus suburbanus Londinensis...
1821	R. Sweet	The Botanical cultivator...
1823-1829	R. Sweet	The British flower garden... (3 vols)

[220]

APPENDIX F

1823	J. B. Papworth	Hints on ornamental gardening...
1824		The Gardener (being pages 158-165 from *The Book of English trades*... New ed)
1824	T. Green	The Universal herbal; or, botanical, medical, and agricultural dictionary... (2 vols)
1828-1844?		Curtis's botanical magazine: General indexes to vols. 1-70 (2 vols)
1829	G.W. Johnson	A History of English gardening
1830	W. Gurney	The Nosegay
1831	G. Lindley	A Guide to the orchard and kitchen garden...
1833	W. Cobbett	The English gardener...
1834-1849		Paxton's magazine of botany, and register of flowering plants (16 vols)
1834	W. E. Allen	A Treatise on... cultivating cucumbers, melons, and sea kale...
1835	J. C. Loudon	An Encyclopaedia of gardening... (New ed)
1836	N. Paterson	The Manse garden (2nd ed)
1838	J. C. Loudon	Hortus lignosus Londinensis; or, a catalogue of all the ligneous plants... of London...
1838	J. C. Loudon	The Suburban gardener, and villa companion...
1838	C. McIntosh	The Greenhouse, hot house, and stove...
1839	G. Childs	Woodland sketches: a series of characteristic portraits of trees... with... descriptions... by Rev. Robert Tyas
1839	C. McIntosh	The Flower-garden... (New ed)
1839	C. McIntosh	The Orchard...
1840	H. Repton	The Landscape gardening and landscape architecture... (New ed by J.C. Loudon)

1841?	J. Lindley	The Ladies' botany... (4th ed)
1841	J. Lindley	Pomologia Britannica... (3 vols)
1842	Mrs. J. Loudon	The Ladies' flower-garden of ornamental annuals
1844	E. Newman	A History of British ferns, and allied plants
1847	C. D. Badham	A Treatise on the esculent funguses of England...
1850	J. C. Loudon	Hortus Britannicus: a catalogue of all the plants... in... Britain (New ed)
1851-1861		The Florist and garden miscellany (4 vols – 1850, 1859, 1860, 1861)
1854	R. Brook	New cyclopaedia of botany and complete book of herbs... (2 vols in one)
1855	J. Lindley	The Theory and practice of horticulture... (2nd ed)
1855	T. Moore	The Ferns of Great Britain and Ireland...
1855	A. Pratt (Mrs. J. Pearless)	The Flowering plants, grasses, sedges and ferns of Great Britain... (5 vols)
1856-1860	E.J. Lowe	Ferns: British and exotic... (8 vols)
1857	R. Deakin	Florigraphia Britannica; or, engravings and descriptions of the flowering plants and ferns of Britain (4 vols)
1858	E.J. Lowe	A Natural history of British grasses
1859-1860	W.G. Johnstone and A. Croall	The Nature-printed British sea-weeds: a history... of the algae of the British Isles (4 vols)
1859	J.E. Sowerby	The Ferns of Great Britain...
1859	R. Thompson	The Gardener's assistant...
1861	W.J. Hooker	The British ferns... systematically arranged
1861	E.J. Lowe	Beautiful leaved plants... in cultivation in this country...

APPENDIX F

1862	W.J. Hooker	Garden ferns...
1864	D. Grant	Treatise on free gardenery
1865	W.J. Linton	The Ferns of the English lake country...
1867-1869	E.J. Lowe	Our native ferns; or a history of the British species and their varieties (2 vols)
1868		Plans of flower gardens, beds, borders, roseries, and aquariums... By contributors to the "Journal of Horticulture"
1868	B.S. Williams	Select ferns and lycopods: British and exotic...
1869	S. Hibberd	The Fern garden... (2nd ed)
1871	S. Hibberd (Ed.)	The Floral world and garden guide
1871	E.J. Lowe	A Natural history of new and rare ferns...
1871	A. Pratt (Mrs. J. Pearless)	The Ferns of Great Britain... (2nd ed)
1872	S. Hibberd	The Ivy...
1872	S.R. Hole	The Six of spades: a book about the garden and the gardener
1872	J.C. Loudon	Loudon's encyclopaedia of plants... (Reprint of the edition of 1855)
1872	A. Smee	My garden: its plan and culture...
1874	D. Wooster (Ed.)	Alpine plants... (2nd ed, 2 vols)
1875	F.W. Burbidge	The Narcissus: its history and culture...
1875	F.G. Heath	The Fern paradise: a plea for the culture of ferns
1876-1880	British Pteridological Society	(Collection of nature prints of British ferns – 4 portfolios)
1876	J. Newton	The Landscape gardener...
1878	W.J. Linton	The Ferns of the English lake country... (2nd ed)

1879-1881	J. Britten	European ferns (orig. issued in 30 parts)
1879	S. Hibberd	The Fern garden. . . (8th ed)
1879	J. Smith	Ferns: British and foreign. . . (2nd ed)
1879	A. Wallace	Notes on lilies and their culture (2nd ed)
1882	E. Newman	A History of British ferns (5th ed)
1882	W. Taylor	Vines at Longleat. . .
1883	F.G. Heath	Where to find ferns. . . (2nd ed)
1884-1888	G. Nicholson (Ed)	The Illustrated dictionary of gardening. . . (8 vols) - Index and supplement (4 vols, 1900)
1885	F.G. Heath	The Fern portfolio
1885	H.S. Miner	Orchids. . .
1885	A.F. Sieveking	The Praise of gardens. . .
1886	A.A. Ernouf	L'art des jardins. . . (3rd ed)
1887-1894	J. Veitch & Sons	A Manual of orchidaceous plants. . . (2 vols)
1887-1905	R. Braithwaite	The British moss-flora (3 vols)
1887	E.V. Boyle	Days and hours in a garden (6th ed)
1888	C.T. Druery	Choice British ferns. . .
1889	C.A. Johns	Flowers of the field (26th ed)
1890	J. Wright	Profitable fruit-growing for cottagers & small holders of land (2nd ed)
1891	E.J. Lowe	British ferns, and where found
1891	J.D. Sedding	Garden-craft old and new
1892	J. Birkenhead	Ferns and fern culture. . .

1892	R. Blomfield and F.I. Thomas	The Formal garden in England
1892	L. Figuier	The Vegetable world...
1892	S.R. Hole	A Book about the garden and the gardener (reprint, with additional material, of *The Six of spades,* 1872)
1893-1895	B.D. Jackson (comp.)	Index Kewensis: an enumeration of the genera and species of flowering plants... (4 vols)
1893	W.J. Linton	The Ferns of the English lake country... (3rd ed)
1894	C.P. Johnson	British wild flowers... Re-issue: to which is added a supplement... by John W. Salter... and... Ferns, horsetails, and club-mosses, by J.E. Sowerby
1895	Hon. A. Amherst	A History of gardening in England
1895	E.V. Boyle	A Garden of pleasure (2nd ed)
1895	H.N. Ellacombe	In a Gloucestershire garden
1895	E.J. Lowe	Fern growing...
1895	W. Watson and W. Bean	Orchids: their culture and management... (2nd ed)
1896-1897	E. Step	Favourite flowers of garden and greenhouse (4 vols)
1896	Hon. A. Amherst	A History of gardening in England (2nd ed)
1896	A.B. Freeman-Mitford	The Bamboo garden
1896	J.H. Veitch	A Traveller's notes... of a tour through India, Malaysia, Japan, Corea, the Australian colonies and New Zealand... 1891-1893
1899	H. Correvon	Album des orchidees de l'Europe centrale et septentrionale
1899	S.R. Hole	Our gardens

1899	G. Jekyll	Wood and garden: notes and thoughts... of a working amateur
1899	E.G. Lodeman	The Spraying of plants... (Reprint)
1900-1902		Gardens old and new: the country house and its garden environment (2 vols) (Country Life Library)
1900-1914	H. Maxwell	Memories of the months... (4 vols)
1900	E.T. Cook (Ed.)	The Century book of gardening...
1900	A.E.P.R. Dowling	The Flora of the sacred nativity: an attempt at collecting the legends and ancient dedications of plants connected in popular tradition with the life of our blessed Lord...
1900	G. Jekyll	Home and garden: notes and thoughts... of a worker in both
1900	J. Veitch & Sons	Veitch's manual of the coniferae... (New ed)
1900	C. Welch	History of the Worshipful Company of Gardeners (2nd ed)

INDEX OF NAMES

Aberconway, Lord (H.D.McLaren) 89
Aberconway, 3rd. Lord 90, 132, 170
Abraham, Thomas 190
Agar, Sir Francis 10, 63, 64, 115, 116
Agriculture, Board/Ministry of 89, 117, 139, 140, 163, 177
Albert, King of the Belgians 140, 141, 142
Alexandra, Princess 10, 99
Alexandra, Queen 92
Alice, Princess, Duchess of Gloucester 10, 12, 13, 76-77, 90, 99, 102, 103, 104, 106, 137, 158, 193
All Hallows by the Tower 165
Allan, Mea 135, 137
Alston, John 184
Amherst, Alicia 7, 26, 88, 110
Amherst, Lord 88, 110
Andrew, Duke of York 15, 100, 106
Anne, Princess (Princess Royal) 13, 77, 104, 104-105
Anne, Queen (statue) 82
Apothecaries, Society of 129, 174, 175
Appleyard, Maj.Gen. K.C. 67, 98, 179, 186
Armourers and Brasiers Company 56
Armstrong-Jones, Antony 99
Ashmole, Elias 134-135
Aubrey, John 135
Bacon, Stephen 183, 184
Bagley, Robert 59
Baker, S.H. 80
Bakers Company 19, 173
Balfour, R.C. 4, 68, 86, 106, 154, 169
Ballard, Ann 106, 128
Ballard, Francis 43
Ballard, Kenneth 128
Banburye, Henry 31
Barbor, William 31
Barker, Alfred 53
Basketmakers Company 20, 174
Batho, Sir Charles Albert 10, 61, 63, 65
Batt, Humphrey 42

Baudouin, King of the Belgians 12, 89, 147, 148-149, 193
Bayer, Charles 59, 63, 68, 92, 93-94, 139, 160, 173
Beale, L.S. 53
Beatrix, Queen of the Netherlands 154-155
Beeson, G.E.W. 64
Belgium 9, 10, 12, 13, 14, 15, 80, 83-84, 86, 89, 90, 102, 139-140, 140-143, 144-145, 147, 147-152, 191, 193
Bell, Sir John 68-69
Bent, Robert 151, 154
Bernhard, Jeffrey 151
Berrall, Julia 26
Berry, Hugh 42
Bewley, John 186
Bickerstaff, Thomas 184
Bishop, W.F. 97
Black, Peter 105
Blades, Sir G.R. 9, 10, 49, 61, 63, 64, 79-80, 139-140, 173
Bleaney, Paul 105
Blick, Charles 93
Board/Ministry of Agriculture 89, 117, 139, 140, 163, 177
Board of Education 161
Bonthuis, R.P. 139
Boone, A.H. 139
Booth, A.B. 91
Bowater, Sir I.F. 67
Bowes Family 56
Bowes Lyon, Sir David 90, 91
Brabant, Duke and Duchess of 145
Bradley, Richard 183
Britain in Bloom 123-124
British Home for Incurables 162
British Petroleum 122
British Pteridological Society 197
Broadbridge, Sir G.T. 10, 61, 65
Brooke-Hitching, Sir Thomas 176
Brown, Alexander 133, 153
Brown, Victor 63, 115, 196

[227]

Buckingham, George Villiers, Duke of 133
Burley, James 35
Burrows, G.W. 50, 53, 110, 176, 194
Burt, George 49, 53
Butchers Company 19, 20
Butler, Rt.Revd. B.C. 186
Butler, Nick 151, 152
Button, Sir Howard 66
Byers, William 42
Byford, Donald 67, 97, 98, 106, 147
Cambrey, Thomas 35
Cants of Colchester 68
Carpenters Company 175
Carrington & Co. 191
Carters Seeds 131
Carton, Alice 77
Carton, A.J. 123, 149
Catesby, Mark 181
Caustone, John de 30
Cawsway (16th century gardener) 28
Chamberlain, Joseph 91
Chambre Syndicale des Horticulteurs Belges 141-142, 143
Chandler, E.G. 62, 71, 98, 106, 123, 170
Chandler, Iris 170
Chandler, Robert 43
Charles I, King 6, 37, 132, 133, 183
Charles II, King 23, 41
Charles, Prince of Wales 14, 15, 90, 100, 104, 105, 106
Chartered Secretaries and Administrators Company 77
Chelsea Physic Garden 104, 129-130, 171, 184
Chester, John 47-48, 49
Cheyne, Charles 129
Chichibou, Princess of Japan 154
Church Gardens Competition 12, 126-127
City and Guilds Art School 120
City Flower Show 14, 121
City Livery Club 77-78
Clarke, Thomas 53
Clarke, William 31
Claus, Prince of the Netherlands 154

Cleary, F.E. 67, 71, 73, 84-86, 121, 122, 123-124, 128, 149, 158, 159-160, 165
Clipstone, John 27
Clockmakers Company 49, 174
Clothworkers Company 19, 22, 42, 91
Clout, Richard 50, 53
Cocker, R.V. 119
Cockson, John 42
Cohen, Sir Brunel 3, 66, 96, 147
Cohen, Christine 121
Cohen, J.B. 105, 136, 152, 170
Cohen, Lt.Col. S.S.G. 66, 97
Cole, Richard 184
Colman, Sir Jeremiah 101
Combmakers Company 53
Cooke, Thomas 43
Cooks Company 19
Coopers Company 19, 20
Corble, George 53, 177
Cordwainers Company 20, 61
Cork, Sir Kenneth 73
Cornwallis, F.S.W. 88
Cranfield, W.B. 197
Cronk, Cecil 190-191
Crosse, C.R. 105, 170
Crosse, Mrs. H.G.P. 168
Crosweller, W.T. 3, 8, 129, 177, 188-189, 197
Crowley, Philip 50, 53, 108, 176
Curtis, James 7, 47-48, 49, 54, 59, 82
Cutlers Company 56, 124
Dean, Edward 145, 165
Delaney, Revd. Peter 165
Denne, Revd. John 185
Denney, G.H. 4, 62, 152, 158, 169
Denny, Sir Lionel 67
Denterghem, Comte de Kerchove de 89, 144-145
Denterghem, Comte Andre de Kerchove de 89, 151
Denterghem, Comte Jacques de Kerchove de 89, 147
Depham, Roger de 30
Dewar, Sir T.R. 69, 88, 195
Disabled Living Foundation 170
Ditchfield, P.H. 19-20

INDEX OF NAMES

Dixon, John 35
Donaldson, Dame Mary 14, 62, 67-68, 76, 77, 85
Doody, Samuel 129
Dowlen, D.E. 4, 98, 169
Drapers Company 20, 22, 28, 114
Driver, Samuel 184
Dron, Sir Thomas 10, 63
Dulwich Congregational Church 127
East Malling Research Station 130
Ebbisham, Lord (G.R. Blades) 9, 10, 49, 61, 63, 64, 79-80, 139-140, 173
Ebblewhite, E.A. 8, 10, 54-55, 56-57, 58, 59, 65, 80, 82-84, 89, 93, 100-101, 110, 111, 139-140, 143, 144, 155, 157, 181, 185, 188, 190-191, 191-192, 196
Edinburgh, Prince Philip, Duke of 95, 96, 99, 155
Education, Board of 161
Edward I, King 27
Edward VII, King 8, 57, 92
Edward, Prince (present) 100
Edward, Prince of Wales (later Duke of Windsor) 10, 89, 102, 104, 193
Edwards, George 51, 188
Elizabeth II, Queen 10, 11, 13, 15, 91, 94-96, 98-99, 100, 103, 104, 105, 155, 193
Elizabeth, Queen (the Queen Mother) 10, 13, 14, 94, 96, 97-98, 99, 100, 103, 104, 105, 106, 130, 136, 168, 169, 193
Elkington & Co. 93, 161
Elliott, Patricia 170
Elliott, Sir Thomas 177
Ernle, Lord (R.E. Prothero) 89, 114-115
Evans, John 149
Evelyn, John 134
Exbury 131
Fabiola, Queen of the Belgians 12, 13, 90, 148, 149, 193
Fairchild, John 181
Fairchild, Thomas 7, 9, 42, 130, 163, 181-187, 197
Fanmakers Company 25, 61, 80, 93

Farmer, Sir William 53, 110, 176
Farrar, Archdeacon F.W. 49
Fears, Constance 90
Federation Horticole Professionelle Internationale 115
Ferguson, Sarah 15, 106
Fester Fothergill & Hartnung 119
Festival Garden 11, 118, 119
Finch, John 45
Fishmongers Company 20, 22, 25, 175
Fitch, E.F. 49, 53
Fitzstephen, William 27
Fleming, J.G. 156
Fletchers Company 48, 73
Floral Awards 120-122
Floralies Gantoises 10, 12, 13, 14, 15, 102, 139, 144-145, 147, 147-152
Flowers in the City Campaign 11, 67, 68, 86, 122-125
Forsyth, William 129
Foster & Cranfield 197
Fowler, J.G. 161
Fox, Sir Murray 123
Framework Knitters Company 84, 192
France 9, 140, 144, 145-146, 147, 153
Francis, Lt.Col. Joseph 142, 143
Fraunceys, Simon 30
Fredericke, Joseph 39
Fresh Air Fund 160
Fruiterers Company 31, 38, 57, 59-60, 64, 175
Furber, Robert 184
Gainsborough, A.G.E.N., Earl 165, 186
Galinou, Mireille 26
Garden Club of Virginia 14, 137, 153, 195
Garden History Society 90
Gardeners Arms Public House 131
Gardeners Company's Day 8, 160
Gardeners' March 14, 180
Gardeners' Pride 10, 180
Gardeners Royal Benevolent Institution (later Society) 7, 11, 12, 116, 157-158, 162, 165
Gardner, F.J.B. 66, 148, 168, 197
Gardner-Thorpe, Col. Sir Ronald 67

[229]

Gascoyne, Sir Crisp 190
Gascoyne, John 190
Gaywood, John 59
George V, King 9, 92, 94, 145, 161
George VI, King 94, 99, 100, 193
Germany 13, 152
Ghent Floralies 10, 12, 13, 14, 15, 102, 139, 144-145, 147, 147-152
Gillett, Cmndr. Sir Robin 73, 86
Girdlers Company 28, 124
Gladstone, William Ewart 24-25, 52
Glasgow, Incorporation of Gardeners of 15, 155-156
Gleed, C.J. 111
Gloucester, Duke of 12, 90, 99, 102, 103-104, 193
Gloucester, Duchess of (Princess Alice) 10, 12, 13, 76-77, 90, 99, 102, 103, 104, 106, 137, 158, 193
Glovers Company 93
Glynde, School of Gardening 89, 113
Goffin, L.L. 111
Gofton-Salmond, Robert 50, 53, 54, 82, 110
Goldsmiths Company 19, 20, 22, 25, 49, 51, 103, 118-119, 125, 126, 164
Gollin, G.J. 76, 82, 98, 147, 195
Gooding, Vicky 168
Goodspeed, Humphrey 42, 43
Goodwell, John 42
Gough, Tom 106, 121
Gould, M.E. 119
Gould, Mrs. P.M. 169
Grace, Princess of Monaco 149
Gray, Christopher 184
Gray, Col. N.G.S. 4, 169
Grene, John 35
Grenfell, Lord 89
Griffith-Boscawen, Sir Arthur 117
Grocers Company 19, 20, 22, 28
Gunmakers Company 25
Gunther, R.T. 133
Gurney, John 74
Gustav VI Adolf, King of Sweden 13, 90
Haberdashers Company 22, 43, 61, 79
Hadfield, Miles 26

Haldeman, D.C. 115, 117
Hall, A.H. 90
Hamilton, Lady 170
Hamond, John 29
Hansford, Benjamin 97, 142
Hanson, Sir C.A. 9, 61, 63, 115
Hardyngham, Sir Gilbert 27
Hare, Robbie 150
Harewood, Countess of 102
Harris, Josephine 195
Harrison, Miss O.M. 110
Harvey, John 26
Hatfield House 133, 195
Hatton, Sir Ronald 130
Haynes, Herbert 159
Heechcock, Robert 31
Helm, William 42
Hench, Mark 31
Henrey, Blanche 26, 90, 181
Henrietta Maria, Queen to Charles I 135
Henry VIII, King 22, 28
Herbert, R.A.E. 90
Herdman, W.A. 88
Heyward, John 31
Hipkins Family 44, 45, 55-56
Hodder & Stoughton 119
Holland 9, 11, 15, 86, 89, 139, 146, 149, 152-153, 154, 183
Hollar, Wenceslaus 134
Hood, William 184
Hooker, Sir W.J. 132
Hookey, F.B. 45
Horners Company 25, 48
Horselydown 7, 42-43
Hosiers Company 20
Hospitals Competitions 11, 12, 125-126
Howard, David 4, 62, 137
Howard, Sir Edward 12, 13, 61, 67, 72, 75, 121, 127-128, 131, 148, 158, 165, 168, 186, 195
Howard, Sir Seymour 11, 61, 66, 97, 100, 102, 195
Huggons, D.A. 4, 73, 105, 138, 168, 192
Hughes, R.P. 196
Hunt, Francis 184
Hunt, Samuel 184

[230]

INDEX OF NAMES

Hurles, John 40
Hurrell, A.B. 106, 153
Hursts (wholesale seedsmen) 49
Huysun, Jacob van 184
Hyams, Edward 26
Incorporation of Gardeners of Glasgow 15, 155-156
Information Technologists Company 25
Inland Revenue 162
Innes, Col. John 136
International Federation of Parks and Recreation Administration 132
Inwood, Sir William 43
Ironbridge Gorge Museum 171
Ironmongers Company 22, 83, 91, 174, 192
Italy 15, 153-154
Ives, George 59
Ivey, F.G. 53, 192
James I, King 5, 6, 30, 33, 34, 50, 132, 155, 183, 188
James II, King 23, 41, 59
James, Aaron 43
James, John 184
James, Moses 184
Japan, Empress of 154
Jeffries, P.V. 158
Jersey 14, 132
Joiners Hall 36
Jones, David 74, 86, 121
Joubert, Sir Philip 178
Jubilee Garden 72-73
Juliana, Queen 11, 89, 146, 149, 152-153, 154, 193
Keeling, J.G. 67, 154
Kemp, L.H. 71, 98, 195
Kent, Duchess of (Katharine Worsley) 10, 99
Kent, Dukes of 99
Kent, William 174
Kerchove de Denterghem, Comte de 89, 144-145
Kerchove de Denterghem, Comte Andre de 89, 151
Kerchove de Denterghem, Comte Jacques de 89, 147

Kettle, Bernard 90
Kew Gardens 89, 90, 119, 131, 132
Killik, Sir S.H.M. 61, 63, 65
Knott, Sir James 112
Kyrle Society 88
Ladies Flower Committee of St. Paul's 14, 106, 127-128
Lambert, Bartholomew 31
Lambert, Maj. George 47-48, 49, 53, 67, 194
Lambourne, William 27
Lang, Jennifer 18
Langford, H.S. 111
Lascelles, Viscount 99
Lawrence, E.K. 111
Lawrence, Sir Trevor 49, 50, 53, 92, 108-110, 111, 161
Leathersellers Company 43
Leaver, Sir Christopher 67
Legge, Bob 150, 151
Leith-Ross, Prudence 137
Leonardslee 90, 131
Leslie, G.F. 106, 153
Lessons, K.W. 126
Letchworth 129
Leverhulme, Lord 114, 116
Lewis, John 189
Ligne, Prince Antoine de 149
Lincoln, Earl of 27
Ling, R.B. 95, 130
Linnean Society 88, 90
Littleton, Sir Edward 6, 8, 36, 69
Lochristi 131, 140
Loder, Sir Giles and Lady 90, 131
London Children's Flower Society (formerly London Flower Lovers League) 67, 164, 168-169
London Gardens Society 67, 103, 119, 121, 125, 126, 164, 167-168
London Hospital 102, 125
Long, Jeremiah 186
Longman, David 4, 77, 98, 104, 105, 107, 123, 128, 150, 151, 169, 187
Longman, Martin 77, 95, 98, 100, 121, 128
Longmans Limited 105, 107, 121

[231]

Loriners Company 174
Lowe, Maj. F.M. 69
Lowe, Obadiah 184
Luke, F.A.B. 96, 100, 103, 130, 146
Lumbert, Bartholomew 31
Luxembourg, Grand Duchess of 154
Lymbery, F.H. 147, 148
MacCormac, Sir William 176
MacGregor, Arthur 135
McKenzie, Maj. Alexander 49, 53
Maclagan, W.P. 67, 169
McLaren, H.D. 89
MacLeod, Dawn 26
McWilliams, Sir Francis 15, 68
Mais, Lord 72
Margaret, Princess 10, 91, 99, 103
Margaretha, Queen of Denmark 154
Marina, Princess 10, 99, 193
Markham, John 28, 31
Marriner, P.D. 67, 151, 155
Marshall, Sir H.B. 59, 60, 61, 62, 63, 92, 102, 161, 178
Martindill, Thomas 186
Martyn, Richard 31
Mary, Princess (the Princess Royal) 10, 89, 99, 101-102, 193, 197
Mary, Queen to George V 8, 9, 92-94, 96-97, 101, 168, 193
Mash, Matthew 42
Mason, Thomas 35
Master Mariners Company 175
Maudsley Hospital 125
Mawson, Thomas 114
Meath, Earl of 88
Medical Rehabilitation Centre (Camden Road) 126
Melton, Richard 35
Mercers Company 20, 22, 24
Merchant Taylors Company 22, 28, 42
Metropolitan Public Gardens Association 7, 12, 67, 71, 73, 85, 86, 88, 122-123, 159-160
Middlesex Hospital 125
Middleton, Roy 120
Miller, Sir James 70, 122, 124
Miller, Philip 129, 184

Milner, Tempest 39
Ministry/Board of Agriculture 89, 117, 140, 163, 177
Mitchell, Christopher 121
Mold, John 35
Molloy, Alfred 186
Monkswell, Lord 88
Moore, H.J. de Courcy 63
Morrall, Thomas 31
Mortimer, John 31
Mullen, R.G. 49, 53
Murrey, Thomas 42
Museum of Garden History 14, 136, 137
Nathan, H.L., Baron 67, 80, 96, 98, 103, 118, 179
Nathan, R.C.M., 2nd. Baron 98, 148
National Allotments Society 117
National Carnation and Picotee Society 93
National Mutual Life Assurance of Australasia 122, 124
National Provident Institution 119
National Rose Society 86, 163
National Society of Horticulture of France 145-146
National Trust 166
National Union of Allotment Holders 115-117
National Westminster Bank 124
Naunton, Sir Robert 6, 34
Needlemakers Company 93
Netherlands 9, 11, 15, 86, 89, 139, 146, 149, 152-153, 154, 183
New Hall (Chelmsford) 133
Newman, Thomas 35
Nicholson, Rosemary 136
Norfolk, Duke of 91
North, Col. J.T. 49, 53
North London Collegiate School for Girls 166
Nussey, Helen 168
Oaker, Thomas 28
Oatlands Palace 133, 134
Ogilvy, Angus 99-100
Osman, C.E. 8, 50, 53, 129, 188
Owen, Janet 74, 77, 128

INDEX OF NAMES

Parish Clerks Company 84
Parkinson, John 133
Partridge, Bernard 141
Paul & Son 161
Paviors Company 48, 61, 80
Payton, R.L. 4, 67, 105, 137, 153, 160, 169
Pearse, J.S. 145
Pearson's Fresh Air Fund 160
Pepperers Company 19
Perry Rise Baptist Church 127
Petiver, James 129
Pewterers Company 28
Philip, Prince, Duke of Edinburgh 95, 96, 99, 155
Phillimore, Joseph 190
Phillimore, Lord Justice 190
Phillips, Capt. Mark 13, 104
Pinmakers Company 53
Piper, Edward 64, 93
Piper and Son 96
Pitts, A.N. 66, 180
Plaisterers Company 175
Playing Cards Company, Makers of 93
Pontifex, Bryan 21
Pool, Thomas 42
Porn, Marcel 77
Portland, Duke of 191
Portugal 13, 90, 152
Potter, J.M.S. 111
Poulters Company 49
Pratt, Richard 129
Price, S.W. 89
Printz, Jean 153
Proby, Henry 39
Prothero, R.E. 89, 114-115
Puppe, Geoffrey 27
Queen Elizabeth's Foundation for the Disabled 166
Rawson Home 170
Red Oaks 11, 158
Reddall, Jill 128
Reddall, L.J. 67, 98, 128, 150, 158
Reid, H.McC. 191
Reid, J. 197
Richard, Prince of Gloucester 13, 104

Richardes, John 31
Richardson, Sir Albert 118
Ritchie, C.T. 176
Roberts, W.T. 64
Robinson, A.J.D. 67
Rockley, Lady Alicia 7, 26, 88, 110
Rogers, A.G.L. 139
Rohde, Eleanour 132
Ross, R.Adm. M.J. 3, 67, 68, 98, 132, 155
Rothamsted Experimental Station 130
Rothschild, Edmund de 131
Rothschild, Leopold de 93, 157
Rowland (17th century gardener) 37
Rowlands, James 51
Royal Agricultural Society 88, 177
Royal Agricultural and Botanical Society of Belgium 151
Royal Belgian Horticultural Society 15, 152
Royal Botanic Gardens 89, 90, 119, 131, 132
Royal Botanic Society of London 8, 88
Royal Gardeners Orphan Fund 8, 12, 116, 157, 158-159, 162, 165
Royal Horticultural Society 9, 46, 47, 49, 50, 52, 83, 84, 86, 89, 90, 91, 108-113, 130, 138, 149, 160-161, 166, 170, 176, 190
Royal Horticultural Society of Belgium 89, 149
Royal Hospital for Incurables 162
Royal National Rose Society 86, 163
Royal Northern Hospital 126
Royce, N.A. 67, 76, 152, 154
Ruddlesden, Eric 180
Rugarth Property & Management 124
Russon, Sir Clayton 132
Saddlers Company 20, 25
Sainsbury, R.J. 64
St. Andrew by the Wardrobe 71
St. Augustine's Abbey 133
St. Bartholomew's Hospital and Priory 72, 159
St. Dunstan in the East 13, 71
St. Giles Cripplegate 185, 187

[233]

St. John the Evangelist (Blackheath) 127
St. John's Clerkenwell 159
St. John's (S.E.15) 127
St. Leonard's (Shoreditch) 184-187
St. Mark's (Greenwich) 127
St. Mary Somerset 73
St. Mary the Virgin (Lambeth) 135-136
St. Michael's Cornhill 186
St. Michael's Hospital 126
St. Paul's Cathedral Flower Committee 14, 106, 127-128
St. Paul's Garden 11, 118, 119
St. Peter's (Deptford) 127
Salisbury, Earls of 133
Salisbury, Sir E.J. 89, 119
Salters Company 22, 25, 174
Salvation Army 170
Samuel, Sir Marcus 7, 8, 53, 60, 61, 62, 189
Savory, Sir Joseph 7, 49, 50, 53, 60
School of Gardening (Glynde) 89, 113
Schot, Adam 27
Schroder, Baron 109, 110
Schroder, Baron Bruno 157
Schweder, J.P. 104, 124, 152, 165
Schweder, Maj. K.E. 97, 130, 197
Scot, John 27
Seamer, Jeremiah 181
Seddon, R.J. 176
Sewell, Col. T.D. 54
Shead, S.G. 97, 101, 113, 140, 141, 177
Shearn, John 148
Shears, Diana 128
Sheffield Park (Sussex) 166
Shepheard, A.J. 48
Shepheard, Beaumont 45, 47-49, 52, 53, 63, 73, 92, 110, 139
Shepheard, Charles 45, 48, 73
Shepheard, P.B. 48
Sheppard, Janet 74, 77, 128
Sherwood, J.E.N. 157
Sherwood, N.N. 49, 53, 63, 88, 108, 139, 161, 194
Shipwrights Company 49, 62
Silkmen and Silkthrowers Companies 53
Silverton, D.W. 158, 162

Simpson, William 43
Singleton, George 184
Skinners Company 20, 22
Slazenger, R. 8, 63
Sloane, Sir Hans 129
Smet, Albert de 143
Smith, Bertram 111
Smith, John 122
Smith, J.R. 116
Smith, Raymond 90
Society of Apothecaries 129, 174, 175
Society of Gardeners 183-184
Solomon, J.H. 63
South London Hospital for Women 126
Southport Flower Show 132
Spalding 11, 130-131
Spectacle Makers Company 61
Spencer, Lady Diana 14, 105
Spencer, William 184
Spencer & Co. 188
Stagg, Peter 71, 74, 86, 121, 123
Stannard, Bishop R.W. 67, 72, 104, 127, 154, 158, 186
Staples, Richard 189
Stapley, J.E. 125
Stationers Company 55, 61, 79
Stearn, W.T. 90
Steele, A.F. 3, 12, 89, 95, 146
Steiner, F.N. 3, 73, 77, 85, 89, 105, 122, 123, 128, 131, 147
Stephenson, Ashley 151, 152
Stepney, Bishop of 185
Stevenson, J.L. 67, 71, 154
Stewart, P.M. 145
Stourhead Park 166
Stow, John 19, 28
Strauss, E.A. 59, 110
Street, Alice 168
Stubbs, George the Elder 43, 44
Stubbs, George the Younger 44, 45
Talbot, C.E. 98, 128, 150
Talbot, J.E. 131, 148
Tallow Chandlers Company 175
Tasker, Sir R.I. 63, 80-81, 94, 102, 161, 164
Taylor, C.E.P. 97, 103, 146, 194

INDEX OF NAMES

Taylor, Sir George 90
Taylor, John 42
Teck, Duke of 8, 88, 92, 101, 178
Teofani, Panajotti 63
Thames Polytechnic 151
Thomaz, H.E. Contra-Almirante 13, 90, 152
Thompson, G.H. 63, 97, 99
Thompson, John 184
Thomson, William 39
Thornton-Smith, E.T. 81-82
Threlford, W.L. 65
Thurston, M.J. 71, 148, 149
Tiarks, H.F. 50, 53
Tichborne, Lord 39
Tin Plate Workers Company 48, 83, 84, 192
Tinley, G.F. 111
Titcomb, Joyce 118
Tradescant, Hester 134
Tradescant, John the Elder 132-137, 153
Tradescant, John the Third 134
Tradescant, John the Younger 6, 14, 106, 132-137, 153, 182, 195
Tradescant Trust 136, 153
Treseders' Nurseries 105
Truro 105
Tucker, John 31
Tulip Time 11, 130-131
Turners Company 19
Tutt, Sylvia 77
Union Discount Company 119
Upward, E.M. 4, 68, 150, 151, 152, 160
Utting, Fred 121
Vacant Land Cultivation Society 116
Van Deurs, Brigitte 13, 104
Vanderpump, Gillian 156
Veitch, Sir Harry 191
Verdun Horticultural Society 144
Villiers, George, Duke of Buckingham 133
Vintners Company 22, 25, 43, 174
Virginia 14, 133, 134, 137, 153, 181, 195
Volkersz, K. 139
Wainhouse, Charles 43
Wakefield, Sir C.C. 61, 63, 97, 143, 161, 178

Wales, Charles, Prince of 14, 15, 90, 100, 104, 105, 106
Wales, Diana, Princess of 14, 105
Walker, I.G. 119
Wallis, Richard 56-57
Walsh, Walter 28
Walworth, Sir William 27
War Seal Foundation 161
Ward, F.K. 89
Warren Nurseries 93
Watford Allotments Protection Society 116
Watlyngtone, John 27
Watney Reed 131
Watson, Sir William 135
Watts, John 129
Weavers Company 19, 20, 57, 174
Webber, Ronald 26
Webster, Very Revd. Alan 127
Weigall, Sir Archibald 130
Weil, Maj. Samuel 144, 189
Weir, John 10, 97, 101, 145, 190, 193, 197
Welch, Charles 3, 47, 49, 52, 53
Welch, Robert 126
Well Hall Allotment Holders 116
Wellard, Revd. Tom 66
Wellham, Doris 107
Welstead, William 184
West Ham Park 74, 123
Weston, Thomas 31
Weston, William 43
Wheatcroft, Harry 71
Whitbreads 125
White, Richard 31
Whiteley, Sir Peter 132
Whitlock, J.W. 97, 118, 119, 130, 165
Whitmill, Benjamin 183, 184
Whittington Garden 71
Wilks, Revd. William 49, 50, 53, 108, 111-112, 176
William and Mary 23, 41
Williams, A.G. 196
Willmott, Ellen 197
Wilson, G. Fergusson 50, 53
Wilson, G. Fox 111

Window Box Awards 11, 118-120
Windsor, Edward Duke of 10, 89, 102, 104, 193
Wisley (R.H.S. Gardens) 50, 110, 112, 130, 170
Wolseley, Viscountess 89, 113
Wontner, Sir Hugh 19, 72
Wood, Gervase 66
Wood, Henry 53, 110
Worrall, Thomas 31
Wortley, Richard 44
Wotton, Edward, Lord 133

Wye College 11, 130, 166-167, 170
Wyon, Allan 189
York, Duke of (later George VI) 10, 99
York, Andrew, Duke of 15, 100, 106
York, Duchess of (Sarah Ferguson) 15, 106
Young, John 191
Young, Sir J.S. 64, 162, 190, 191
Young, Thomas 31
Young Gardeners 68, 151, 152
Zinkeisen, Anna 98